The Lord Who Is Half Woman

The Lord Who Is Half Woman

Ardhanārīśvara in Indian and Feminist Perspective

Ellen Goldberg

State University of New York Press

In memory of my beloved teacher, Swami Vinit Muni

(1938–1996)

Published by
State University of New York Press, Albany

Printed in the United States of America

For information, address State University of New York Press,
90 State Street, Suite 700, Albany, NY 12207

Production by Kelli Williams
Marketing by Anne M. Valentine

Library of Congress Cataloging-in-Publication Data

Goldberg, Ellen, 1954–
The Lord who is half woman : Ardhanārīśvara in Indian and feminist perspective / Ellen Goldberg.
p. cm.
Includes index.
ISBN 0-7914-5325-1 (alk. paper) — ISBN 0-7914-5326-X (pbk. : alk. paper)
1. Ardhanārīśvara (Hindu deity) 2. Śiva (Hindu deity) I. Title.

BL1218 .G65 2002
294.5'2113—dc21 2001049305

10 9 8 7 6 5 4 3 2 1

Contents

List of Illustrations

In water I am the taste, Kaunteya, in sun and moon the light, in all the Vedas the syllable om, in the ether the sound, in men their manhood. In earth I am its fragrance, in the sun its fire, in all creatures their vitality, in the ascetics their austerity. Know, Partha, that I am the eternal seed of all beings, I am the thought of the thinkers, the splendor of the splendid.

—*The Bhagavadgītā*

Enlightenment is the eradication of all marks. Enlightenment is without duality, since therein are no minds and no things. Enlightenment is equality, since it is equal to infinite space.

—*The Holy Teaching of Vimalakīrti*

Acknowledgments

My research for this book was sponsored by scholarships and grants from the Social Sciences Humanities Research Council, Ontario Graduate Scholarships, the University of Toronto and the Center for the Study of Religion, and EPROC (Toronto South Asian Business Community). I have used libraries in Toronto and in India for the bulk of my research, and I have traveled thousands of miles throughout India to see images of Ardhanārīśvara in their pan-Indian context.

The instruction and the guidance I received from Swami Vinit Muni, Swami Om Shivatva Muni, and most importantly Swami Arundhati over the past twelve years are deeply present in each phase of this research. There are no words to convey my gratitude for their overwelming patience, love, trust, and wisdom. I also want to express my thanks to Cecilie Kwait and Lama Namygyal Rinpoche for their discerning and eloquent transmission of Buddhism.

There are many friends and colleagues without whose help and efforts this research would not have been possible. In India, I would like to mention my dear friends, Dr. Bharat and Yukti Gupt, whose generosity and kindness helped me survive my first field trip to the Śiva caves at Amarnath, Kashmir. Also, my friends, Sri Kant and Nikki Verma, who transported me throughout Himachal Pradesh to visit the Ardhanārīśvara Temple in Mandi, via Dharamasala and Kulu, on my second field research trip.

At the University of Toronto, I must extend my thanks to various readers and advisors who shared their expertise and sound advice: Dr. Naren Wagle, director of the Department of South Asian Studies and professor of History; Dr. Joseph T. O'Connell, associate professor, Center for the Study of Religion; my dear friend and colleague, Dr. Marsha A. Hewitt, professor of Ethics, Trinity College; Dr. Anthony Warder, professor emeritus, who strongly disagreed with the feminist analysis but still led me to a keener understanding of the Ardhanārīśvara *stotram*; and T. Venkatacarya, Department of Linguistics, University of Toronto. I also must thank Dr. Leona Anderson, Department of Religious Studies, University of Regina, for her careful reading of my doctoral dissertation, as well as my current department at Queen's University for the support and encouragement they have shown me since joining the Department of Religious Studies in 1995. Finally, Dr. Eva Neumaier-Dargyay provided critical dialogue from time to time on the subject of Hindu and Buddhist *yoga-tantra* during my stay at the University of Alberta that has remained with me and prompted me into deeper critical analysis of the field.

For this book I drew primarily on collections of Ardhanārīśvara from the American Institute of Indian Studies (AIIS and ASI), Gurgaon, India, and I must thank Mr. Sharma and all of the staff who provided me with photographic archives and copyright permissions. I also used the French Institute at Pondicherry extensively for images of Ardhanārīśvara, and I thank Mr. Murugesan for his help, Dr. Dennis Depommier, director of the Institute, and the staff for providing me with photos and copyright permissions to reproduce images of Ardhanārīśvara. John Hurst at the British Museum and Shaula Coyle at the Los Angeles County Museum of Art guided me through the procedures of copyrights and acquisitions and assisted me in acquiring images of Ardhanārīśvara that I published from their collections. Dirk Bakker also provided his beautiful photographs of Ardhanārīśvara that are reproduced here with his generous permission.

At SUNY Press, I must thank my editor, Nancy Ellegate, who supported this project from the very beginning, and the anonymous readers whose fair and helpful comments have become the inspiration for a revised approach. Thanks are due to Kelli Williams, production editor, and Michelle Lansing, copy editor, for all their efforts and assistance in the preparation of the manuscript.

On a personal note, my gratitude and love to friends and family who lived through and encouraged me in the process, particularly Anne Howard, Susie Kent, and my sister Gayle Shulman, who were there when it all began; Adele Cohl and Lori McGoran, who always asked about my work and cheered me on; Shelane Donoghue who inspired me; my dear friend Dr. Rolf Sattler, who challenged me to think deeply about nonduality; and my beautiful dog, Molly, who often heard me work out theories and ideas on our walks in the park. Finally, my inexpressible thanks to Shelley Cohl—without her love, support, and sacrifice, this book would not have been possible.

Introduction

The influence of Ardhanārīśvara on Indian society has never been thoroughly studied. My hope in this book is that a more sustained and focused examination of one of the most popular images of Śiva in various modalities of Indian culture and history will inspire other such investigations. The iconographical aspects of Ardhanārīśvara have attracted scholars to look at the image primarily in the context of Śaiva art (i.e., as an aspect of Śiva), and as an example of dual or composite iconographic representation in that field. So far, this does not address the complex theological, philosophical, and social implications inherent in the male and female aspects of the image, nor does it probe the psycho-spiritual context of the image in other contributing avenues of Indian tradition, such as *haṭhayoga* and *bhakti*.

The reason I have chosen to examine the androgynous motif of Ardhanārīśvara in various aspects of Indian tradition is that it has not been dealt with from this perspective in any other known text. Feminist theory has debated the assumptions of androgynous motifs in Western literary traditions, but aside from the aforementioned studies of Ardhanārīśvara in Śaiva art, and Wendy Doniger's phenomenological study of androgynes in Indian tradition and beyond, this image has yet to receive its recognition.

The fact that a feminist analysis is appropriate for this image is evident in the name given to the figure "Ardhanārīśvara." This epithet does not translate as "half-man, half-woman," as Frederique Marglin (1989) suggests, but rather as the "lord who is half woman" (Marglin 1989, 216). This immediately suggests a gender hierarchy in the sense that the status of the male Śiva half, is privileged by the title *"īśvara"* (god, lord, master), whereas the female Pārvatī half with whom Śiva shares his body, is simply designated by *"nārī"* (woman). In other words, the name does not convey an equivalent status for both halves.

The time has come for a careful study of the complex signs of gender proposed by a dual image of the transcendent. Although in some instances the image has been used to promote the notion of women's equality, it is necessary to look at the specific ways in which male and female have been constructed and defined according to this motif in Indian tradition to see if in fact the image is a positive, emancipatory ideal for women, and for men for that matter. To this end, we will look at four specific avenues of conceptual representation of Ardhanārīśvara. The significance of such models will become evidently clear when we begin to recognize that they constellate to form clusters of received knowledge or homologous structures of parallel significance in Indian tradition.

To study the image of Ardhanārīśvara is to look into the way Indian tradition considers gender. Hence, one task of this book is in a sense to see how "woman" and "man" are made. For it is undoubtedly human society that constructs and converts its symbols into reality through the multivalent avenues of human expression, ancient and contemporary. In this sense, the mythology of the divine androgyne Ardhanārīśvara falls into four distinct areas of Indian culture, namely, iconography, *haṭhayoga*, *bhakti* (devotional) poetry, and mythology.

As well, we see in Western feminist theories that the varied mythology of the androgyne that has been inscribed in philosophy, theology, psychology, and literature has typically been understood as a positive symbol of plenitude and wholeness from a male-identified perspective. However, the more recent debate on androgyny since its use in first-wave feminism by authors valorizing the writings of Virginia Woolf stakes out a very different position with regard to the usefulness of the image of the androgyne for the contemporary feminist concerns of women. As such, this debate informs our study of Ardhanārīśvara insofar as it enables a dialogical approach between East and West.

What becomes significant in the Western context is that foremost among the uses of the androgyne motif is its application to a primarily male model that desires primal wholeness, but in many Western literary encounters with this motif, we find that such a "fictional" or "dreamlike" vision unfolds into an ultimate desire for death. In other words, the absorption of the female into the male in the end leads to the male subject's own death or annihilation. However, in Indian accounts of this narrative, the ideas of death and immortality take on entirely new cultural meanings and are valorized through the praxis-oriented technologies of *haṭhayoga*. The radical duality of the world order and its attendant reality of suffering, separateness and rebirth necessitate a programmatic strategy for overcoming and dislodging such cyclical subjectivities of human becoming and point the way to a significantly more peaceful strategy for wholeness and transcendence in which the androgyne motif, exemplified by Ardhanārīśvara, participates. In such a state of consciousness the radical duality of binary thinking, and the pain engendered by it, collapses in successively absorptive stages until complete and total unity is achieved by the self. Such a dance of transformation is performed not only by Śiva Naṭarāja, also referred to in our study as Ardhanārīnaṭeśvara, but by each and every enlightened consciousness. The entrance into difference with the motif of splitting or separation that we see over and over again in Indian mythology is reversed by the advanced practitioners of *yoga* in an attempt to recover the perfect symmetry of transcendence portrayed in form by the figure of Ardhanārīśvara.

This is why a study of this type is so vital. It is precisely this utopian dream of perfect symmetry that is being analysed. The theoretical (and theological) model of perfect symmetry that Ardhanārīśvara represents in Indian tradition depends largely upon sustained models of essentialized categories of male and female in order for the social aspect (*dvaita*) of the image to succeed. However, the crucial paradox underlying this immensely important figure is its inclusion of the disruption of stable categories of gender and difference at all relative levels in the transcendental realization of *advaita*. That is the message that this image ultimately delivers. The fusion of masculine and feminine in the androgynous "dream" or "fiction" represented by Ardhanārīśvara is precisely that, a partial attainment (*sabīja samādhi*) *en route* to transcendence, where all forms ultimately collapse and erode in the mystery and fluidity of organic singularity.

For this reason, where Western models of androgyny often have demonstrated an unachievable promise or hope of fusion and wholeness, Indian models of sacred androgyny not only suggest that they are the "real" and all else is "illusion," indeed, they rely on such classical structures as constitutive of reality, truth, knowledge, and enlightenment. Duality and its attendant models are in turn considered "unreal," "ignorance," and they suggest a "relative," "conditioned," or "conventional" understanding at best. Transcendence of form (*rūpa*) by the enlightened practitioner implies intuitive and experiential knowledge of the successive stages of Ardhanārīśvara through the psycho-spiritual technologies of *haṭhayoga* praxis.

In three chapters of this book I examine the image of Ardhanārīśvara and interpretations of the image as found in Indian iconography, *haṭhayoga* theory, and *bhakti* poetry. In chapter 1, I begin with an analysis of the traditional diagnostic features of Ardhanārīśvara as discerned in the pan-Indian tradition of temple *mūrtis* and sacred canons of Indian art from Nepal to Tamil Nadu. I develop a typology of the image, and I illuminate gender issues in the images various iconographical motifs.

A feminist critique of this image is necessary given the gender implications of several of its diagnostic features and the lack of feminist analysis of the image to date in sources on Indian iconography. No doubt, dual deities are prevalent in Indian tradition dating as far back as the Ṛg Veda. A reworking of this dual deity motif is found in the *puruṣa-prakṛti* imagery of Sāṃkhya-Yoga, the Vedāntic notion of *ātman-māyā*, and even Buddhist notions of *samsāra-nirvāṇa*. As early as the Kuṣāṇa period, Ardhanārīśvara appears as the quintessential Śaiva expression of this motif in iconographic form, well before variations develop in the *purāṇas*.

In chapter 2, I look at the image of Ardhanārīśvara as a paradigm of *haṭhayoga* realization. I explain how the image is portrayed in *haṭhayoga* theory and show that the image continually draws upon homologous patterns in Indian thought. I also propose the idea that the professional practitioner of *haṭhayoga* experiences this deity as a process that moves through three successive stages from gross to most subtle, culminating in the *sahasrāra cakra* in the crown region of the head, even though the *cakra* theories of *haṭhayoga* put forth, for instance, by Western scholars of *yoga* as early as Arthur Avalon (1972), have situated the image of Ardhanārīśvara in the *viśūddha cakra* only. However, in the third stage, the practitioner's experience of Ardhanār-īśvara as "self" transcends form (*arūpa*).

In *haṭhayoga*, divine reality is polarized into male and female. From this paradigm, (i.e. Ardhanārīśvara), the practitioner learns the means (*upāya*) to enlightenment. By cultivating or generating the transcendental aspects of the androgynous divine, the relative reality of being gradually collapses, and along with this go any indications of duality, inequality, hierarchy, caste, class, ego, and so on. Since such theoretical discourse signifies "the true nature of reality" for the tradition and its adept practitioners, the implications of this ideology in the broader discourse on androgyny and gender need to be made clear. Indeed, the image of Ardhanārīśvara in Indian *haṭhayoga* points to a doctrine of ultimate singularity (*advaita*) that is impossible to capture in language and theory, and the subtle markings of subjectivity are not only disrupted by it, but also heralded.

In chapter 3, I look at the image of Ardhanārīśvara in Śaiva *bhakti*, or devotional poetry. I provide a translation and an analysis of the *Ardhanārīnaṭeśvara stotra* as a classic example of devotional iconography that evokes the image of the divine androgyne and sculpts the half-female, half-male form through the medium of metaphor and simile. In *haṭhayoga*, god/dess is polarized into the divine active *(śakti)* and divine inactive *(śiva)*, and this is abundantly clear in their respective portraits in the *stotra* tradition, as the dance of Ardhanārīnaṭeśvara reveals.

In chapter 4, I situate two important studies of androgyny in a dialogical framework as I examine the concept from a feminist perspective, East and West. In particular, I look at how disparate culturally mediated theories/traditions can inform each other and raise some questions about their own use of the symbol.

In chapter 5, I look at the female/Pārvatī/Śakti half of the image of Ardhanārīśvara and the ambivalent messages offered. As I mentioned, god is polarized into the divine feminine or active pole, Śakti, alongside the divine masculine or inactive pole, Śiva. Śakti is inherent in god; just as Śiva is inherent in god, they are inseparable, like moon and moonlight. But what implications does this have for the concerns of Indian feminism? Is this imagery positive from the perspective of "real" women, or does it in some way necessitate subordination? Clearly, the theological motif of androgyny refracts the cultural norms of men and women and often presumes a hierarchical and patriarchal structure. However, there are ways to read the symbol of the divine androgyne that show alternate and countervailing interpretations. For this reason, I provide a discussion of Śakti as it has been seen at varying times, unmasking the culturally mediated interpretation of theological categories and their shifting meanings, as well as several instances of reversed iconography that attest to this reading in the temples of South India.

Sacred iconography presents the theological understanding of the unfolding of the divine in human reality. The iconography of Ardhanārīśvara represents the gross or most obvious physical form of the deity (*pratimā, mūrti, rūpa*) only, for ultimately Śiva-Śakti has no form. In the final process of *layayoga* the advanced practitioner sees that there is no god and no goddess (i.e., no form, *arūpa, śūnya*). Hence, Ardhanārīśvara as *rūpa* attempts to articulate a potential balance in the world of form between *prakṛti/śakti* relative to *puruṣa/śiva*. The difficulty from a feminist perspective is that this balance is not necessarily rendered as social equality between masculine and feminine, even though *prakṛti* and *puruṣa* have come to signify male and female in Indian thought. It is this very ambivalence that is the subject of our study.

Chapter 1

Ardhanārīśvara in Indian Iconography

> Without a form, how can God be meditated upon? If (He is) without any form, where will the mind fix itself? When there is nothing for the mind to attach itself to, it will slip away from meditation or will glide into a state of slumber. Therefore the wise will meditate on some form, remembering, however, that the form is a superimposition and not a reality.
>
> —*Viṣṇu Saṃhitā*

Introduction

This chapter is particularly concerned with an analysis of the *mūrti* (image) and *rūpa* (form) of Ardhanārīśvara[1] in the canons of Indian iconography and point outs, through various emblems and traditional ornamentation, the gender implications of the diagnostic features used by the Indian *śilpins* of the past and present.[2] There are, to date, no systematic studies dealing with the image of Ardhanārīśvara as such, therefore, my data must be collected from scattered sources. This chapter draws primarily upon the principal canons of Indian iconography, the substantial canonical commentaries of Ardhanārīśvara in Indian iconography by art historians such as T. A. Gopinatha Rao (1967), J. N. Banerjea (1956), M. E. Adiceam (1967), and two recent studies of Ardhanārīśvara by Raju Kalidos (1993) and Neeta Yadav (2000), since they provide the most thorough accounts of the image in the context of sacred art. I also use the theories of Doris Meth Srinivasan and her unparalleled insights into Śaiva art to locate Ardhanārīśvara within the broader category of Śiva *mūrtis*. To conclude, I offer an iconographical analysis of seventeen illustrations of the image of Ardhanārīśvara. Here I examine how applications of and commentaries on the image have traditionally portrayed the gendered diagnostic features of the divine androgyne. In the context of this interpretive investigation, I provide information that will help place the image in its historical context as well as outline the details of the critical feminist theory used throughout this analysis.

General Background Information

In Indian tradition, Ardhanārīśvara reveals a seemingly perfect, indissoluble unity, complete in himself/herself. The theological and philosophical presuppositions of Śaivism and the metaphysical underpinnings of the image in that tradition celebrate the ultimate singularity and nonduality of Śiva and Śakti in the form and figure of Ardhanārīśvara. For the precise purpose of examining the iconography of Ardhanārīśvara, it is necessary here to briefly discuss some of the theoretical and speculative ideas that lie behind the image, in particular, the relationship between form (*rūpa*) and formlessness (*arūpa*) in Indian art. The main reason for this, as contemporary art historian Vidya Dehejia (1997) reveals, lies in the fact that "so much of Indian sculpture was produced in order to embellish a sacred scripture" (Dehejia 1997: 1).

One crucial element in discerning the interrelationship between transcendence and materiality in Śaivism lies in an unfolding tripartite structure that, according to Srinivasan, explains in theological terms how the formless (*niṣkala, arūpa, aliṅga*) deity manifests through a progressive, three-stage process into material form (*sakala, rūpa, liṅga*), or *mūrti*. The *niṣkala-sakala* form of Śiva, or the subtle form of god known as *liṅga* or Sadāśiva, lies between the *arūpa* and *rūpa* stages.[3] This aniconic image has been referred to more recently in Indian iconography as *yoni-liṅga* and points to the highest expression of the unmanifest whose ultimate and singular essence is considered beyond attributes (*guṇas*), such as time (*kalā*), space (*ākāśa*), action (*karma*), and name and form (*nama-rūpa*) and, as we will show, it is similar to the iconic form of Ardhanārīśvara, particularly in the *haṭhayoga* tradition.

Śaivism (referred to here as an umbrella term pertaining to a constellation of somewhat diverse theological teachings) constructs and incorporates parallel iconographical themes and mythological narratives to represent underlying theological doctrines and beliefs.[4] According to Srinivasan, Parabrahman or Paraśiva are names given to the formless or unmanifest aspect (*brahman, niṣkala, arūpa, aliṅga*) in an unfolding tripartite system. Maheśvara identifies the fully manifest form (*sakala, rūpa, mūrti*),[5] and Sadāśiva (*niṣkala-sakala, arūpa-rūpa, mukhaliṅga*) lies in the intermediary space arising between the two, as the creative aspect of the emerging transcendent begins to manifest parts or form (*kalā, rūpa*).[6] When expressed in theological and iconographical terms, the evolutionary descent of the transcendent proceeds from the formless Paraśiva (*niṣkala* or theological equivalent of Brahman) and moves toward full manifestation (*sakala, mūrti, rūpa*) in the form of Maheśa by way of Sadāśiva (*sakala-niṣkala*). This sequential, triadic assumption of form or *mūrti* is refracted not only through the lens of Śaivite theology, but also through Indian iconography. In this sense, the fully materialized *rūpa* of Paraśiva is Maheśvara, whereas Sadāśiva designates "the godhead on the way to full manifestation" (Srinivasan 1990, 108–10; 1987, 338; 1997, 272).

The positioning of Ardhanārīśvara in this threefold schema is not addressed explicitly by Srinivasan, nonetheless, an iconographic and a theological patternization is set out that can be applied to our specific analysis by articulating this basic structure. In terms of the canons of Indian iconography, Ardhanārīśvara is recognized as a composite, fully manifest, anthropomorphic form of Paraśiva emerging, similar to Maheśvara, in the third stage of the evolutionary descent. As such, the *rūpa* of Ardhanārīśvara as fully manifest and human bears structural and status equivalency with Maheśvara in visual and iconographic terms as well as in aspects of his/her basic theological presuppositions.

It also must be registered that although Ardhanārīśvara and Maheśvara often display a different theological message in visual terms from Sadāśiva, all three bear close resemblance with one another in terms of theological categorization and dual diagnostic attributes. When viewed in this context, Ardhanārīśvara (alongside Paraśiva, Sadāśiva, and Maheśvara) is a vital part of a progressive evolutionary triptych or a visual, iconographic unfolding of the formless Brahman and, as such, is closely aligned with Maheśvara. Similarly, the equivalent functionary role of Maheśvara and Ardhanārīśvara as overseers of the creation, maintenance, and destruction of the world is evident in their respective mythic narratives and partial female natures. Consequently, iconographic texts such as the *Viṣṇudharmottara* situate the formulae for maintaining the diagnostic accuracy of Ardhanārīśvara *mūrtis* within the broader categorization of Maheśvara. Stories from the Śaiva *purāṇas* explain that Ardhanārīśvara appeared when Brahmā meditated on the form of Maheśvara. However, Ardhanārīśvara also is referred to as the Īśana form of Sadāśiva, and it is not uncommon to find parallel references to Ardhanārīśvara as Sadāśiva in *haṭhayoga* and iconographic sources. From these varied accounts, we can conclude that

Ardhanārīśvara as an iconic *niṣkala-sakala* form bears a subtle resemblance to, and can be closely aligned with, Sadāśiva. Ardhanārīśvara also displays a distinct resemblance to Maheśvara, particularly in functionary roles.

If one explicit purpose of Śiva *mūrtis* is indeed symbolic representation and embellishment of theological norms and doctrines, as Dehejia suggests, then it also is on these grounds that images of Ardhanārīśvara must be understood and assessed. Briefly, a theological message of cosmogonic and cosmological speculation is conveyed by the *mūrti* of Ardhanārīśvara. That is, Ardhanārīśvara, as found in myth and symbol, explains the biological fact of human origin. Through the form of Ardhanārīśvara, Śaiva iconography illustrates that as the ineffable void (*śūnyātā, brahman*) proceeds from "transcendence to materiality" (to borrow a phrase from Srinivasan), or from formlessness to form, the dual or composite aspect of deity becomes ever apparent in his/her symbolic concretization of reality. Hence, we find not only a male but also a female nature in the theistic equivalent of Paraśiva/Brahman that comprises no less and no more than half of the anthropomorphic form (*mūrti, rūpa*) of Ardhanārīśvara. As such, Śiva is described and portrayed in his/her explicit anthropomorphic androgynous aspect as the "god who is half woman." This bipolar representation provides the internal coherence necessary to partake of the primordial role and function of cosmogony.

This is a significant point that Nikky-Guninder Kaur Singh (1993) raises in her investigation of the essential role that the feminine aspect of the transcendent plays in Sikh religion. Indian tradition, which includes among its diverse theological expressions a bipolar god/dess, offers women and men images of divine reality that orthodox, male, monotheistic traditions do not. Critical issues pertaining to the maleness of god and the pervasive and exclusive use of male god language in Judeo-Christian religions seriously affect Western theologians' feminist sensibilities. Masculine identity as the presiding singular reference to ultimate reality denies for women a sacred feminine norm or an equivalent. Jewish and Christian feminist theologians, such as Judith Plaskow (1991), Rosemary Radford Reuther (1983), and Elisabeth Schussler Fiorenza (1994), argue that the invisibility of a countervailing feminine divine undermines women's equal representation and participation in society and divinely sanctions the invisibility and exclusion of women as equals in religious community and family life. Recognition of a bipolar god/dess in Indian tradition offers an alternative and inclusive image of divinity. However, the question as to whether this inclusion actually affects the status of "real" women remains to be seen.

Iconography also functions in Indian tradition as a meditational and devotional aid (*dhyānamūrti*) for worshippers and, consequently, it must be understood as a dynamic and an integral part of the pan-Indian traditions of *yoga* and *bhakti*. This first chapter addresses the idea of the progression of the sacred from transcendence to materiality in iconographical terms. This direction or movement toward the assumption of form is precisely what differentiates god/dess from human (Srinivasan 1997, 142). Srinivasan writes:

> [T]he predominant movement of god's unfolding is downward, even though life as we know it grows upward. A baby grows tall. Grasses and flowers shoot up. A tree climbs high. . . . . Trees, like longings, originate from earth. Not so does god. His otherness is conveyed in many ways. One is his downward progression from transcendency to materiality. (Srinivasan 1997, 142)

For humans, however, the process is reversed. When we probe the image of Ardhanārīśvara in *haṭhayoga* theory in a later chapter, the experience of the adept becomes the focal point, as she/he becomes an embodied form of Ardhanārīśvara through the reversal process of *sādhana* (spiritual praxis). This, in turn, effects a dynamic inversion of the triarchic evolutes on the part of the living *yogin/ī*, or a return of the *yogin/ī's* consciousness to an unmanifest state (*laya*) by recognizing one's essential identity with Ardhanārīśvara. In this sense, Ardhanārīśvara presents a map or meditational aid for the *yogin/ī*. The *yogin/ī* as *rūpa* undergoes a process of return or involution (*nivṛtti*) in which manifestation or evolution reverses, thereby leading the adept practitioner to a state of transcendence called Śivatva, or the equivalent of the *niṣkala* aspect of Śiva. It is in this particular application that Indian iconography functions alongside and parallels other ritual technology and spiritual practices such as *mantra, pūjā, yantra,* chanting, *āsana* (postures), *mudrā, prāṇāyāma,* and so on to effect an experience of perfect union (*yoga siddhi*).

Ardhanārīśvara and Indian Iconography

It is important to understand what the canons of Indian iconography tell us about the broad-ranging body of traditional emblematic features of the androgynous god/dess before we consider particular illustrations of Ardhanārīśvara from various Indian sites. In general, sources of Indian iconography include archaeological, epigraphical, and numismatic data, as well as diverse literary material. The latter is particularly abundant and usually draws its descriptions from three main Sanskritic sources: *śilpaśāstras, purāṇas,* and *āgamas*. Kalidos (1993) observes that texts of this latter type are usually "committed to a particular cause, i.e., the delineation of an iconographical theme, and thus present stereotyped and cooked-up material rather than account for a narrative of the quasi-historical type" (Kalidos 1993, 102). This being the case, most of the textual iconographic descriptions of Ardhanārīśvara appear in the literature as so-called recipes and are rather formulaic in their orientation. Our primary purpose is to cite from a few sources that specifically mention Ardhanārīśvara to demonstrate the formulaic methods used to convey the distinctive diagnostic features of the image across time and place and to develop a clear typology of the diagnostic language used to render and conceptualize a coherent tradition and formal patternization of Ardhanārīśvara images. Hence, this section draws primarily on the cursory descriptions offered by traditional canons of Indian iconography, studies by Rao (1968) and Adiceam (1967), and the empirical data of my own field research into pan-Indian Ardhanārīśvara images to create an overall typology of the stylistic discourse that clearly depicts recurrent and continuous iconographic patterns of identification often shared across regions.

A broadly conceived analysis of the diagnostic features of Ardhanārīśvara images indicates that the standard bipolar human body of the deity (*dehārdhavibhāgina*) is differentiated along the traditional central vertical axis (*brahmasūtra*)[7] into male and female, as the name Ardhanārīśvara (the Lord who is half woman) suggests. As stated earlier, the right half of the image is male, and the left half of the image is female. From top to bottom, the image usually is depicted with one face, though some variations can be seen. The male right half can display the following diagnostic features: a *jaṭāmākuṭa,* sometimes shown ornamented with snakes, crescent moon, the goddess Gaṅgā, and/or jewels; smaller right eye; half moustache; and male physique, including flat male chest, broad right shoulder, wider waist, and more massive thigh.

Three possible earring styles can be discerned on the right/male side, namely, *nakra-kuṇḍala* (common), *sarpa-kuṇḍala,* or an ordinary *kuṇḍala,* whereas a female-style earring called *vāḷikā* is worn in the left ear (Rao 1968, 324). The *Vāstuśāstras* also refer to *patra kuṇḍala* and *śankha patra kuṇḍala,* worn by Umā, and a fourth style, *ratna kuṇḍala,* worn by Śiva. Dissimilar earrings are one of the most noticeable diagnostic emblems demarcating the dual male and female nature of the deity and can be discerned on Śiva *mūrtis* such as Naṭarāja, Caturmukhaliṅga, and so on. In fact, this significant identifying feature becomes one of the primary means of identification for busts of Ardhanārīśvara (see Figure 1.2).

One distinct diagnostic emblem found specifically on North Indian images of Ardhanārīśvara is the half *ūrdhvareta* (ithyphallic) feature on the right male side. South Indian Ardhanārīśvara images do not bear this marking. Perhaps this is the reason Rao does not account for it in his commentary, which considers primarily South Indian sources. Furthermore, the entire right/male side must be ornamented with the requisite and customary accessories suitable for a male/Śiva image. These include draped garments (e.g., *dhotī*) made of silk (*kauśeya*), cotton (*kārpāsa*), or tiger skin usually covering the body from the waist to the knees, *mekhala* (belts), jewelry, and so on. However, it also is important to note that clothing (*vastra*) is not always discernible on sculptural images from early periods, as we often encounter many that are damaged. In addition, two unusual features mentioned in the canons of Indian iconography suggest that the right/male side should be covered with ashes, and the *rudra* aspect, which is depicted as red in color, could be evident. Other right-side colorations include gold or coral, however, in actuality, these features are rarely encountered.

Several diagnostic features are shared jointly by the male and female sides. They include navel,[8] ornaments on the chest, wrists (*kankana*), upper forearms (*keyūra*) and ankles (*bhujangavalaya* on right side), neck pieces (*hāras*), rings, and belts (*mekhala*). A shared elliptical-shaped halo (*prabhamaṇḍala, prabhavali*) often illuminates the entire deity from behind the head, though the shape of the right and left halves may vary. The sacred thread (*yajñopavīta*) worn by the *dvijātis* (twice born) appears on deities from the Gupta period onward and is sometimes observed on Ardhanārīśvara in the form of a serpent (*nāga yajñopavīta*) crossing the upper torso of both the male and female sides of the deity. When indicated, the third eye (*trinetra*) of Ardhanārīśvara is constructed in several ways. It is shown as either a full or half eye situated slightly to the right side on the forehead on the male half, as a full third eye directly in the middle of the forehead and shared by both the male and female sides, or as a half third eye directly in the middle of the forehead above or below the female dot (*bindu, tilaka*). The entire body stands variously in *tribhaṅga* pose, that is, there are three bends, in the head (it leans to the left), torso (it leans to the right), and right leg (emphasizing the fuller left hip), or in *sthanamudrā* (straight posture), sometimes indicated on a pedesal, such as a *padmāsana* (lotus seat). The latter stance also is called *samapāda*. Seated images of Ardhanārīśvara are not as common in the canons of Indian iconography but do have a significant representation nonetheless.

An important feature of any Ardhanārīśvara image, and one that we will consider in more detail further on, is the number of arms. Typically, the deity is figured with either two, four, or three arms. As we will see, two-armed Ardhanārīśvara images were the earliest representations. In this case, the deity holds the right male hand in *abhaya mudrā* (sign or gesture of reassurance and fearlessness), and the left female hand holds a mirror (*darpaṇa*) or *nīlotpala* (flower). If there are four arms, probably a later development, they are usually divided at the elbows, the front right hand is held in *abhaya mudrā,* and the rear right hand holds the *paraśu* or *triśūla*. We also witness canonical variations on the right male side, such as *varada mudrā, ṭaṅka, akṣamālā* (rosary), *daṇḍa, khaḍga* (sword), *khatvaṅga* (club), *vajra* (thunderbolt), *kapāla* (skull), and *pāśa* or *aṅkuśa* (noose), sometimes in the form of a snake. References to six or more armed images are rare but can be found in South Indian sources.

Although some *purāṇic* and iconographical accounts, such as the *Viṣṇudharmottara,* refer variously to Umā, Śivā, or Gaurī, the left female side is commonly identified as Pārvatī and is distinguished by what I call "female indicators." Beginning with the top of the head, the female/left/Pārvatī side of the image shows a *karaṇḍa makuṭa* or *dhamilla* (a braided hairstyle or bun, sometimes laden with jewels and ornamentation).[9] Earlier we mentioned that on the left/female side of the forehead is a half *tilaka* or dot (*bindu*) corresponding to the half third eye on the male side. The *bindu* also can be placed in the center of the forehead above or below the male third eye, or a third variation is no *bindu* at all but rather a shared third eye centrally situated in the middle of the forehead. In rare instances, the *bindu* is strategically placed in the center as the only forehead marking (see Figure 1.8). The left eye, unlike the one on the right, can be larger, and it is typically outlined with collyrium. A female-style earring, as mentioned above, is worn in the left ear. When color is indicated, the left half of the body is covered either in saffron or is parrot-green, though this diagnostic emblem is seldom employed in practice. Rarely do we notice nose ornamentation (*vesara*) on the female side of early images of Ardhanārīśvara, as this seems to be a later custom.

The central feature of the left/female half is a woman's breast that is characteristically round and well developed. The waist is usually smaller and the hip fuller than the corresponding male half. The ornamentation identifying the female half includes earrings, jeweled *hāras,* draped silk clothing to the ankles, saffron body powder, anklets, bracelets, belts, necklaces, and red lac (henna) coloring on the left foot or hand. Depending on whether the image has four arms or two, the following variations are seen. On later four-armed images of Ardhanārīśvara, one left arm is bent and rests on Śiva's vehicle Nandin, and/or is held in *kaṭaka mudrā*. The other left hand typically holds a *darpaṇa* (mirror) or a *nīlotpala* (lotus flower or *puṣpa,* sometimes hanging at her side). Alternatively, the female left hand carries a *kamaṇḍalu* (waterpot), a *vīṇā,* a *ḍamaru* (drum), or a small parrot perches on the left wrist. On three-armed images of Ardhanārīśvara, the right male side always has two arms, whereas the female side has only one. Both are shown with variations of the attributes outlined above.

Mudrās in Indian art are suggestive of the states of consciousness or the specific psychology, character, or emotion of a given deity (*bhava*) and find corresponding expression in the traditions of Bharata's *Naṭyaśāstras*.[10] In this context, *mudrās* are symbolic gestures that crystallize or convey a particular underlying sentiment. To understand this codified system of hand gestures, one requires technical background not only in Indian religion but in Indian classical dance as well. While such a reading is well beyond the limits of this particular work, the overall significance of *mudrās* in Indian iconography is that they give voice to seemingly silent deities. Hence, what is of import to this particular analysis is to identify the symbolic voice encoded in the specific hand gestures that we see on Ardhanārīśvara images in Indian tradition.

The *Vastuśāstras* enumerate three varieties of not less than fifty-six *hastas* or *mudrās* in all. However, the principal *mudrās* pertaining particularly to the right male side of Ardhanārīśvara are *abhaya* (variously referred to as *śāntida,* and *varada), cinmudrā,* and *kaṭyavalambita hasta.* In *abhaya mudrā* the right male hand of Ardhanārīśvara is shown with the palm turned upward facing the devotee, and fingers straight, in a gesture of fearlessness and reassurance. This hand gesture is quite common, and we also see it on well-known Kuṣāṇa images of Śākyamuni Buddha. According to Zvelebil (1985), it is the right hand gesture "*par excellence*" (Zvelebil 1985, 35). The *varada mudrā* elicits a meaning similar to *abhaya mudrā,* and is alternately used. It implies the bestowal of favors or boons onto the devotee by the deity. Characteristic of this *mudrā,* the hand faces downward with palm turned toward the devotee, and fingers are held straight. *Cinmudrā* is similar, but in this *mudrā* the hand is held closer to the right chest, and the thumb and forefinger touch. In some examples, we see the left female hand of Pārvatī in *kaṭyavalambita* or *katisamsthita hasta* or *mudrā* (posture of ease). In this pose, the left hand is held by the side of the body resting on the leg or thigh. Just as Zvelebil referred to *abhaya* as the *mudrā par excellence,* Coomaraswamy acknowledges *katisamsthita mudrā* as the "most excellent" *mudrā* in ancient and medieval India (Coomaraswamy, cited in Shukla 1996, 125). However, Coomaraswamy makes no specific reference here to images of Ardhanārīśvara.

Embodied deities also appear in various postures (*sthānas, āsanas*). Nine principal postures are enumerated in the *Viṣṇudharmottara*. Generally, Ardhanārīśvara can be seen standing in three different poses, technically referred to as *samapāda, ardhasamapāda,* and *tribhaṅga*.[11] One description of *tribhaṅga* offered by A. N. Tagore specifies that the *brahmasūtra* or medial axis passes through the left or right pupil, the midsection of the chest, the navel, and follows downward to the heels (Tagore, cited in Shukla 1996, 132). In addition, there are three bends in the body, in the hips, shoulders, and head (hence, the term *tribhaṅga*, meaning three bends). This implies that the head leans either to the right or left. The alternative postures *samapāda* and *ardhansamapāda* suggest balance, symmetry, and equipoise in the body, as the two halves are divided equally along the *brahmasūtra* from the navel to the crown of the head. The weight and proportions of the body are distributed on the left and right sides equally, and there are no bends whatsoever in the body to differentiate the rounded volumes of the female form or shape. We find this posture on early Indian coins, seals, and some four-armed anthropomorphic images of Ardhanārīśvara. *Tribhaṅga* pose, according to Banerjea, is less common than *samapāda*, though our findings suggest that it is actually quite common, because *tribhaṅga* is the typical posture for female deities, hence, this stance is depicted on the female half as normative.

Iconographical Texts

Specific accounts of the formal diagnostic features of Ardhanārīśvara are given in the canons of Indian iconography. The *Viṣṇudharmottara* (eighth century), for instance, besides being the prominent treatise on the rules of *pratimālakṣaṇa*, contains references on *dharma*, medicine, dance, archery, astrology, astronomy, temple architecture, and the efficacy of *mantra* and, similar to other texts of this genre, provides only brief, formulaic descriptions of the rules of composition (*rūpa*). Structured in the form of a dialogue between the mythical King Vajra and the sage Mārkaṇḍeya, the *Viṣṇudharmottara* proclaims the greatness of Lord Viṣṇu and therefore belongs to the genre of Indian literature known as *upapurāṇas*. The third *khaṇḍa* on the ancient Indian arts of *pratimālakṣaṇa* is considered exemplary and is cited here specifically for this reason.

The *Viṣṇudharmottara* (*adhyāya* fifty-five in the third *khaṇḍa*) gives a simple description of the iconographic attributes of Ardhanārīśvara under the collective heading Mahādeva. It identifies Ardhanārīśvara as the Īśana form of the *pañcamukha* Mahādeva, and refers to him/her as Īśanarūpam, as well as the Gaurīśvara form of Śiva. In accordance with the typology of diagnostic features articulated above, it records that Īśana should have one face, two eyes, and four arms. The right half of the deity holds a rosary (*aksamālā*) and trident (*triśūla*) and is adorned with snakes (*nāgas*), the attributes of Śiva. The left half of the body is Śiva's consort (*vāma-ardhadayitātanuḥ*), who holds in her two hands a mirror (*darpaṇa*) and a lotus flower (*nīlotpala*). According to this account, the composite form represents the nonduality (*abhedābinnā*) of *prakṛti* and *puruṣa*.[13]

The *Viṣṇudharmottara*, like other canonical sources of Indian iconography, offers only a brief description of the image of Ardhanārīśvara. What is equally significant in the formulaic account given is a single reference to worship and meditation, suggesting that this is only possible when there is a form. In other words, Mārkaṇḍeya reiterates the reciprocal relationship, stressed at the outset of this chapter, between the form of the deity as portrayed in the *mūrti* and the higher realms of experience of the adept in meditation. Here, form is considered inspirational, and meditation on the *mūrti* brings the adept closer to an experience of nondual reality (i.e., Ardhanārīśvara, or *prakṛti-puruṣa).* As iconographical treatises characteristically suggest, religious images function primarily as aesthetic, devotional, and meditational aids, and as such they convey both an "extrinsic" theological doctrine and an "intrinsic" meaning for the devotee (Maxwell 1989, 3; Srinivasan 1997, 14; Shukla 1996, 45). In this latter sense, the *mūrti,* insofar as it follows time-honored prescriptive guidelines, functions as a map in the process of worship or *sādhana.*

It also seems that the *Viṣṇudharmottara* and other *śilpa* texts represent a compilation of recipes or formulas from older texts which, as Kalidos (1993) and Kramrisch (1924) show, have been lost to us by the ravages of time. The research that Bruno Dagens (1989) has conducted on the *Śaivāgamas* led him to conclude that Indian *śilpa* treatises[13] such as the *Mayamata* and the *Vāstuśāstras,* which deal primarily with Indian temple architecture and, to a lesser extent, Indian art, have for the most part extrapolated their formulaic descriptions from preexisting monuments (Dagens 1989, 151). In other words, Dagens argues that image precedes text, and this is clearly the status with images of Ardhaṇārīśvara. As such, the *śāstra* tradition for Dagens offers nothing more than a guide for the image maker and presents "a short, factual, and non-optional list of compulsory requirements needed to identify the god" (Dagens 1989, 153). Dahmen-Dallapiccola draws a similar analogy between the *śilpa* tradition and Western cookbooks that offer recipes for unexperienced cooks (Dahmen-Dallapiccola 1989, xv). According to these interpretations, the iconographic textual tradition is understood as subservient to practice. The *śilpin* has the liberty to modify the image according to his/her creative and aesthetic imagination, but only within the limits of tradition. As we will see in chapter 2, this is precisely what Eliade concludes in his comparative study of iconography and *yoga.*

Moreover, the prescriptive accounts of Ardhanārīśvara given in various iconographical texts preserve an orthodox tradition of *brahmanical* theology and philosophy. Ardhanārīśvara is generally listed as the *saumya* and *śanta* (benevolent and peaceful) forms of Śiva alongside other orthodox *brahmanical* Hindu images. That is, the *mūrti* portrays an ideal, or what R. N. Misra calls a "symbol-symbolized continuum" (Misra 1989, 175). Consequently, the *śilpaśāstras* are an integral link in a much larger cultural system of homologues or a network of correspondences in which the *mūrti* is understood as a "concretized" or "reconstituted" form of the unmanifest deity (ibid.). When viewed from this perspective, the *śilpaśāstras* function to uphold and embellish already existent theological and philosophical traditions through prescribed canonical forms. The significance of the *rūpa* seen in this context lies primarily in how it relates and/or is integrated with other forms of Indian religious practice, such as *yoga* technique, *dhyāna*, *pūjā*, and *darśana*.

Of course this raises several important issues regarding the purpose or function of iconography in India. Most icons are used primarily as objects of worship, and although the modes of practice vary to some extent throughout the subcontinent, the use of images is pan-Indian. The word "*pratimā*" has as its basic connotation the idea of "likeness" (Shukla 1996, 25). Bhattacharyya (1980) uses the term *echo* to convey the idea of symbolic representation of divine attributes. *Mūrti* reflects only the manifest aspect (*saguna, sakala*, etc.) of the deity, whereas *pratimā* refers to the actual living "likeness"of deity. This is clearly consistent with Srinivasan's theory of Saivite iconography, discussed earlier. The purpose of the canons of iconography, however, is simply to codify prescriptive formulae for maintaining a system of correct proportions and attributes of a particular *mūrti* for use in worship, whatever form that worship may take. Therefore, adherence to correct rules and practices of measurement and form, as the research of John Mosteller (1987, 1988) reveals, is central to effecting and maintaining the orthodox tradition of manifest sacred images particularly for the *brahmanical* elite. In this way, the precise implementation of a specified artistic tradition ensures continuity and the programmatic transmission of conventional form (*rūpa*) across time and place.

It is from this dynamic and varied *śilpa* tradition that our information on the prescriptive dimension of Ardhanārīśvara iconogrphy derives, at least in part. However, Maxwell (1989) warns us that applying *śāstric* iconographical passages to specific images is ultimately "doomed to failure," because in the final analysis, these texts are not the "key" to understanding the iconography (10). As I mentioned, Maxwell, like Dagens, Bose, and V. Dehejia, to mention only a few contemporary commentators on Indian iconography, see iconographical canons as being designed primarily to elaborate, preserve, and embellish convention and tradition rather than create it. Indeed, as Maxwell observes, "many of the most exciting and communicative examples of Indian art are far beyond the reach of seemingly precise *shastric* injunction" (Maxwell 1989, 11).[14] Some of the figures of Ardhanārīśvara that we will look at later in this chapter are certainly examples of inspired works of sacred art that reach well beyond formulaic design. One such example is the masterful tenth-century Chola bronze from Tiruvenkadu. The vibrant imagery in contemporary Indian poster art also maintains the basic codes of the diagnostic tradition, though it far exceeds its preserved vision. One explanation for this is that iconography primarily derives its aesthetic inspiration from the adept *yogins*, *yoginīs*, saints, and sages of Indian religions.[15]

Although the *śilpaśāstras* are relatively silent on the social function of art, they do provide cultural archetypes, or what Maxwell calls "inherited symbol clusters" of received "cultural intelligence" (Maxwell 1989, 11). It is in this sense that the image of Ardhanārīśvara must also be understood or assessed. Maxwell's point is important and will bear close reinvestigation as the feminist analysis of this study unfolds. For now, it is clear that instructions regarding *śāstric* precepts originate from *brahmanical* sources that not only codify the iconographical tradition but also legitimate it. Maxwell is arguing this when he writes:

> If we rely exclusively upon surviving *shilpashastric* texts to interpret Indian art, we will never understand it, since these texts are manifestly those of a small group composed not of artists but of their social superiors, the priestly gaurdians of cultural tradition. (Maxwell 1989, 15)

In other words, the dominant social class preserves the normative way to perceive a deity through *śāstric* iconographical rules and encoded traditions.

Still, Maxwell recognizes the necessary and requisite spiritual practices on the part of the *śilpins* to adeptly execute the empirical and aesthetic form that the deity assumes. For this reason, he urges the art historian to regard the *śilpin* tradition, and its inherited body of literature, as a distinct category that may not only be "divorced from the realities of image making," but in a broader sense is actually "mediating," "legitimating," and "recording" their perceived norms and practices (Maxwell 1989: 12). It is in this sense that the *śilpa* tradition operates as a storehouse of legitimated cultural norms under the power and supervision of its priestly/male guardians (15).

What we can conclude from this in the final analysis is that the *śilpa* tradition indicates and records the traditional norms as put forth by the male elite for maintaining the so-called perceived integrity of the image across time and place. Sheldon Pollock (1989) provides corroborating evidence of this and argues that the *śāstric* tradition in India typifies the "desire to codify" and "textualize" the iconographic tradition (15).

The *brahmanical* tradition extends rules to incorporate all domains of human activity and, in its overall purpose, he claims, the *śāstras* teach people typically "what they should and should not do" (18–19). In other words, they impute prescribed "human" and "divine" moral imperatives (18). This does not, however, discount the skill and multiple talents[16] required by the *śilpins* to produce Indian works of sacred art, nor compromise their significant role as aesthetic visionaries articulating the symbolic forms that eventually become the form and substance of the codified *śilpa* tradition.

With this view clearly in mind, we can look at a few samples of some of the formulaic descriptions of Ardhanārīśvara found in Indian iconographical works. These so-called recipes are consistent with the typology discussed earlier and are in keeping with the *brahmanical* codified tradition of the *śilpaśāstras*, though we do notice some variation. The examples chosen represent both commonalities and differences in Ardhanārīśvara images across time and place.

1. A typical, albeit abbreviated, description of Ardhanārīśvara given in the *Mānasollāsa* states that the right male chest should be flat, and the left female side should indicate a female breast. The hairstyles should differ, with jatted locks on the right, and a female hairstyle or bun on the left. The forehead (of the single face) is marked by a half third eye on the left.

2. The *Skanda Purāṇa* does not add much to this overall description except to indicate, in an unusual reference, that the vehicles (*vāhanas*) of the fish (*matsya*) and bull (*vrisabha*) should be shown with their respective deities. As we will see in an examination of the images themselves, variations on the depiction of *vāhana* are evident, but nowhere have we found this particular formation executed.

3. The *Matsya Purāṇa*, which is one of the three oldest of the eighteen *mahāpurāṇas*, provides generous material on Indian iconography. Indeed, its elaboration on iconic representations is one of its special features. Iconographical details in the *Matsya Purāṇa* (MP) are treated in as many as ten chapters. Ardhanārīśvara is addressed specifically under the various anthropomorphic forms of Śiva, alongside other composite or so-called syncretic deities, such as Umā-Maheśvara and Hari-Hara (MP 260.2-11). Typically the prescription of Ardhanārīśvara in the *Matsya Purāṇa* proceeds along traditional lines. The deity is half male and half female. A partition is made in the hair, with the right male half indicated by plaited hair and crescent moon, and the left female half beautifully coiffed. This hairstyle differential indicates the bipolar division of male and fe-

male along the *brahmasūtra*. The forehead is centrally marked by a shared *tilaka*. The right male ear wears an earring made from the serpent Vasuki, whereas an ordinary earring marks the left female ear. The right hand carries a skull (*kapāla*) or a trident (*triśūla*) and the left a mirror (*darpaṇa*) or a lotus flower (*nīlotpala*). From this brief description, we can ascertain that the deity is featured with one face and two arms. The right male half of the body is covered in tiger skin and serpents and displays genitals, whereas the left female side of the body is fully covered in cloth and various jewels. There is an unusual reference to the right foot, which rests on a lotus, and the left foot dyed in red lac is adorned with jewels and women's ornaments.

4. The *Mayamata* (36.81b–89a) delineates Ardhanārīśvara as a three-armed figure, holding a *kapāla*, a *triśūla*, or an ax in the right hand and an *utpala* (flower) in the left. The iconographic description mentions that a rosary adorns the left side of the chest, and the *yajñopavita* is arranged on the right. The right arms are muscular, and the left side is marked by a female breast. The two-footed deity is standing on a *pīṭhapadma* (lotus pedestal). The right half is described as Īśa and the left as Umā. Three-armed figures raise important questions regarding gender and will be discussed in more detail further on in the chapter.

5. The *Śilparatnakośa* by Sthāpaka Nirañjana Mahāpātra is a seventeenth-century Orissan *vāstu* text (not to be confused with the South Indian *Śilparatna* of Śrīkumara). It focuses primarily on temple construction based on the underlying correspondence between the structure of the temple and the human form (*puruṣa*), that is, macrocosm and microcosm. Of particular interest to our study is that it provides programmatic evidence of the Mañjuśrī type of *yantra* temple construction deriving from the geometric substructure or diagramic form of the *śrīcakra* or *śrīyantra* (S. 363–96). Consequently, this *śilpa* treatise offers one of the few textual examples identifying the integration of the dynamic female principle, Śakti, and the static male principle, Śiva, to create a temple structure that parallels other iconic and aniconic idiomatic forms of Ardhanārīśvara.[17] The second *khaṇḍa* (part) of this technical treatise pertains specifically to temple sculpture or images (*pratimālakṣaṇa*) and mentions Hara-Pārvatī by name only. Iconographic details are not given (S. 316).

6. South Indian *śilpa* treatises, such as *Śilparatna* (1.3.57), *Śrītattvanidhi*, *Sārasvatīyacitrakarmaśāstra* (*Adhyāya* 23), *Kaśyapaśilaśāstra* (*Paṭlam* 72), *Agastyasakalādhikara* (*Adhyāya* 12), *Aṃśumad-bhedāgama*, and *Supraphedāgama*, to name just a few, present the *pratimālakṣaṇa* of

Ardhanārīśvara as contiguous with the overall typology mentioned earlier (Rao 1968; Kalidos 1993; Kandasamy 1994; Adiceam 1967; Yadav 2000). The body is divided along the right male left female axis. The right half has a broader shoulder and virile chest, and the left half has a voluptuous breast. In several descriptions, Nandin appears in front of the image or at the side of Umā/Pārvatī. The image stands primarily in the *tribhaṅga* posture. The Śiva half is described as white or ash colour, and the Pārvatī half is gold or saffron. Most texts describe the deity with two and a half eyes, that is, a half third eye is placed on the right Śiva side, complemented by a half *tilaka* on the Pārvatī side. Hairstyles and ornamentation is also consistent with other *śilpa* materials. We find the sacred thread is common to both sides, or the alternate feature of a garland of skulls on the right half, and a necklace of jewels around the left half of the neck. Śiva is also portrayed dressed in tiger or elephant skin, whereas Pārvatī is wearing beautiful clothes of the finest fabric. The *Āgamas* indicate a three-armed Ardhanārīśvara, with two arms on the right Śiva side. Other representations show two and four armed images as normative. There is an atypical reference to Śivārdhanārīśvara in his *rudra* form with eight to sixteen arms. Adiceam (1967) charts these characteristics in more detail in her typology of South Indian Ardhanārīvara images.

Ardhanārīśvara is just one example among many described briefly in the complex texts on the religious art of India, and an analysis of its textual and iconographic descriptions and terminology will yield, as Maxwell argues, only a partial understanding of the image itself. In other words, the descriptive language used in the *śāstras* to convey the seemingly singular and normative forms of the icon is only part of the making of an image. A stylistic analysis can only convey part of the message that is central to its success as a cultural iconic archetype. Overall, one sees in the *śāstric* tradition on Indian arts in general and the descriptions of Ardhanārīśvara in particular a formulaic discourse. The intent is probably one of legitimation, as well as preservation, embellishment, and perpetuation of tradition. However, it also must be remembered that the correlation between iconography and Indian culture is at once philosophical and theological, and this must be central to any explication or understanding of Indian images. The aphoristic and repetitious style of the *śilpa* texts enabled memorization and, as Dahmen-Dallapiccola (1989) shows, an easy way to pass on "the secrets of the trade" from one generation to the next (40). In this way, parallels are drawn with other Indian traditions that relied on memorization and oral transmission, including dance, and *yoga*. Clearly, Indian iconography is highly religious and aesthetic in nature, but this must not mystify the political and social forces also at work within the tradition. Perhaps this will be understood best in the analysis of specific examples of Ardhanārīśvara from various regions of the Indian subcontinent.

An Examination of Seventeen Images of Ardhanāriśvara

Before we begin in this section to look at specific images of Ardhanārīśvara it is important to understand the critical feminist theory that is being applied, and its appropriateness, given the ambivalence of the status of the female half and the close association of the feminine with nature in Indian tradition. The female-nature equation in Indian tradition does not necessarily imply the same ideological assumptions that it does in some Western feminisms. In the Indian context, the association of the feminine with nature is a sign of divinity and auspiciousness imbued with the qualities of fertility, prosperity, creativity, abundance, power, wisdom, and growth. The term *prakṛti,* which in essence has come to be synonymous with the feminine, has as its basic meaning "original or primary substance," "nature," "fundamental form," and so on, according to Monier Williams. By extension, it has come to represent the active or dynamic principle inherent in Indian cosmogony, as well as a female cosmological principle. As such, it is concerned with origins and associated with powerful images of motherhood, giving life, nourishment and nurturing, wealth, energy, purification, creativity, healing, and so on.

As well, the half-male, half-female image of Śiva under examination here belongs to a rich and stylized pantheon of Indian sacred art and, consequently, the function of this imagery must be thoroughly examined in its theological context. It is important, I think, to understand that in many cases religious imagery of the feminine is not necessarily an oppressive force in women's daily experience but rather a positive factor providing personal empowerment and agency. Nonetheless, the asymmetry of power and privilege at times embedded in the image must be acknowledged.

Consequently, I intend to use a feminist analysis at certain points to probe the gender issues and associations raised by the images of composite male-female form in various media of Indian tradition. Ardhanārīśvara, as I mentioned, is certainly informed by more than just the canons of Indian iconography. Although there are a variety of textual accounts of Ardhanārīśvara from *śilpaśastra, purāṇas, yoga* treatises, and *bhakti* literature, as well as Śaiva and Śakta theology, social convention, law codes, family values, and so on also inform the construction, interpretation, and application of the image at the level of "mortal" men and women. In other words, the visual legacy of Ardhanārīśvara deriving from varied sources constellates to establish the paradigmatic diagnostic features used to recognize, identify, and legitimate the image of Ardhanārīśvara in Indian tradition. Thus we find a range of types of Ardhanārīśvara images that also varies in the degree to which gender hierarchy is present, though I would agree with Kalidos (1993) that the overall impression of the referential typology in specific cultural terms places the advantage primarily, but not always, on the right-male side (bearing in mind that Ardhanārīśvara is an image of Śiva). Indeed, only when we look at a countervailing image (see Figure 5.1) referred to by Kalidos as Ardhanārī or Kaṇṇaki, as we will see in chapter 5, is the privileging reversed. As such, this marks a shift in the emphasis of worship from the god Śiva to the goddess Śakti-Devī and may or may not portray a corresponding shift in human gender relations.

Ardhanārīśvara is not "human" or "mortal." As an iconic form, Ardhanārīśvara is typically employed in a religious or sacred context. For this reason, it is important not to collapse this image into mundane or secular terms. Rather, it is instructive to perhaps consider this image as a description of divine reality operating in the human realm or, as Srinivasan outlines, as the third stage in a triadic process of divine emanation. This explains why we are concerned here both with the physicality of iconography as a sacred Indian art form, as this aspect of analysis is necessary to establish the typology of Ardhanārīśvara images, but also, and perhaps more importantly, how this image has been historically formulated to convey religious significance and to encode philosophical and metaphysical presuppositions in a language that is essentially gender identified. Overall, the pairing of Śiva and Śakti/Pārvatī in one androgynous form represents several ancient Indian cultural narratives all compressed into one highly nuanced image. Looking at the androgynous metaphor reminds us again and again that this is not in any strict sense a model for human physicality *per se* but rather that Ardhanārīśvara represents an archetype or a paradigm of sacred human knowledge. Moreover, Ardhanārīśvara offers an interpretation of our essential and subtle natures as defined by Indian *haṭhayoga* traditions. As such, Ardhanārīsvara encodes a description for attaining emancipation and representing divinity at the subtle level of metaphysics. In this way, the body of the divine androgyne Ardhanārīśvara becomes a symbolic cultural landscape, formulating, regulating, and legitimating religious and ideological presuppositions including gender, on the one hand, while also providing a diagnostic paradigm for mapping the transformation of human consciousness through the subtle conjunction of the male and female symbolic form, on the other hand. In other words, the image of Ardhanārīśvara enables the professional practitioner to approach more closely the *haṭhayoga* view of *sādhana* as a vehicle for self-knowledge (*ātmavidyā*, *jñāna*), but this must not idealize, romanticize, or mystify our attention to and critique of the implications that this motif has on human society.

As we have seen, it is clear that Indian sacred art is subject to regulation and control. Normative values, that is, male *brahmanical* values, are concretized by the *śilpins* in the artistic production of sacred images. With this in mind, it follows that not only are philosophical and theological doctrines encoded in the production of sacred images in India, but social relations and regulations also are most certainly codified and fixed in these standardized models of the bipolar sacred. For this reason, an interpretation of the divine androgyne that also is informed by feminist imperatives is long overdue. Hence, one purpose of this book is to identify and point out the gender implications in the representation of male and female and to question systematic, seemingly normative, and traditional typological patterns of subordination when and if they appear to place authority and privilege on the right-male side.

Although we will consider this in more detail later in chapter 5, in this section it is my overall contention that the image of the divine androgyne, like the earlier "pairs" of Vedic religion, portrays the female half in largely ambiguous ways. Śakti-Pārvatī is both goddess and woman (*nārī*) in her embodied or physical union with Śiva, though most often it is her womanliness that is emphasized in the iconography. For instance, the *śilpa* texts enumerate various emblems for mundane female figures who could best decorate sacred sites. Of these, three of the prerequisite diagnostic features assigned to ordinary women by the *śilpin* texts are canonically echoed as standard fare by the left-female/Pārvatī side of Ardhanārīśvara, including mirror, lotus flower, and anklets, and the fourth diagnostic feature, the parrot, is cited in texts and encountered in sculpture, though less often (Dehejia 1997, 19, 7–8). Yet Pārvatī, in her mythology and heroic imagery as the triumphant woman who is not only a goddess but the counterpart of Śiva, offers Indian society a powerful image, and it is here, in the role of heroine-goddess, that she speaks most eloquently to worshippers about the human experience. Consequently, I propose a feminist reading that considers the concepts associated with this so-called composite image and acknowledges Pārvatī-Śakti's ambivalence as both goddess and woman (*nārī*) in her embodied iconographic union with Śiva.

Although there is no lack of images of Ardhanārīśvara in sources on Indian iconography, this image has yet to receive its recognition. I make an effort here also to correct this deficiency by presenting an examination of seventeen images of Ardhanārīśvara from different regions and periods in Indian tradition. I have selected these images from over 100 examined because, in my estimation, they represent a broad cross-section of the various ways in which the half-male and half-female image of Ardhanārīśvara has been portrayed in Indian art over the centuries. The sacred image of Ardhanārīśvara is universal in the Indian context, from Kashmir and Nepal to Tamil Nadu but, to be sure, variations can be seen throughout the following examples. The illustrations are arranged both chronologically and by region. I begin with the earliest images of Ardhanārīśvara from North India, followed by classic examples of well-known, rock-cut reliefs, and South Indian images, and I conclude with later North Indian images, including Nepal. This brief survey attempts to cover both commonalities and marked representational variations realized over time and place.

The Earliest Images of Ardhanārīśvara

The earliest images of Ardhanārīśvara date from the Scytho-Kuṣāṇa period. The oldest of them (Figure 1.1) is a small, mid-first-century C.E. red sandstone Kuṣāṇa stele currently located in the Government

Figure 1.1 Kuṣāṇa stele, mid-first-century C.E. Courtesy of the American Institute of Indian Studies, Gurgaon, India.

Figure 1.2 Bust of Ardhanārīśvara. Gosna Village, Mathurā, third century. Courtesy of Dirk Bakker, photographer.

Museum, Mathurā.[18] This magnificent relief, measuring seven and a half inches wide by ten inches long, has been called "a veritable Brahmanic "iconographic document"" (Srinivasan 1997, 19). It shows Ardhanārīśvara standing on the right in a group of four alongside two males and one female who are all of equal height, identified, respectively, as Viṣṇu,[19] Gaja-Lakṣmi, and (possibly) Skanda. The specific image of Ardhanārīśvara portrays the emblematic central axial divi-

Figure 1.3 Ardhanārīśvara. Kuṣāṇa, Mathurā, late second-third century. Courtesy of the Los Angeles County Museum of Art.

sion (*brahmasūtra*) of right half male and left half female. It is a two-armed figure, with the right hand held in *abhaya mudrā,*[20] or a gesture of fearlessness, and the left uncharacteristically raised. The prominent breast and fuller hip are indicated on the left female side. The half *ūrdhvareta* feature and half moustache, common in early North Indian Kuṣāṇa images of Ardhanārīśvara, mark the right side. The male *jaṭā* hairstyle is clearly discernible on the right half of the image, and the sparse ornamentation is appropriate to the stylistic standards of the period.[21]

Other early images of Ardhanārīśvara from this period include a second-century torso from Mathurā, presently housed in the National Museum, Delhi, identified as Ardhanārīśvara specifically by the single female left breast. A bust of Ardhanārīśvara (see Figure 1.2) from Gosna Village, Mathurā, dating from the third century, renders the identification of Ardhanārīśvara through male and female identified ear ornamentation only. What is most significant about this striking image is the accuracy and immediacy of these symbolic identifiers to effectively counterpoint the male and female sides and thereby to generate an image of Ardhanārīsvara. Another unusual feature of this image is that the eyes are closed. The headdress is differentiated by two distinct styles, and a simple necklace adorns the male and female sides. A third eye is placed directly in the center of the forehead.

The third Kuṣāṇa image of Ardhanārīśvara examined (Figure 1.3) is a late second–third century C.E. image from Mathurā, Uttar Pradesh, which stands twelve and one-eighth inches high. This rare image of Ardhanārīśvara, currently housed in the Los Angeles County Museum, presents the androgynous aspects of Śiva carved on a grainy or mottled red sandstone *liṅga*. The Indian *śilpa* tradition enumerates a variety of materials used by *śilpins* to construct images. Variously employed, an image could be made from any available element or material such as wood, earth, gold, silver, copper (i.e., metal), ivory, or stone. Just as sandstone was used in Bihar, and stone in Amaravati, to make sacred images, a type of red mottled sandstone was generally used in Mathurā, as all of the above examples illustrate.[22]

The appearance of this notable figure contains several essential iconographical features. For instance, the figure is differentiated along the vertical axis into male and female—the right side is male, and the left side is female. Again, this is one of the central diagnostic features of all known anthropomorphic Ardhanārīśvara images. The unique feature of this particular image is that it is possible to see its entire composition, front and back. Viewed from the back, the observer can distinguish only the slim *liṅga* or columnar form emphasizing the prominence of the male identified Śiva aspect of the deity.

On the right/male side the image is identified by the following ornamentation: *jaṭāmakuṭa;* slightly different shaped eye; half moustache; broader right shoulder; wider waist; flat chest; and, one testicle and half *ūrdhvareta* feature pointing upward to the right. In addition, one of the three traditional-style earrings usually worn by Śiva's male half is noticeably absent in this sculpture.

The left/female side contains the following iconographical features: *karaṇḍa-makuṭa;* larger left eye; *kuṇḍala* (common earring); well-developed female left breast; curved hip; slimmer waist; and fuller thigh. Consistent with all Ardhanārīśvara images, the female genitals are not indicated, whereas they are clearly depicted on the right male half. Instead, we see finely sculpted draped garments gesturing to the historical and regional conventions of female form and dress.

A single strand of pearl-shaped beads worn around the neck is common to both the male and female halves of the image. The figure is two-armed, and both arms are adorned with bracelets. The right arm is raised in the traditional *abhaya mudrā* and also holds a small *akṣamālā,* while the left arm, extended next to her side in *kaṭyavalambita mudrā,* carries a downward-facing *nīlotpala* flower. As stated, *śilpa* texts list the *nīlotpala* as one of the defining attributes of a woman in Indian sacred art.

Overall, the three examples from the Kuṣāṇa period discussed here mark some of the earliest images of Śivārdhanārīśvara preserved in Indian sacred art. They provide ample evidence that this motif was well-known to formal iconographic styles of this period and region. Accounts indicate that Śiva, under the label Oesho, appeared in his androgynous form on some late Kuṣāṇa coins (e.g., the gold coin of Kaniṣka III), attesting to the prominence and popularity of the image during this early period (Williams 1967; Joshi 1984; Yadav 2001). A single reference to a cave temple in the Western Ghās as early as the second century C. E. reports a two-armed "colossal statue" of a half-male and half-female deity. The markings, however, do not conform precisely to our typology, but the image has been recognized as an early Ardhanārīśvara form (Yadav 2001, 14). Art historians generally cite passages from the *purāṇas* to explain Ardhanārīśvara images, with the given provision in Banerjea's case that supporting mythological evidence is limited.[23] However, the above Kuṣāṇa illustrations from the first century C.E. would indicate that images of Ardhanārīśvara developed well before their *purāṇic* explanations evolved, and provide evidence that the earliest surviving images of Ardhanārīśvara were two-armed.

The next North Indian image (Figure 1.4), dating from the late fifth century C.E., Nachnā, Madhya Pradesh, is identified as Ardhanārīśvara primarily by the larger left female breast. Currently housed in the Feroze Mistry Collection, Mumbai, India, this austere image, carved in local sandstone, is divided vertically into right male and left female by a few distinct features. The hairstyle on the left side is composed of small tight curls arranged in a knot or bun. This feature contrasts with the unusually long, loose, or unbound *jaṭāmakuṭa* seen on the right

Figure 1.4 Ardhanārīśvara. Nachnā, Madhya Pradesh, fifth century. Feroze Mistry Collection, Mumbai, India. Courtesy of Dirk Bakker, photographer.

male side. There are two different-style earrings indicated on the right and left sides of the deity. Also, the female torso is slimmer at the waist and leg from the knee downward, whereas the left hip and upper thigh are fuller than the right/male side. The deity stands in the *tribhaṇga* pose, with shared *prabhāmaṇḍala* behind his/her head. The right half leans on Nandin (though the head of this figure has been destroyed), whereas no vehicle is provided on the left female side. The most noteworthy feature of this image is the unique method used by the *śilpin* to depict the deity's four arms. In most images where Ardhanārīśvara is shown with four arms, they are typically divided at the elbows. However, in this rendering, all four arms derive from the shoulder. Unfortunately, the lower arms have been destroyed, making it impossible to identify the articles carried by this unusual image of Ardhanārīśvara. This image is representative of early Madhya Pradesh sculpture in its smooth execution and sturdy, compact form.

Rock-Cut Images of Ardhanārīśvara

The next three figures of Ardhanārīśvara are classic examples of Deccan rock reliefs.[24] The first illustration (Figure 1.5) is from the Śiva cave temple at Elephanta (originally known as Gharapuri). This well-known early Cālukyan image of Ardhanārīśvara is situated directly to the right of the massive three-headed figure of Śiva Maheśvara. In this three-dimensional carved relief, dating from approximately the sixth century C.E., several standard features of Ardhanārīśvara are immediately recognizable. The image is divided vertically into male and female, right side male and left side female. The left side is distinguished by the larger female breast, and the contours of the body outline the curvature of the female waistline, hip, and thigh, emphasized by the pronounced *tribhaṅga* pose. The right shoulder is more boldly extended than the left. Other prominent features include two different earring styles and four arms. The upper left arm carries a mirror, and the lower left arm hangs in *kaṭyavalambita mudrā* and holds what remains of a stem, the top portion of the object, most certainly a lotus flower, having been destroyed. The upper right arm holds a serpent, and the lower right arm leans gently on Nandin, Śiva's *vāhana* (vehicle). While the upper part of the body of the image is bare, the bottom half, from just below the waist, is all but destroyed, making it impossible to compare the articles of clothing on the right and left halves of the image, or to ascertain the presence of the *ūrdhvaliṅga* feature.

If we accept the identification of the third face of the central image of Maheśvara at Elephanta as Umā, then it is possible that this particu-

Figure 1.5 Ardhanārīśvara. Elephanta Caves, sixth century. Courtesy of the American Institute of Indian Studies, Gurgaon, India.

lar image of Ardhanārīśvara forms part of an important triptych that acknowledges the inclusion of the feminine creative aspects of Śiva's nature in all three of these central *mūrtis*. In other words, the image of Ardhanārīśvara is situated in the left niche of the southern flank of the west *kanika* on the back wall of the cave next to the colossal three-faced image of Maheṣa containing the *ugra* (Rudra), *saumya*, and *vāmadevī* (Umā) aspects of Śiva. To its right is the Gaṅgādhara *mūrti* (descent of Gaṅgā). This image and its corresponding mythology foreshadow the image of Śiva in the aspect of Ardhanārīśvara. Collins (1988) makes the point that the Ardhanārīśvara *mūrti* and the other two images collectively portray essential features of Śiva that illustrates his/her manifest feminine nature. That is, the Ardhanārīśvara and Gaṅgādhara *mūrtis* are connected to the active role of generation, or the combined feature of primordial parenthood. Gaṅgā carries the sperm of Śiva, though Schneider (1987) disagrees that this motif has anything whatsoever to do with fertility (329). Collins claims that the androgynous aspect of Śiva, rendered by the Ardhanārīśvara *mūrti*, creates by his/her innate or internalized ability, whereas the Gaṅgādhara *mūrti*, in which the feminine is situated external to Śiva, that is, atop his head, creates by a more "active role in the world" (Collins 1988, 76). Hence, both of the images that flank the central and focal image of the cave temple illustrate Śiva's necessary relationship to, and identification with, the dual aspect of the male and female cosmogonic pair.

The next image of Ardhanārīśvara (Figure 1.6) from the rock-cut cave temples at Bādāmī (situated in the west wall of the Mukhamaṇḍapa) is similar in many ways to the preceding image. This sixth–seventh-century image of Ardhanārīśvara, similar to the Elephanta image, is a substantial sandstone rock relief that shows a proclivity toward a broader and more massive style. Like the preceding image, the deity is divided into his/her male and female sides along the vertical axis. The image contains various traditional iconographical motifs that are located on the male and female sides of the deity. On the right/male side, these include *jaṭāmakuṭa*, *sarpa-kuṇḍala*, two arms with a serpent encircling the upper portion of the lower right arm of the deity, half moustache, third eye, *paraśu* with a coiled serpent, single bracelet around the forearm and lower right wrist, and Nandin (Śiva's vehicle).

The left/female side of the deity contains the following details: *headdress*, *kuṇḍala*, two arms, upper left arm carries a *nīlotpala* flower, and lower left arm is bent forward and rests in front of the prominent left breast holding a *vīṇā* (also in the front right arm). Other diagnostic markings are a slim waist, a full hip, and a female garment that drapes just above the ornamented left ankle.

Features common to both the male and female sides of the image are *yajñopavīta* (sacred thread), necklaces, belts, garments befitting the styles worn by both gods and goddesses, and *prabhāmaṇḍala*. Furthermore, the deity is shown standing in a slight *tribhaṅga* pose on a platform ornamented with eight small figures. Several unusual features of this Ardhanārīśvara image include the *vīṇādhara* aspect and the placement of a second Devī (female attendant) carrying a vessel in her left hand. To the right of Ardhanārīśvara, standing beside Nandin, is an

Figure 1.6 Ardhanārīśvara. Bādāmī Caves, sixth–seventh century. Courtesy of the American Institute of Indian Studies, Gurgaon, India.

emaciated human figure who may represent the devoted *ṛsi* Bhṛngī. Above the deity to the right we see a *deva* and his consorts. The figures shown above the left side of the head both appear to be female, whereas the figures to the right of the deity appear to be male and female. The male on the right is clearly differentiated by the sacred thread worn across the upper half of his body.

A later development that resembles the images of Ardhanārīśvara at the Elephanta and Bādāmī caves is the Gujara-Pratihara image of Ardhanārīśvara (Figure 1.7) from Abaneri that dates from the ninth century C.E. This standing figure, like the two preceding images, is a scrupulously detailed three-dimensional carved stone relief that portrays, along a vertical axis, the half-female and half-male body of Ardhanārīśvara in the *tribhaṅga* pose. The four arms of the deity display various emblems, such as a trident with an encircling serpent in the upper right hand, an unusual depiction of a small, fully open lotus flower in the lower right, and a mirror in the upper left. The hand of the lower left arm is empty and is shown leaning gently on the enlarged female left hip. Among the types of ornamentation that differentiate the male and female sides of the deity are two distinct and elaborate hairstyles, as well as two different styles of earrings, a *sarpakuṇḍala* and a *vāḷikā,* respectively. Delicately carved features indicating the deity's clothing, held by several *mekhalas* (belts) common to both sides of the deity, reveal a lion skin worn by the male side and a draped fabric falling just above the ankle on the female side. Single bracelets adorn the two left and two right wrists. Nandin, Śiva's vehicle, carries a small human male attendant on his back, and a small female attendant of equal size stands on her own to the left of Pārvatī. The striking Abaneri rock reliefs are somewhat more ornamental in their style but are consistent with the normative standard of medieval rock-cut sacred art and adhere to traditional representations of Ardhanārīśvara.

Orissa

The next illustration (Figure 1.8) from the Simhanātha Temple, Barmba, Cuttak, Orissa, belongs to the eighth century C.E. It displays several unusual features and unique regional artisitic production, and it is included in our examination for this reason. The normative standard of Ardhanārīśvara male and female features is represented in this image by the differentiated hairstyles and bipolar right-left division. It is an ornate, four-armed image holding a *gadā* in the upper right hand and an unidentifiable object in the lower right hand. The upper left hand holds a mirror and the lower left hand a downward-facing flower. Ear ornamentation is dissimilar, emphasizing the male and female sides, also indicated by the larger left breast and flat male right chest. Draped clothing styles are beautifully sculpted in such a way as to integrate the male and female sides into one unified form. Jewelry and accesso-

Figure 1.7 Ardhanārīśvara. Abaneri Caves, ninth century. Courtesy of the American Institute of Indian Studies, Gurgaon, India.

ries are patterned on canonical norms. Attendants stand balanced and equal in height on either side of the deity.

What distinguishes this image of Ardhanārīśvara carved on the sanctum of the west *jaṅghā* from other sculptures is the *aghora mukha mudrā*, that is, the wrathful and terrifying nature of the deity. This is clearly discerned by the sharp, penetrating position of the eyes. We rarely come across this feature either in canonical or sculptural accounts of Ardhanārīśvara. In addition, the left female side indicates a nose ring. This also is not shown on earlier images. Atypically, a *bindu* rather than *trinetra* is placed in the center of the forehead, attesting to

Figure 1.8 Ardhanārīśvara. Simhanātha Temple, Barmba, Cuttak, Orissa, eighth century. Courtesy of the American Institute of Indian Studies, Gurgaon, India.

the rising popularity of Śaktism in Orissa. Curiously, the left rather than right shoulder is broader and more massive. There also is an intimation of a reversed bend in the mid-region, as the male hip swings to the right in a more pronounced and extended way. The left side is slender and shows no characteristic female curvature whatsoever. Overall, this is a remarkable example of Eastern Indian Ardhanārīśvara design.

Other South Indian Images of Ardhanārśvara

The earliest representation of Ardhanārīśvara (Figure 1.9) illustrated here is from Mahābalipuram (city of Mamalla), Tamil Nadu,[25] and displays the simplicity and slender proportions characteristic of this location and period. Openly carved in granite on the Dharmarājaratha, it is a monolithic, rock-cut monument dating from the seventh century C.E. This Pallava image of Ardhanāīśvara sculpted in Toṇḍaimaṇḍala style stands erect in *samapāda* or *sthāna mudrā* (straight posture) and is split vertically into right side male, left side female. Where the early Kuṣāṇa images typically portrayed Ardhanārīśvara with two arms, the Pallava form illustrated here is equally balanced, representing the deity with four arms divided at the elbows. The upper right arm holds the traditional *paraśu*, and the lower right arm is typically raised in *abhaya mudrā*. On the left female side, the upper arm is held in *kaṭaka mudrā* to facilitate a small parrot perched on the wrist adorned with numerous bracelets. The front arm hangs down resting the elbow at the hip in *kaṭyavalambita mudrā*. The left foot is noticeably adorned with an ankle bracelet (*karā*). These emblems are consistent with canonical formulations of the image. Two different hair and earring styles, representative of the male and female aspects, demarcate the right and left sides along the traditional *brahmasūtra*. Also, the left hip is characteristically larger, though not as pronounced as some of the other Ardhanārīśvara figures I examine, and the left waistline is proportionately smaller. The sculpted clothing and drapery also identify the right male and left female aspects of the deity, and a common necklace joins the two halves.

A second illustration (Figure 1.10) from Mahābalipuram, Chengalpattu District, Shore Temple, from the same period, shows an unusual rock-cut image of a four-armed Ardhanārīśvara positioned on an *āsana* (seat). Here, Ardhnārīśvara plays the *vīnā* with his/her two-bracelet adorned left arms divided at the shoulders. Since this is a seated Ardhanārīśvara, the right leg is raised and bent, leaning on the left thigh. The front right arm holds the base of the instrument, and the upper right arm is held uncharacteristically, that is, bent at the elbow and held up by the side of the head. This diagnostic feature cannot be accounted for in the canonical literature. No other accessories are held, but a trident is carved into the rock site. Headdress, earrings, left breast, and stylistic adornment are clearly discernible.[26]

Figure 1.9 Ardhanārīśvara. Mahābalipuram, Tamil Nadu, seventh century. Courtesy of the American Institute of Indian Studies, Gurgaon, India.

Figure 1.10 Ardhanārīśvara. Mahābalipuram, Tamil Nadu, Chengalpattu District, Shore Temple, seventh century. Courtesy of the French Institute of Pondicherry.

Chronologically, the South Indian Chola style[27] of art follows the Pallava period, and with it we witness a change in the representation of Ardhanārīśvara images. The first sculpture illustrated (Figure 1.11) from Kundalaiyatrur Kattumannarguditalu, South Arcot District, Śiva Vallabeśvara Temple, is a four-armed Ardhanārīśvara figure standing in *tribaṅga mudrā*. Typically, the right and left sides are male and female, respectively. Of the two right male arms, the back right hand holds a *paraśu*, and the front hand rests comfortably on the forehead of Nandin, who straddles the entire figure. The upper left female hand holds a lotus flower, and the front left arm hangs in *kaṭyavalambita mudrā*, resting on the upper thigh. The dress and ornamentation of the two halves of the body are consistent with canonical sources and follow the male-female vertical split, indicating a larger left breast, full hip, slim waist, slightly broader right shoulder, male chest, draped clothing appropriate to male and female, different earrings, headdresses, and sacred thread across the body from left to right. The most striking feature is the way in which the image is highlighted by placing Ardhanārīśvara on a flat pedestal with a lofty *triśūla* rising from its platform. This period motif also can be found on the Ardhanārīśvara *mūrti* at Bṛhadīśvara Temple (three-armed, eleventh–twelfth century), Tanjore, and Sri Rajakombeera Temple, Tiruchchirappali District (four-armed).

The next Chola image of Ardhanārīśvara (Figure 1.12) is a bronze from Tiruvenkadu, dating from the ninth century C.E., currently preserved in the Madras Museum. This three-armed image standing in the *tribhaṅga* posture demonstrates clearly one iconographical feature that privileges the male half of the divine androgyne, that is, the right/male side has two arms, whereas the left/female side has only one.[28] In her commentary of this image, Nicole Balbir suggests that this feature contributes to the work's overall beauty (Balbir, cited in Śivaramamūrti 1974b, 79). However, I would argue that this apparent absence of symmetry is a testimony to the codification of power and privilege at times associated with the male right Śiva side of the deity. This feature exhibits in anthropomorphic form what is indicated by the name "Ardhanārīśvara" in Indian tradition. As mentioned earlier, the name "Ardhanārīśvara" is used to convey a somewhat different status for the male and female deities fused in this composite image. Here we wish to point out, once again, that the name does not translate as "half-man, half-woman,"[29] as Marglin (1989) suggests, but rather as the "lord who is half woman" (216). This immediately suggests a gender hierarchy in the sense that the status of the male Śiva half is "*īśvara*" (lord, god), whereas the female Pārvatī half is simply designated "*nārī*" (woman). The name, in other words, does not convey the same status for both halves. Pārvatī must heroically win her status as divine through *tāpas*, whereas Śiva is eternally transcendent.

Another discernible feature of this image is Śiva's full third eye (*trinetra*), situated directly in the middle of the forehead and shared by both the male and female sides. Interestingly enough, this particular

Figure 1.11 Ardhanārīśvara. Kundalaiytrur Kattumannarguditalu, South Arcot District, Siva Vallabeśvara Temple, Chola Period. Courtesy of the French Institute of Pondicherry.

diagnostic feature stands in stark contrast to the asymmetry portrayed by three arms. In this iconographical motif lies a recognition of the divine wisdom and status emanating equally from both the male and female sides of the deity. Iconographical variations of this diagnostic emblem will be pointed out from time to time in this analysis, but generally the dot located on the female left side refers, in the historical

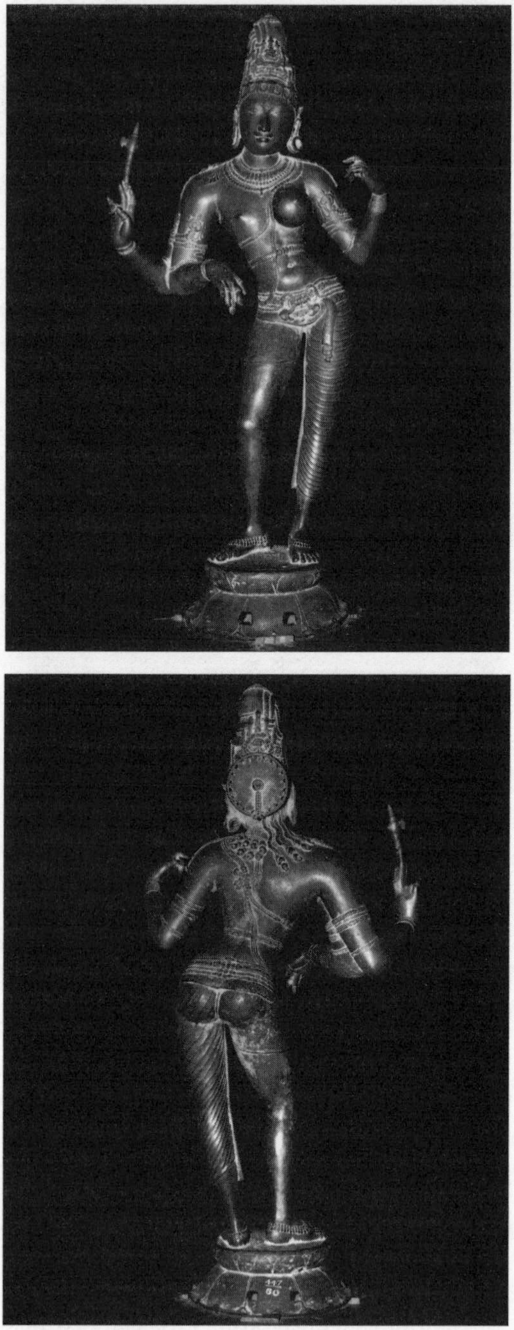

Figure 1.12 Ardhanārīśvara. Tiruvenkadu, ninth century. Madras Museum. Courtesy of the French Institute of Pondicherry.

realm of real men and women, to the marital status of the female, whereas the third eye variously shown on the male right side or, as in the case presented here, shared in the middle of the vertical axis, attests to Śiva's and Pārvatī's divinity or transcendence as *īśvara* and *iśvarī*, respectively. This diagnostic feature in its variations marks the ambivalence and inclusiveness of Pārvatī's human/divine (*nārī/devī*) status. In this sense, usually if any mark is to be discerned on Śiva's male half, whether common to both sides or not, it is always the mark of divine wisdom or, in some instances, the mark of ashes collected from various funeral pyres signifying the yogi *par excellence* who, donning the snake around his neck or *triśula,* as the image often shows, conveys that the body has transcended worldly life (*prakṛti*). On the left female side we see either a third eye or a dot. Hence, the type and location of the markings on the forehead of the image, similar to the number of arms, could be read as a subtle diagnostic indicating status, that is, lord and wife/woman, just as the name Ardhanārīśvara implies.[30]

Other than these obvious and significant differences, the image is consistent with alternate iconographical representations of the deity, such as vertical demarcation between left female and right male, larger left breast, broader right shoulder, different hairstyle and ear ornamentation, and clothing characteristic of male and female styles. It is important to mention that several features portrayed in the aforementioned images are absent in this one, namely, trident, serpent, mirror, and lotus. The only emblem that Ardhanārīśvara holds is the characteristic *paraśu* in the upper right hand. I also have included an illustration of this striking sculpture viewed from the back. Rarely do we have an opportunity to view the image in full view, however, here we can discern the ornamentation and detailed composition in both positions. We can see the delicate formation of the two arms as they join from the elbows on the right male side, the elaborate joint headdress fluidly adorning the back of the head, with necklaces, bracelets, and clothing draping the back of the body. Also we see the sacred thread just under the right side of the male musculature. The *tribhaṅga* pose seen from the back emphasizes the rounded, well-shaped buttocks of the male and female halves, respectively.

Later North Indian and Nepalese Images of Ardhanārīśvara

One engaging quality of the image of Ardhanārīśvara is its keen attempt at equality. June McDaniel (1992) claims that anthropomorphic images such as Ardhanārīśvara celebrate an embodied male and female side by side as evidence of a strong egalitarian impulse in Indian tradition. The doctrine of *rūpa/svarūpa* that she discusses in this context presumes that the "true state of the human male and female is in the union of the divine couple (*jugal milana*) in an eternal relationship of love" (28). The next three images of Ardhanārīśvara from the tenth century onward could be said to provide such evidence of this egalitarian *rūpa/svarūpa* impulse.

The first illustration (Figure 1.13) examined is one of many images of Ardhanārīśvara from Nepal. Nepalese images of Ardhanārīśvara are assignable to the tenth to eighteenth centuries.[31] The earliest of these is a copper alloy image from the Paśupati Temple compound circa.1000 C.E., which is currently preserved in the Nasli and Alice Heeramaneck Collection, Los Angeles County Museum of Art. The noticeable feature in this image is the remarkable fluidity between the male and female form conveying a sense of symmetry and balance. This image stands erect with straight head in the *samapādasthanaka* pose (straight posture), thirty-three inches high. It has four arms, two on each side separating at the elbows. An unusual feature is that the upper two arms are bent in parallel gestures. The lower left arm holds a small atypical water pot, and in the upper hand there may be a mirror (Pal 1985, 96). In the right hand is an unusual, downward-facing *triśūla*, but as we can see, the lower right arm is broken at the elbow.

This image of Ardhanārīśvara is not only the earliest Nepalese sculpture to have survived but, according to Pal, it also is one of "the largest and most beautiful bronzes known" (Pal 1985, 96). Pal attributes this to the deity's half-shut eyes, lending the image a sense of elegance and "grace" reminiscent, he says, of the earlier Gupta period. Other noteworthy features of this image include the intricately carved hairstyles adorned with gemstones, the semiprecious necklaces shared by both male and female halves, and the delicate finery worn by the male and female sides of the image. The male and female aspects of the deity are clearly differentiated by the expressive outlines of their respective torsos, including larger left hip, smaller waist, and the prominent female breast. A sacred thread and necklaces jointly adorn the male and female halves.

Similar to the preceding Nepalese image, the next black schist image of Ardhanārīśvara (Figure 1.14) from the eleventh century C.E., Rajasthan, also stands perfectly straight in the *samapādasthanaka* pose, leaning neither to the left nor the right. Multiple attendants accompany the deity, males on the right and females on the left, carved in equal proportion. Several strands of jewels adorn the neck of the composite god/dess, as well as a single bracelet around each wrist. The figure has two arms, one on each side, but the left shoul-

Figure 1.13 Ardhanārīśvara. Nepal, tenth century. Courtesy Nasli and Alice Heeramaneck Collection, Los Angeles County Museum of Art.

der is curiously broader than the right, whereas in most of the previous illustrations this feature when indicated was reversed. Each hand conveys an emblem, namely, a *triśūla* in the right hand and a *nīlotpala* flower in the left. The body of the goddess is denoted by the well-developed female left breast. However, the voluptuous contours

Figure 1.14 Ardhanārīśvara. Rajasthan, eleventh century. Courtesy of the Los Angeles County Museum of Art.

of the female hip and waistline, often found on other images, are noticeably absent here; indeed, the right hip appears unusually larger. The differentiated earrings, elaborate headdresses, *prabhāmaṇḍalas*, and clothing styles appropriately mark the male and female sides of the image. The male half wears a *sarpa-kuṇḍala*, and the female half wears a *kuṇḍala*, typical of the goddess. On the right side of the forehead is Śiva's third eye and on the left side Pārvatī has a dot, indicating their status.

In the next illustration (Figure 1.15) the animated quality of Indian poster art from Mumbai captures the imagery of the male and female forms of Ardhanārīśvara.[32] Reproduced here in black and white, the original poster by H. R. Raja portrays the image of Ardhanārīśvara in vivid colors that capture striking physical differences between Śiva's male and female sides, perhaps more than any of the other illustrations. The image is divided into male and female along a straight vertical axis. On the right male side, Śiva is identified by numerous diagnostic indicators, including *jaṭāmakuṭa, trinetra, tilaka, rudrākṣamālā, paraśu, triśūla*, a two-sided drum (*ḍamaru*), serpent, horn, bells, and his vehicle Nandin. He is dressed in a loin cloth made from tiger skin. The image is two-armed, with the lower right raised in *abhayamudrā*. On the left female side, Pārvatī is identified by her elaborate hair ornamentation, ordinary *kuṇḍala*, jeweled necklace, upright lotus flower, lion vehicle, henna on the hands and feet, and distinct female form.

In this contemporary work are several unique features. First, the male and female sides of Ardhanārīśvara are demarcated by their contrasting complexions, a feature we will see again in Indian devotional poetry. In the original poster the male half is blue, and the female half is golden. Second, the image is contextualized against a Himalayan backdrop, depicting the meditation abode of Śiva atop Mt. Kailasa. Also, a luminous *prabhāmaṇḍala* shines in equal proportion behind the head of Ardhanārīśvara, as Gaṅgā flows out of the top right side adorned with a crescent moon.

The image of Ardhanārīśvara is one of the most celebrated syncretic motifs in Indian art. This image and the next two demonstrate this quality of syncretism most explicitly. Although there are compositional variations in the following image of Ardhanārīśvara, it does bear a striking resemblance to the contemporary poster by H. R. Raja. This painting from Rajasthan (Figure 1.16) dates from the late eighteenth to early nineteenth century and is currently preserved in the British Museum. In this image, like the one preceding it, the deity is portrayed in vivid color, hence the vertical division between the male and female is clearly evident in the demarcated shades of their skin tones. However, in this portrait, unlike the one described above, the male half is depicted with white skin and the female half with red. The deity has four arms. The right upper arm holds a *triśūla*, with a horn, sack, and a small drum attached to it, and the lower right arm rests on the right leg, a diagnostic feature we have not encountered

Figure 1.15 Ardhanārīśvara. Contemporary Poster Art, Mumbai, India.

previously. The left upper arm holds a small noose, and the front left arm is bent. The third eye is shared, as it is situated in the middle of the forehead on the vertical dividing axis between male and female. The different hairstyles are demarcated clearly by a golden-colored *jaṭā*

Figure 1.16 Ardhanārīśvara. Rajasthan, late eighteenth to early nineteenth century. Courtesy of the British Museum.

on the right, with Gaṅgā flowing from the top, and on the left a tiara is placed in long, black hair. Two different earring styles are worn and, like the preceding image, the left nostril is adorned with a ring, typical of later styles of female accessorization. Two features are noteworthy. The deity is seated on an *āsana* made from deer and lion skin, while Nandin appears in the forefront, and the garments that convey the male and female aspects of the deity are differentiated by the design in their fabric and by the drape of cloth over the left shoulder revealing the female breast.

The most visible expression of syncretic tendencies in Indian iconography is demonstrated in the following image (Figure 1.17) of Ardhanārīśvara and Hari-Hara from Madura, India (Rao 1968; Bhattacharyya 1980; Singh 1973; Banerjea 1956; Shukla 1996; Kandasamy 1994; Kalidos 1993). By juxtaposing the principal deities of the Śaiva and Śakta schools in one composite form, the image of Ardhanārīśvara signals a reconciliatory current evident among ideological movements. Other hybrid icons, such as Hari-Hara,[33] indicate this same tendency toward unification and are based on the Ardhanārīśvara model.

To amplify the relationality between syncretic figures, I have included this illustration from an eleventh-century temple in Madhura of Ardhanārīśvara and Hari-Hara standing side by side. This figural juxtaposition clearly acknowledges the common theme of syncretism. Viewed from this paired perspective, comparative associations with more broadly conceived dual deities or binary two-in-one pairs, such as *prakṛti-puruṣa*, *māyā-brahman*, and *ātman-brahman*, which come from Vedic literature,[34] are required.

What becomes clear is that a sacred tradition of dual or androgynous deities is intricately interwoven into a complex and diverse mythological, philosophical, and iconographical religious tradition dating back in some instances as far as the early Vedic period. One of the earliest of the Indo-European Aryan motifs of an androgynous deity is the Ṛg Veda sky-earth deity Dyāvā-Pṛthivī, who generates the universe through an act of splitting into two distinct halves. Another example is the Asura Bull-Cow, Viśvarūpa, who appears as an androgynous self-generating principle (Ṛg Veda 3.38.4). Puruṣa, the cosmic man, who creates the universe in the *Puruṣasūkta*, gestures to an androgynous principle (RV 10.90). In a later Vedic text, the *Bṛhadāranyaka Upaniṣad* (1.4.3–4[35]), we find a single body (*ātman*) shaped like a man. Desiring a companion, he procreates the universe through an act of splitting the body into two halves, male/husband (*patī*) and female/wife (*patnī*). Moreover, if we follow Srinivasan's thesis that Rudra also is identified with Puruṣa in the *Kauṣītaki* (6.1–9) and *Satapatha* (6.1.3.17) *Brāhmaṇas*, then we can clearly see that the seeds of Śiva's androgynous motif are strategically placed throughout Vedic literature preparing, as she says, "an overall understanding of the advent of the *śaiva* Ardhanārīśvara concept and form" (Srinivasan 1997, 57). In subsequent *purāṇic* versions of androgynic or two-in-one creation myths, Śiva as Ardhanārīśvara becomes the quintessential androgyne and is seen variously paired in anthropomorphic and emblematic representations alongside a female principle, or Śakti, usually identified as Pārvatī or Umā. In Hari-Hara images, Viṣṇu simply replaces the function and role of Śakti.

Figure 1.17 Hari-Hara. Madura, India. Courtesy of the American Institute of Indian Studies, Gurgaon, India.

The Hari-Hara motif in Indian art, which traces its origins to the early Kuṣāṇa and Gupta periods, evolves into a figure of some importance and presents definite iconographical parallels to Ardhanārīśvara. Structured on the Ardhanārīśvara model, Hari-Hara sets the two prominent deities of the Brahmanical pantheon, Viṣṇu and

Śiva, side by side in one syncretic reconciliatory image.[36] Although there is little specific mythology associated with Hari-Hara, the form is mentioned briefly in various *purāṇas*. For instance, in a dialogue between Mārkaṇḍeya and Brahmā from the *Harivaṃśa*, Mārkaṇḍeya says that there is no difference between Śiva, who exists in the form of Viṣṇu, and Viṣṇu who exists in the form of Śiva—together they are an Ardhanārīśvara (cited in Rao 1968, 54). Any distinction or difference between them is simply attributed to *avidyā* (human ignorance). The *Viṣṇu Purāṇa* states that there is no difference between Viṣṇu and Śiva, and the *Vamana Purāṇa* claims that Viṣṇu and Śiva are one.[37]

Together these examples suggest the underlying theological idea that Śiva does not exist without Viṣṇu, nor does Viṣṇu exist without Śiva; yet, it is curious that Śiva, by being placed on the right-hand side of the dyadic iconographic form, is given prominence in these principally Vaiṣṇava texts. Surely analogies and images such as these offer instructive ways to explain and think theologically about the interdependence of divine polarity in Indian tradition, that is, the interrelationship between the dynamic or oscillating aspect of divine reality manifesting as creation or matter (*prakṛti*), and variously represented by Śakti or Viṣṇu on the left, and the static pole or formlessness (*puruṣa*) represented by Śiva on the right.

However, it also is important not to overlook the fact that such placements can simultaneously cloak subtle forms of gender privileging that imply hierarchy and, of course, rival sectarianism. Let me elaborate on this point further. The image of Hari-Hara in the *purāṇas* recalls the dual character of Ardhanārīśvara. As such, the syncretic form of Śiva and Viṣṇu parallels the dual form of Śiva and Śakti/Pārvatī. Śiva and Viṣṇu, like Śiva and Śakti/Pārvatī, are typically represented in their cosmogonic roles as primordial parents. In the Hari-Hara modification, Śiva remains on the right side in the male aspect or principle of destruction/transformation, whereas Viṣṇu takes the creative "left hand" or female aspect (*vāma* or *strī*). In this regard, Raju Kalidos (1994) says the position of Viṣṇu is subordinate by aligning him with the feminine (275).[38] As Kalidos shows, the left-hand position usually is associated with "something low," "not worthy of being accorded a commendable status of equality," "weakness," "frailty," "baseness and degradation," and so on (287). In this sense, the association of Viṣṇu with the female left-hand side denigrates Viṣṇu and proclaims the superiority of Śiva. By the time the so-called syncretic image of Hari-Hara appears in Indian iconography in the second century C.E., the subordination of the left-hand female side is already implicit in the composite image of Ardhanārīśvara. As Kalidos observes, all so-called syncretic images simply continue the Ardhanārīśvara phenomenon by subtle forms of hierarchy.

I would suggest that in this particular image, and other composite forms modeled on it, the forces of the privileged right male side have not only established a subtle polarized sectarian polemic but have cast this sectarianism in gendered terms. This gendering is in fact a requirement for the sectarian project to succeed. The uneven exchange of power between men and women in traditional patriarchal cultures provides the perfect metaphor for domination and subordination at the level of sectarianism. Kalidos hints at the social and sectarian implications of this throughout his study of Hari-Hara images, but the full articulation of the subtle gender bias implicit in the image has yet to be put forth. Clearly, this strategy of privileging the right-hand side is part of the inherited legacy deeply encrusted in the nomenclature of the form of later syncretic images of Indian tradition, and is not only modeled on male and female gender relations but indeed functions and succeeds because of it.[39] Moreover, the possible autochthonous origins of Indian goddess worship later associated with the image of Ardhanārīśvara could certainly add to her placement on the left side, as such an identification becomes explicit in the later stages of development.

To date, most scholars of Indian iconography have been rather inattentive to the possible sociological and gender implications of the male and female positioning in their commentaries of dual or syncretic images and infer that the real import of composite images such as Ardhanārīśvara or Hari-Hara forms is that they demonstrate the inseparability or oneness of the male and the female in cosmic creation. While this is clearly a fundamental point, it does not address the implied hierarchical privileging that, whether joined with Viṣṇu, or with Pārvatī, Śiva typically represents the male and dominant aspect of the pair, signified by his position on the right-hand side of the figure. The female principle, or *prakṛti tattva*, situated on the left-hand side (*vāmadeva/vāmadevī*), is variously represented in the subordinate position by either Viṣṇu or Pārvatī. As a general formula, the imaging of Hari-Hara follows the diagnostic form conveyed by the androgynous image of Śiva and Pārvatī, in which the role of male/*puruṣa* dominates.[40]

Chapter 2

Ardhanārīśvara and *Haṭhayoga*

> There are, indeed, two visible appearances (*rūpa*) of *brahman*—the one has a fixed shape, and the other is without a fixed shape; the one is mortal, and the other is immortal; the one is stationary, and the other is in motion; the one is Sat and the other is Tyam.
>
> —*Bṛhadāranyaka Upaniṣad*

Introduction

Haṭhayoga[1] maintains that the nature of reality is ultimately *advaita* or nondualist (Śiva Saṃhitā (SS) 1:85–88; Haṭhayogapradīpikā (HYP) 4:7; Gheraṇḍa Saṃhitā (GS) 3:37–42, 7:12–13). That is, in language and symbol, the tradition of *haṭhayoga* portrays ultimate reality as the union or inseparability of masculine and feminine form. Śiva and Śakti are not two separate entities, according to *haṭhayoga* tradition, but rather they are mutually interdependent and coexistent, like the moon and moonlight, sweetness and milk, or fire and heat.[2] Śiva (as Paramaśiva) is *prākāśa* (pure light), and Śakti is *cit* (pure consciousness) or *vimarsa* (reflection), ergo, in Indian iconography Pārvatī carries a *darpaṇa* (mirror) in her left hand. The metaphysical symbol of a bipolar god/dess, and the absolute assimilation and unity between male and female principles, conveys the normative Śaiva understanding of ultimate reality, as well as the essence of the inner self. The Āgamic system of *haṭhayoga* describes this as *sāmarasya* or *saṃyoga*, implying the conjunction or mutual interpenetration of Śiva and Śakti where they stand together as a single, undivided whole.[3]

Through the dynamic process of evolution (*pravṛtti*), undifferentiated reality bifurcates or splits into a dichotomous subject-object duality. One of the most vivid portrayals of, and responses to, this epistemological problem in Indian iconography is the composite image of Ardhanārīśvara. Most *yoga* treatises mention Ardhanārīśvara rarely by name. For this reason, the image of the divine androgyne has been largely overlooked in studies of *yoga* theory. However, Ardhanārīśvara is Śiva-Śakti: the divine hierogamy and the paradigmatic motif for the *haṭhayoga* attainment of *sabīja samādhi*.[4] In this sense, Ardhanārīśvara articulates not only the *saguṇa* or *sakala* iconographic form of Śiva-Śakti but also a direct discovery or state of consciousness realizable by professional *yoga* practitioners. Ineffable *nirguṇa* or *niṣkala* Śiva-Śakti corresponds to the attainment of *nirbīja samādhi* and can only be gestured to in *haṭhayo*ga tradition as *arūpa* (not form), neuter, beyond time and space, and as emptiness (*śūnyatā*) or *brahman*.

To adept practitioners, the image of Ardhanārīśvara in Indian *haṭhayoga* tradition signals experiential awareness of the interdependent play of divine reality, that is, the mutual identity and simultaneous singularity expressed as the cosmic dance of transcendence and materiality, formlessness and form, and divine being (*sat*) and nonbeing (*asat*). Consequently, in the penultimate state of *sabīja samādhi,* the adept recognizes or unveils his/her own true nature as divine, nondual, and androgynous or, in other words, as Ardhanārīśvara. In fact it is not until the adept practitioner reaches this stage and recognizes herself/himself as Ardhanārīśvara (or Śiva-Śakti) that the goal of *sabīja samādhi* has been realized. From this point, one can proceed to the final stage of the path (*rāja yoga, nirbīja samādhi, layayoga,* etc.), wherein no form (*arūpa*) whatsoever (including sex and gender) remains.

Haṭhayoga treatises, like the *tantra śāstras* with which they are nearly related, reveal not only a masculine (*Śiva*) and feminine (*Śakti*) presence inherent in all creation through a vast system of homologues, they also insist on the transcendence of gendered forms expressed as neuter (e.g., *brahman*). While the concept of duality, often structured on a gendered model, usually pertains to the functions of creation, preservation, and destruction of life, neuter designates the *yoga* attainment of undifferentiated consciousness (*advaita,* nonduality), which is not to say the absence of male or female, *per se,* but rather an indissoluble union and ultimate singularity. This experience of absorption is characterized as "pure consciousness,"[5] and it is variously referred to in *haṭhayoga* treatises as *mahapralaya, turīya, śūnyatā, nirvāṇa,* and so on. The attainment of pure consciousness through the realization of the ultimate nonduality of Śiva-Śakti, or the so-called masculine and feminine principles in the macrocosmic and microcosmic mind-body complex of each individual, informs the entire approach of *haṭhayoga* practice. This describes a subtle process of personal self-transformation that not only recognizes but ultimately attempts to systematically deconstruct the relativity (and, to some extent, the insubstantiality) of historical gender designations. Hence, *yoga* (i.e., union) actually begins in the penultimate stage of *sabīja,* or *samprajñāta samādhi,* when the essence of nondual consciousness articulated by the image of Ardhanārīśvara is unveiled and established.

Consequently, in this chapter we consider how the image of Ardhanārīśvara in the tradition of *haṭhayoga* signifies the attainment of *sabīja samādhi,* which in turn propels the adept practitioner to the final stages of *nirbīja samādhi.* To support this analysis we look at several theories of *haṭhayoga* to show how Ardhanārīśvara presents a metaphysical paradigm for the nondual cognition of the ultimate,[6] and to explain how the image of Ardhanārīśvara is portrayed in *haṭhayoga* ideology. I suggest, based on careful textual, historical, and interpretive analyses, that the final stages of *yoga* (i.e., *sabīja* and *nirbīja samādhi*) actually begin when the *yogin/ī* experiences Ardhanārīśvara. Couched in classic *haṭhayoga* terminology, this occurs when the *prāṇa* or *Śakti* of the individual practitioner reaches the *viśuddha* and *ājñā cakras* and begins its ascent through the uppermost regions of the *suṣumṇā nāḍī* to its final destination in the *sahasrāra* (thousand-petalled lotus). We also continue our examination of how various networks of culture, in this instance *haṭhayoga* theory, portray the half-male and half-female genders of Ardhanārīśvara, and offer a feminist critique of *advaita.*

Typically, the primary *haṭhayoga* treatises to which we refer in this chapter, such as the *Haṭhayogapradīpikā* (HYP), *Śiva Saṃhitā* (SS), *Gheraṇḍa Saṃhitā* (GS), *Gorakṣa Śataka* (GoS), and *Gorakṣa Paddhati* (GP), represent Śiva as the highest reality. The initiated practitioner who is to some extent guided by these manuals aspires to attain experiential knowledge of, and union with, Śiva (SS 5:205; GS 3:37–42). To this end, the *sadhaka/sadhikā* practices a daily, ritualized program of powerful, prescriptive psycho-physical and spiritual techniques (*sādhana, upāya, upāsana*) that could include *yama, niyama, āsana, mudrā, satkarman, bandha, prāṇāyāma, pratyāhāra, dhāraṇā,* and *dhyāna,* eventually leading to the various levels of *samādhi* (or *śūnyatā*). Such practices, usually learned under the guidance of a realized *guru,* progressively navigate the practitioner to a gradual and direct experience of one's own essential nondual nature.

However, identity with Śiva in these treatises always presupposes that Śiva and Śakti are essentially one (GS 7:12-13; HYP 4:58–59). Physical microcosm and divine macrocosm are both Śiva-Śakti. In other words, Śiva is eternally Ardhanārīśvara, as Śivaramamūrti asserts. *Yogaśāstras* describe this recognition in myriad ways, such as *yoga citta vṛtti nirodha, rājayoga, unmanā, manonmanī, laya, śūnyatā, aśūnya, advaita, jīvan mukti, sahajāvastha, nirvāṇa,* and *turīya,* to name only a few, but the idea most often conveyed in *haṭhayoga* treatises and Indian iconography is Śiva-Śakti. How the aspirant theoretically attains this unitive state of pure consciousness through ritual praxis has been well documented in *haṭhayoga* texts. For this reason we draw on several of these primary texts in this chapter, as well as on practical discourses on the subject of *haṭhayoga,* to demonstrate how the image of Ardhanārīśvara has been variously represented in this tradition.

Yoga Body and Praxis

In this section we focus specifically on two central issues. First, the relationship between *haṭhayoga* practice (*sādhana, upāsana*) and Indian iconography and, second, the *yogic* body as it relates directly to the state of consciousness portrayed by the form and figure of Ardhanārīśvara. The goal of *haṭhayoga sādhana* (*upāya*) is a direct, sustained realization of the nonduality of human consciousness imaged as Ardhanārīśvara or Śiva-Śakti. *Sādhana* is praised in the tradition of *haṭhayoga* as the only means (*upāya*) by which to attain this, and as a way to overcome the suffering (*duḥkha*) caused by the fractured nature of, or seeming duality inherent in, human existence. *Haṭhayoga* manuals, for all intents and purposes, are *sādhana śāstras.* They explicate an arduous system of psycho-physical disciplines intended exclusively for the initiated. *Yoga* offers its practitioners various methods and ritual techniques, including visualization practices, *maṇḍalas, āsanas, prāṇāyāma, yantras, mudrās,* and so on, to enable the *yogin/ī* to overcome or to put an end to suffering (*duḥkhānta*).

Visualization techniques and meditation exercises, according to Eliade (1969), awaken "one's inner forces" (207). This depends, however, on the practitioner's ability to internalize a particular deity or image in accordance with appropriate iconographical features. The aspirant must visualize the image according to precise ritual instructions or, as Eliade writes, "project it on a sort of inner screen through an act of creative imagination" (ibid.). This ensures not only the proper transmission of iconographical details but also a codified body of experience. The aspirant thereby follows strict guidelines based on consistent depictions of the prescribed and intended imagery. As Eliade writes:

> There is no question here of the anarchy and inconsistency of what, on the level of profane experience, is called "imagination"; no question of abandoning oneself to a pure spontaneity and passively receiving the content of what,

in Western psychology, we should term the individual or collective unconscious; it is a question of awakening one's inner forces, yet at the same time maintaining perfect lucidity and self-control. (ibid.)

In this sense, Eliade suggests that a mutually contingent and willful relationship exists between *yoga* practice and the codes or canons of Indian iconography. That is, a perfect correspondence is expected between the symbol or deity that is being visualized and the image that is awakened within the subtle body of the practitioner. Following formulaic guidelines set forth in the somewhat standardized Indian iconographic tradition, Eliade argues that the practitioner must "visualize what has been 'seen' and prescribed and codified by the masters, not what his personal imagination might project" (208). Consequently, each visualization exercise (*dhāraṇā*) must comply precisely with the rules of Indian iconography in order for the practitioner to claim a legitimate experience of the internal hierogamy, or to behold the deity within by *jñāna* or direct knowledge, as opposed to discursive thought.

To illustrate his point further, Eliade offers visualization instructions for a *sādhana* on the Tantric Buddhist goddess Candamahāroṣaṇa. According to these ritual instructions the practitioner visualizes the absolute emptiness of the goddess Candamahāroṣaṇa in his/her meditation. With specific reference to Benoytosh Bhattacharyya's translation of *Sādhanamālā*, Eliade explains how the disciple visualizes the deity. These instructions are typical of Tantric Buddhist *sādhanas*. For instance, the aspirant imagines a red solar disc seated on an eight-petalled lotus located in the heart center (*anāhata cakra*) of Candamahāroṣaṇa. From this lotus the seed syllable (*bīja*) *hum*, black in color, arises. From the seed syllable *hum*, light rays emanate in the ten directions illuminating all *buddhas*, *bodhisattvas*, *gurus*, and the goddess Candamahāroṣaṇa. The light dissolves into the heart, at which point the practitioner and goddess become one.[8]

Here we are instructed in the Buddhist tantric *sādhana* on Candamahāroṣaṇa, but we could easily substitute the directions given in this particular *sādhana* with an account of the iconographic details of Ardhanārīśvara found in temple *mūrtis*, Indian poetic iconography, or *yoga śāstras* to illustrate the primary techniques of visualization that Eliade provides. A description of the *viśuddha cakra* in the *Ṣaṭcakranirūpaṇa*, or one of the *dhāraṇās* (visualizations) recommended in the *Gheraṇḍa Saṃhitā* or *Śiva Saṃhitā* (e.g., GS 6: 1–22; SS 4:1–5), or even the *śrīyantra* diagram depicting a series of intersecting upward (male) and downward (female) facing triangles would serve equally well to illustrate the interplay between the codified traditions of Indian iconography and *yoga sādhana*. These instructions, such as the ones offered by Eliade, provide explicit details such as posture, *mudrā*, location, emblems, and symbols required by the practitioner to summon or visualize the form or presence of a particular deity, such as Ardhanārīśvara, correctly.

Though identification with the deity constitutes a fundamental goal of *haṭhayoga*, it is significant to note that there are few *sādhanas* available specifically on Ardhanārīśvara. There are *stotras* (hymns of praise), *bhakti* poems, *mūrtis*, and so on, but few *sādhanas* mention Ardhanārīśvara specifically by name. *Haṭhayoga* treatises offer only scant descriptions of the *cakras* to describe Ardhanārīśvara, yet I would argue that this deity figures more prominently in the broader tradition than these textual descriptions suggest. Accounts that do exist typically run parallel to, but in large measure augment, traditional canons of Indian iconography. They supply all of the requisite, subtle, iconographical, diagnostic components rendering the practitioner capable of visualizing the deity through meditation (*dhāraṇā, dhyāna*), such as lotus, triangles, seed (*bīja*) syllables, location in the body, and external descriptions of the deity. Significant psychological determinants provide the correlation between the iconographic schema and the actual meditation or visualization exercises and, as Eliade claims, what is seen internally must correspond to what is presented in the *sādhana* or *mūrti*. However, I also am suggesting that there are subtler ways of understanding the image of Ardhanārīśvara in the *yogic* body than by simply visualizing or willfully conjuring up a precise vision of prescribed iconography.

Nonetheless, visualization techniques offer a valuable perspective on the relationship between *yoga* praxis, iconography, and a tradition of systematic correspondence. That is, the *dhāraṇā* should invariably resonate in its external formulaic design with the canons of Indian iconography. Parallel developments such as this operate in Indian *yoga* tradition to preserve and maintain tradition as well as to inform the practitioner of his/her progress and stage. It also provides, as I mentioned earlier, a type of inner guide or meditation map for the practice of *sādhana*. In other words, the symbol confirms an inner experience or an arising state of consciousness. However, it is important to acknowledge that as long as a projected symbol (*nyāsa*) appears, the ultimate goal of *yoga* (i.e., *śūnyatā, turīya, brahman, advaita, nirbīja samādhi*, etc.) remains unattained.

Descriptions of Ardhanārīśvara are given in *haṭhayoga cakra* theory, but there are often ambiguities and variations in the testimonies and textual accounts of *cakras* and their respective deities. How can we account for this? Gopinath Kaviraj (1968), in his discussion of the *cakra* system according to Goraksanāth, claims that conceptual accounts are primarily the result of the individual consciousness (or the subconscious) of the *yoga* aspirant and therefore often vary from individual to individual and from school to school.[8] As such, it is worthwhile noting that even though the rituals, *sādhanas, dhāraṇās,* and canons of Indian iconography are broadly informed by the so-called "secrets" of *yoga,* there certainly can be subtle variants of one and the same image in their pan-Indian formulation (and this is clearly discernible in the illustrations of Ardhanārīśvara, presented in chapter 1). Another simple explanation to account for this lies in the purely experiential and often preliminary nature of *yoga* praxis.

Embodied praxis, including *dhyāna* (meditation) as well as numerous other techniques such as *āsana, mudrā, prāṇāyāma,* and so on, is prescribed initially in *yoga* treatises simply as the purificatory ritual technology necessary to progressively navigate the adept practitioner to unveil subtler and subtler states of consciousness until *yoga* is fully attained, and the cessation of the dualistic, verbal, and categorizing mind is established. In *haṭhayoga,* this epistemic realization is further characterized by the attainment of immortality signified by a divine body (*jīvan mukti, divya deha, kāya siddhi*) purified by *yogic* fire (*yogāgni*). In fact, in the *haṭhayoga* theory-praxis continuum, the human body is valorized in ways unknown before in the history of Indian spirituality. Accordingly, longevity, strength, spiritual perfections (*siddhis*), a human physiology homologous to the cosmos, and the acquisition of a divine body beyond the grasp of death are just some of the promises of *haṭhayoga sādhana* (HYP 4:13, 27, 70, 74). Since final liberation is believed in Indian tradition to take many lifetimes, a perfect body, free from pain, old age, disease and, most importantly, one that has attained immortality, can be extremely advantageous in the final orientation of the *yoga* spiritual practice. Hence, *haṭhayoga* conjoins the alchemical quest (*rasāyana*) for the elixir of immortality, or *amṛta.*[9]

Haṭhayoga treatises inform us that the individual body of the *yogin/ī* constitutes the sacred space or inner temple wherein the interfusion and mutual penetration of male and female energies, signified by the image of Ardhanārīśvara and numerous homologues, occur (SS 2:1–36; 5:132–39). A type of inner copulation or unitive experience arises spontaneously (*sahaja*) in *sādhana* during the internal practice of various *mudrās* and *bandhas,* such as *vajrolī, sahajolī, yoni, śakticālanā mudrā, jālandhara bandha* (HYP 3:82–123; SS 4:53–58; 4:1–11). In advanced stages of *sādhana,* the life force or *prāṇa-Śakti* of the *yogin/ī* penetrates the subtle energy centers, is absorbed into, and attains ultimate union with Śiva in *sahasrāra/nirvāṇa cakra* in the crown of the head. The *prāṇa* or *kuṇḍalinī-Śakti* of the *yogin/ī* that lies dormant at the base of the spine in the *mūlādhāra cakra* must be awakened, harnessed, and subsequently drawn upward through the *suṣumṇā/śūnyatā nāḍī* (central nerve or medial channel) to its final destination in the cranial vault. This helps explain why textual accounts of *yoga mudrās* are often charged with vivid erotic implications.[10]

In her study of Kashmir Śaivism, Lilian Silburn (1988) describes in some detail how the adept use the impetus of sexual (i.e., spiritual) energy to access a state of pure cosmic consciousness and then unite within oneself by mirroring the actions of the divine pair (138). However, before such a union is possible, the *yogin/ī* must undergo an intense process of bodily purification, rejuvenation, and transubstantiation through ongoing *yogic* ritual and technique. Through this work, each of the six primary *cakras* (*mūlādhāra, svādhisthāna, manipūra, anāhata, viśuddha, ājñā*), and each of the three *granthis* (*brahmā, viṣṇu, śiva*) of the subtle body, is purified, penetrated, and transformed. Then and only then can Śakti achieve final union with Śiva in the *sahasrāra padma*. In other words, a pure and completely unobstructed pathway in the subtle body from the *mūlādhāra cakra* directly to the *sahasrāra cakra* must be prepared by the aspirant if Śakti is to reach "her" final destination with Śiva in the *sahasrāra*.

In *haṭhayoga* theory, energy (*prāṇa*, Śakti) flows in the body through the *iḍā* (moon) and *piṇgalā* (sun) *nāḍīs*. The central *nāḍī* located between the *iḍā* and *pingalā* is known as *suṣumṇā* or *śūnyatā nāḍī*. With the assistance of advanced *haṭhayoga* techniques such as *śakticalana mudrā, khecarī mudrā, vajrolī mudrā, mūla bandha, jālandhara bandha,* and *uḍḍīyāna bandha*, either willfully or spontaneously arising during *sādhana*, the *yogin/ī* is able to stimulate, harness, and then unite the flow of energy in the right and left channels (*piṇgalā* and *iḍā*) at the *brahmadvāra* (door of *brahma*) and compel it through vigorous and forceful effort (*haṭha*) to ascend through the *suṣumṇā nāḍī* to the cranial vault in the crown of the head (*sahasrāra cakra*). This is what is actually intended by the term "*haṭha*" *yoga*, that is, the union of the sun (*ha/pingalā*) and moon (*tha/iḍā*) by force (*haṭha* techniques).

Haṭhayoga texts align the nature or essence of the three central *nāḍīs* (nerves), that is, the *iḍā, pingalā,* and *suṣumṇā,* with the moon (*chandra* or *soma*), sun (*sūrya*), and fire (*agni*), respectively. However, the interfusion of these referents has a deeper significance. They actually indicate the transformation of the material body (*śarīra*) into an immortal or a divine body. In order to understand this more fully, and its implications for our discussion of Ardhanārīśvara, we must appreciate that here we are dealing with the subtle body and its corresponding symbolism based on an elaborate system of gendered homologues. The *yogin/ī*, by unifying what appears to be complementary fundamental pairs (e.g., positive/negative, hot/cold, sun/moon, *prāṇa/apāna*, right/left, etc.) symbolized in *haṭha yoga* texts by the natural flow of energy in the *iḍā* and *piṇgalā nāḍīs*, strives, like the alchemist, to overcome the seeming duality of life (Śakti) and death (Śiva) through the attainment of immortality.

However, procedurally, it is far more complex than this. *Haṭhayoga* theory, like the Rasāyana school of Indian alchemy, postulates that the *soma* and *sahasrāra cakras* secrete an elixir of immortality (*amṛta*) from the moon center (*candracakra*). If the *yogin/ī* can transmute this nectar and prevent its consumption by the sun (*sūrya, manipūra cakra*), then a divine (*divyadeha*) or perfect body (*kāyasiddhi*) can be attained. Certain techniques, such as *khecarī mudrā,* facilitate this retention (HYP 3:32–53; SS 4:31–37). *Haṭhayoga* treatises, however, often give obscured instructions for various practices, such as *vajrolī, amarolī,* and *khecarī mudrā,* as well as misleading descriptions of various *bandhas* (locks), such as *mūlabandha, jālandhabandha,* and so on, which arise spontaneously in the adept's body during advanced stages of *sādhana* to seal (*mudrā*) or immobilize breath, seed, mind, and so on. These practices and their textual descriptions, I would argue, are kept explicitly esoteric to maintain not only the secrecy of the *haṭhayoga* tradition but also to secure its oral transmission within a specific lineage. To this end, we find that *haṭhayoga* treatises give abbreviated instructions and, in some cases, inaccurate or obscure directions to ensure and maintain the strict codes of secrecy and proper transmission from *guru* to disciple.[11] The implications of secrecy are compounded by the inability to transfer experience from one person to another. In other words, techniques can be disclosed, but their effects cannot.

It also should be pointed out that to comprehend the complex symbolism and so-called hidden secrets encoded in the image of Ardhanārīśvara, we must first understand that in *haṭhayoga* tradition, sun/*pingalā* and moon/*iḍā* denote the relative duality of female (ovum, *rajas,* etc.) and male (semen, *bindu,* etc.). The *suṣumṇā nāḍī,* or central channel, unites and consolidates the flow of *praṇa* from the *iḍā* and *piṇgalā,* hence, as Swami Kṛpalvananda (1995) discloses in his commentary of the *Haṭhayogapradīpika,* the *suṣumṇā* is not actually a third or separate *nāḍī* but rather the union of the *iḍā* and *piṇgalā*. This implies a distinct analogy or homology between the subtle physiology of the *yogin/ī* and the image of Ardhanārīśvara. In other words, the *suṣumṇā nāḍī,* like the image of Ardhanārīśvara, unites, or should we say, reunites, the homologous designations gendered as female (*piṇgalā*) and male (*iḍā*) within the subtle body of the practitioner. Once unified, this field has the nature of *agni* (fire).[12]

As I mentioned earlier, the separation, or splitting of masculine and feminine principles, pertains specifically to the creation, preservation, and destruction of life, whereas neuter usually designates potential reunification or attainment of undifferentiated consciousness (*yoga*), which is not to say the absence of male or female but rather absolute singularity and indissoluble union. The image of Ardhanārīśvara, like the description of the subtle physiology of the *suṣumṇā nāḍī*, reflects this doctrine of the interplay between union and separation. Das Gupta writes:

> In the yogic texts in general the moon and the sun represent the two elements underlying physical existence,—viz., the element of creation and preservation and the element of change and destruction. The moon as the principle of non-change and immortality resides in the region of Śiva and the sun as the principle of change and destruction resides in the region of Śakti. The moon and the sun are thus associated with Śiva and Śakti. (Das Gupta 1976, 239)

In this sense, the *iḍā* and *piṇgalā nāḍīs* denote feminine/Śakti and masculine/Śiva, respectively, as well as sun (*sūrya*) and moon (*candra*) in their unfused or split state, whereas the *suṣumṇā nāḍī* (fire/*agni*) represents their union and is depicted as androgynous. It is the subtle body iconographic equivalent of the *brahmasūtra* or central axis indicating the "razor's edge" or "middle way" between the male and female halves of the anthropomorphic form of Ardhanārīśvara. *Yoga sādhana* requires the adept to discover through direct experience the reciprocal fusion or absorption of Śiva (masculine, *iḍā*, moon, bull, semen, etc.) and Śakti (feminine, *pingalā*, sun, ovum, cow, etc.) to attain undifferentiated consciousness and absolute emancipation (*śūnyatā*). According to *haṭhayoga* treatises, this begins once the *prāṇa* of the *yogin/ī* reaches, and becomes steady in, the *viśuddha* and *ājñā cakras*, or the designated locus of Ardhanārīśvara in the subtle body of the practitioner.[13]

The powerful ritual techniques of *haṭhayoga sādhana* arouse *prāṇa*, Śakti, and *kuṇḍalinī* in the *mūlādhāra cakra* and lift "her" like a hydraulic pump through the six major energy centers in the subtle body, so "she" can unite with, or return to, her beloved Śiva in the *sahasrāra cakra*. This occurs once the *iḍā* (male) and *piṇgalā* (female) *nāḍīs* have coupled at the second *brahmadvāra,* located in the *ājñā* cakra. In his commentary of the *Haṭhayogapradīpikā*, Kṛpalvananda explains that for the *yogin/ī* the most important section of the *suṣumṇā nāḍī* begins in the *ājñā cakra* and ends in the *sahasrāra*, for it is here that the flow of male and female energy, symbolized as Śakti (sun) and Śiva (moon), actually begins to comingle and becomes one. This is signified by the form and figure of Ardhanārīśvara in *haṭhayoga cakra* theory.

Couched in the twilight language of *haṭhayoga* (called *sandhyābhāsā*), we see that the entire process involves the union of sun, moon, and fire, but its deeper significance for our study of Ardhanārīśvara lies in the further symbolism of sun and moon as the union of male and female (fire), for this is precisely what is being transmitted by the image of Ardhanārīśvara. By awakening, conveying, and uniting Śakti with Śiva in the *sahasrāra cakra,* the subtle androgynization process of *haṭhayoga* (union of sun and moon, male and female, etc.) becomes fully internalized by the adept practitioner. Consequently, the *yogin/ī* comes to gradually recognize himself/herself as a subtle form of Śivārdhanārīśvara.

The various ritual exercises of *haṭhayoga* not only promote holistic health, longevity, calm, and tranquility, but, more importantly, they guide the *yogin/ī* toward insight and wisdom into the metaphysical mysteries of the cosmos portrayed iconographically by the subtle image of Ardhanārīśvara. Eliade, Doniger, Jung, and others have referred to this condition in Western psychotherapeutic or alchemical terms as *conuinctio oppositorum,* or the conjunction of opposites (Jung 1977; Eliade 1969; O'Flaherty 1980; Dyczkowski 1989). Eliade writes:

> Tantrism multiplies the pairs of opposites (sun and moon, Śiva and Śakti, *iḍā* and *piṅgalā,* etc.) and, as we have just seen, attempts to "unify" them through techniques combining subtle physiology with meditation. This fact must be emphasized: on whatever plane it is realized, the conjunction of opposites represents a transcending of the phenomenal world, abolished of all experience of duality. (Eliade 1969, 269)

Practitioners of *haṭhayoga* are guided in the advanced stages of *yoga sādhana* to unify and embody fully the so-called feminine-Śakti and masculine-Śiva poles of their inner nature and subtle being. Indeed, the desired goal of *haṭhayoga* ascetic and spiritual practice could be conceived of as a recognition or reintegration of the two cosmic principles formulated as Śakti and Śiva (or *yoni/liṅga,* sun/moon, *nāda/bindu,* ovum/semen, etc.) within the disciple's own body, similar to the comparative Western notion of *conuinctio oppositorum.*

Through the various techniques mentioned above, the practitioner "forces" his/her personal energy (Śakti) to open the closed door of the *suṣumṇā* to deliver the goddess Śakti to Śiva in the *sahasrāra cakra* (HYP 3:5). *Haṭhayoga* theory portrays this extensive process as the resorption of primordial being (Śakti) into non-being (Śiva). Hence, it is perceived as involutionary (*nivṛtti*) rather than evolutionary. Through this very method of dissolution (*mahāpralaya*), the primordial androgyne, namely, Ardhanārīśvara, is experienced. Eliade writes:

> In the language of the Nātha Siddhas, it is the reabsorption of the cosmos through the inversion of all the processes of manifestation. It is the coincidence of time and eternity, of *bhāva* and *nirvāṇa;* on the purely "human" plane, it is the reintegration of the primordial androgyne, the conjunction, in one's own being, of male and female—in a word, the reconquest of the completeness that precedes all creation. (Eliade 1969, 271)

The so-called coincidence of opposites of ultimate reality experienced in the *yogin/ī's* body-mind-spirit, and exemplified by the image of Ardhanārīśvara in *haṭhayoga* tradition, is induced through the ritual and performative techniques of *sādhana*. The *yogin/ī* endeavors to reverse the process of evolution expounded by the *tattva* doctrine in Sāṃkhya-Yoga by anticipating processes that occur at death (HYP 4:106, 111). The *Śiva Saṃhitā* explains, for example, how the attained *yogin/ī* reverses the order of evolution, materialization, and emanation through a process in which she/he dissolves into undifferentiated or *brahman* consciousness, element by element. This hierarchical inversion or retrogressive process begins in the body of the practitioner with the densest element *bhū* (earth) and moves progressively to the element *ākāśa* (space), designated the purest and most subtle, until individual consciousness merges with *brahman* in the ineffable void/*śūnya* (SS 1:69-78). In other words, during *sādhana*, the *yogin/ī* draws his/her energy (*Śakti*) from the root cakra (*mūlādhāra*), whose element is earth, to the *viśuddha cakra,* whose element is space. This is precisely why the presiding deity of the *viśuddha cakra* is occasionally identified as Sadāśiva or Ardhanārīśvara.[14] Once the *viśuddha cakra* is attained by the *yogin/ī* and the five elements (earth, water, fire, air, and ether, signified by the five heads of Sadāśiva) have been purified, *prāṇa-Śakti* can ascend into and reach the *ājñā cakra,* where the final stages of *yoga* actually begin.

The *Śiva Saṃhitā* announces that ignorance (perceived here as duality and separateness) begins to dissolve, and individual distinction (*asmitā*, I-am-ness) is transcended, once the adept's *prāṇa* or Śakti is established in the *ājñā cakra* (SS:1:78, 85–88). From this point, the *yogin/ī* lifts his/her life force to the crown *cakra* (*sahasrāra, brahmarandhra*) to completely absorb in (*laya*), or reunite fully with, Śiva. In this stage, there is no perception of gender, time, space, and so on. There is only the conscious reflection (*darpaṇa, buddhi*) of authentic identity. The *Yogasūtras* (YS) define this process of introversion, or what we could refer to as primordial androgynization, not only as a reversal of the movement of *pravṛtti* to the state of *nivṛtti* but as *cittavṛttinirodhaḥ* (YS 1:2). It involves, according to Das Gupta,

> firstly, the retrogressive process of turning the cosmic manifestation back to its original form of rest, and this is effected by the yogins by rousing Śakti and uniting her with Śiva in the Sahasrāra. The combination of the sun and the moon implies secondly the yogic practice in which the male and the female unite and the combined substance of the seed and the ovum is sucked within by the yogin or the yogini, as the case may be, through some secret yogic processes. (Das Gupta 1976, 238–39)

In theory, the *yogin/ī* achieves reunion through the practice of advanced *haṭhayoga* techniques, such as *śakticalanā mudrā, vajrolī mudrā, khecarī mudrā*, *kevala kumbhaka*, and so on, which facilitate purification. Indeed, the ultimate aim of *haṭhayoga* purification could be described as the dissolution of being into non-being, signaled initially by Ardhanārīśvara, the image of duality in union *par excellence*. Once this is established, *rājayoga* begins in the crown *cakra* of the head, hence, the term "*rāja*" (HYP 1:1; SS 1:2).

Most studies of this subject have not questioned the gendered nature of the esoteric cosmo-physiology postulated in the *haṭhayoga* paradigm of Śiva-Śakti, nor its attendant iconography. According to our analysis of the subtle body in the *haṭhayoga* system, Ardhanārīśvara, as a relative or conventional paradigm for *haṭhayoga* attainment, sanctifies an elaborately constructed, gendered vision of the universe based primarily on *advaita* precepts. It claims the complementarity of maleness and femaleness in a nondualist, dyadic unity; however, according to *haṭhayoga*, the abstract concepts that the male and female sides of Ardhanārīśvara connote sometimes suggest otherwise. That is, the polyvalent system of homologues represented by the image of Ardhanārīśvara becomes increasingly complex and pervasive, until the entire *haṭhayoga* symbol system as an attempt to describe *samsāra* and *nirvāṇa* can, to a great extent, be rendered by this single, androgynous motif or image.

The base location of Śiva in the *sahasrāra* and Śakti in the *mūlādhāra* is only one of many illustrations of how interpretations of *haṭhayoga* theory have tended to overlook the privileged maleness of the androgyne. Other binary structures, such as left and right, negative and positive, red and white, vowels and consonants, *samsāra* and *nirvāṇa*, to name only a few examples, are modeled on a similar polarization of gendered homologous structures which, at points, give priority to the male half. In other words, the image of Ardhanārīśvara in the *haṭhayoga* tradition still fundamentally conceptualizes the male and female human mind-body-spirit matrix in male-identified terms and, as such, risks displacing its emancipatory goals of nonduality with potentially hierarchical gender ideology.

Ardhanārīśvara in *Haṭhayoga* Iconography

One focus of *haṭhayoga*, as we have mentioned, is its system of *cakras* and their *yantras* or diagrams. *Haṭhayoga* manuals provide a guide to these *cakras*, indicating their characteristics and attributes, such as location, color, form, *bīja* (seed syllables), *vāhana* (vehicle), and so on. For the most part, *haṭhayoga* is fundamentally a praxis-oriented experiential tradition, and the philosophy and metaphysics it promulgates are transmitted orally from *guru* (attained master) to disciple in spite of the current proliferation of modern treatises and commentaries on the subject. As Kaviraj says: "The truth is, the facts of transcendent life are, as a rule, so little known to the outside world" (Kaviraj 1968, 115). As such, its highest secrets are opened only to the initiated, and this is emphasized repeatedly in *haṭhayoga* treatises. For instance, the *Haṭhayogapradīpikā* advises that one who desires "*siddhi*" (perfection) should keep "*haṭha vidyā*" (knowledge) "secret" (HYP 1:11; 3:9; SS 1:19; 5:168; 206–07; GS 1:18). Bearing this in mind, as early as 1913, Western scholars studied these esoteric texts and commented on the *haṭhayoga cakra* systems. Avalon (1972), Briggs (1989), Pott (1966), Eliade (1969), and Danielou (1955), to name only a few pioneers in this field, situated Ardhanārīśvara in the *viśuddha cakra* located at the base of the throat or, more specifically, at the laryngeal and pharyngeal plexus where the spinal column and the medulla oblongata join.

Haṭhayoga treatises generally give the *viśuddha cakra* as the site or locus of Ardhanārīśvara. Typically, it is portrayed as a sixteen-petalled lotus,[15] along with sixteen corresponding syllables (*a, a, i, i, u, u, ru, ru, lu, lu, e, ai, ao, auo, am, ah*). The seed syllable "*ham*" is placed in the center of the *candra maṇḍala* or its specified diagram, the circle. Its element is *ākāśa* (space), and the quality of the *element* is *śabda* (sound). Consequently, it is commonly referred to as the communication center. It is sky blue or smoky in color. As we have already mentioned, Ardhanārīśvara, sometimes in the form of Sadāśiva, is portrayed as the presiding deity.

It also is important to note that the seat of *citta* (consciousness) is located between the eyebrows in the *ājñā cakra*, and the seats of matter (*prakṛti*) are distributed according to density in hierarchically ascending order along the five centers (*cakras*) from the base of the spine (*mūlādhāra cakra*) to the throat (*viśuddha*). There also are several lesser known *cakras* that lie between the *ājñā* and *sahasrāra cakras*. In some systems, they include *sūryacakra, agnicakra, candracakra, lalanācakra, somacakra,* and *kalācakra*. In this way, each *cakra* is linked to the evolution of the *tattvas* of Sāṃkhya philosophy. For instance, the four *cakras* rising from the *ājñā* correspond in the Sāṃkhya system to *manas, ahaṃkāra, buddhi,* and *prakṛti,* respectively. In other words, the *sūryacakra* corresponds to *manas, candracakra* corresponds to *ahaṃkāra, agnicakra* corresponds to *buddhi,* and *sahasrāra* corresponds to (pure) *prakṛti*. The *ājñā cakra,* however, is commonly given as the collective frame of reference for the seat of mind in the *cakra* system.

Being different from the *viśuddha cakra*, the iconography of the *ājñā cakra* illustrates a diagram containing two petals and the seed syllables (*bīja*) *ha* and *ksa*. In the center of the circle is a *trikoṇa* (a female-identified triangle with apex facing downward ▼) displaying the "3" portion of the diagrammatic version of the *praṇava* (*auṃ* or *oṃ* symbol ॐ). Directly above the *trikoṇa* is the *ardhacandra bindu* (half moon and dot, ँ). It is possible that the *ardhacandra bindu* gestures in its diagrammatic form to the three *cakras* mentioned above, that is, the *sūrya*, *candra*, and *agni cakras*. In this sense, these combined symbols imply the underlying union of the *iḍā*, *pingalā* and *suṣumṇā nāḍīs*, referred to in *haṭhayoga* texts as *triveṇī* or *prayāga*, a process that the *yogin/ī* experiences in the primary or beginning stages in the *mūlādhāra* or root *cakra* and again in more advanced stages in the *ājñā cakra* (SS 5:132–44). This well-known term, *triveṇī* or *yukti triveṇī*, refers to the geographic confluence of the Yamunā, Gaṅgā, and Sarasvatī rivers (*nāḍīs*), but in *yoga* theory, these rivers are homologous with the three main *nāḍīs* of the subtle *yogic* body, namely, *iḍā*, *piṇgalā*, and *suṣumṇā*, respectively. When applied in *haṭhayoga*, the term *triveṇī* refers to the place of union of these three rivers/*nāḍīs* in the subtle body of the practitioner. The initial experience of *triveṇī* occurs in the *mūlādhāra*, but the second and lesser-known *triveṇī* is slightly above the *ājñā cakra* in the second *brahmarandhra* (upper portion of *suṣumṇā*), and it is sometimes referred to as Vārāṇasī or *brahmadvāra* (SS 5:100, 132–44). We refer again to this symbol in the context of *nāda yoga* and its relation to the image of Ardhanārīśvara further on in the chapter.

We also see a comparison emerging between the *śrīcakrayantra*, depicting the state of Śiva-Śakti in the *sahasrāra*, and Ardhanārīśvara. The *śrīcakra yantra*, like the *sahasrāra cakra*, conveys in aniconic form the belief in the interpenetration and complementarity of the masculine and feminine principles of ultimate reality. Pupul Jayakar (1990) states that the *śrīcakrayantra* is considered a "manifestation of the half-male, half-female forms, the Ardhanārīśvara" (123). In the symbol of the *śrīcakrayantra*, this is conveyed by the intersection of nine upward and downward facing triangles signifying the male and female cosmic principles Śiva and Śakti. For Jayakar, abstract representations involving geometric configurations such as the *śrīcakra* are an intrinsic part of the collective Indian unconscious and coexist in the pan-Indian context alongside anthropomorphic expressions of the deity.

Even in some descriptions and illustrations of the *sahasrāra*, union between Śiva and Śakti is figured diagrammatically by the *trikoṇa* and *yoni* to indicate the absolute inclusion of the feminine principle in *yoga* attainment and cosmology (SS 5:122, 145). There also are illustrations that depict the transcendent state of consciousness attained by the *yogin/ī* in the *sahasrāra* and the extended realm above as figured anthropomorphically by the androgynous motif of Ardhanārīśvara. For instance, a famous gouache on paper dating from seventeenth-century Nepal portrays the *sahasrāra cakra* with a *trikoṇa* and a divine couple in an amorous posture. The transcendent realm above this is presided over by Ardhanārīśvara (Rawson 1973). This is evident from the various identifying diagnostic features contained in the image, such as vertical division into two separate complexions, a half moustache on the right, two different shaped eyes, *triśūla* in the right upper hand and flower in the left upper hand, different earring styles, and two distinct types of clothing.

Consequently, we see that there is some ambivalence about where and when Ardhanārīṣvara or Śiva-Śakti is encountered, though typically in the *haṭhayoga cakra* system the *viśuddha* and *ājñā cakras* are the primary loci (Kaviraj 1968, 234). *Yantras,* or sacred diagrams, experienced by the adept during *sādhana,* are imbued with esoteric meaning. Indeed, that is their primary purpose. The deity, element, location, *bīja,* and so on operate as a discrete language that discloses to the individual practitioner their stage of development, but the ultimate, underlying, theological implication is that Śiva is eternally one with Śakti. However, according to *haṭhayoga* theory, Śiva is most evidently Ardhanārīśvara once the disciple has attained a certain stage of meditation proficiency and the initial stages of *advaita* begin. This starts in the *viśuddha cakra* and continues until the final stages of self-realization in the *sahasrāra*. As the *Śiva Samhitā* explains, in the initial stages of the final phase of the involution of *prakṛti,* all thoughts of a personal self/ego (I, *ahaṃkāra*) begin to dissolve, and individual consciousness (*citta*) is absorbed in the *mahāśūnya,* or the great nothingness (SS 5:160, 172–74). This can only occur once Śakti has been raised to the *ājñā cakra,* or the realm of *buddhi* (portrayed in Indian iconography by Pārvatī's *darpaṇa*), and commences the crowning journey (i.e., *rājayoga*) upward through the subtle *suṣumṇā nāḍī* (SS 5:155, 7:5–16; HYP 4:5–7).[16] Although many Western scholars following Avalon identify Ardhanārīśvara as the presiding deity of the *viśuddha cakra* (see, e.g., Eliade 1969, 243; Pott 1966, 11; Danielou 1955, 131), I am proposing, as *haṭhayoga* manuals suggest, that Ardhanārīśvara as Śiva-Śakti is actually experienced in three progressive stages, from gross (beginning) to subtlemost (advanced), that is, from the *viśuddha* to the *sahasrāra*. However, iconography can only render the perceived *sakala* aspect.

Consequently, the *Haṭhayogapradīpikā* implies that in the final stages of *yoga* (i.e., *samādhi*), there can be no possible grounds for sexism, misogyny, racism, *hiṃsa,* and so on, precisely because the *yogin/ī* is no longer conscious of a "self-centered" identity nor clings to labels, hierarchy, duality, senses, and so on (HYP 4:106–13). This includes sex and gender designations as well. Indeed, the symbol of nonduality, complementarity, and equality that Ardhanārīśvara postulates (depending, of course, on variations of the expression), could stand as a potent one in Indian tradition for the unity and ultimate dance of interdependence between *samsāra* and *nirvāṇa* (e.g., Ardhanārīnaṭeśvara).

Inside the Tradition

Since I began this examination of Ardhanārīśvara in 1989, I was fortunate to have an opportunity to study and practice with Swami Vinit Muni. During that time, we worked together on a translation of his *guru's*, Swami Kṛpalvananda's, commentary of the *Haṭhayogapradīpikā* (1994). In his oral exegesis of the text, Swami Vinit Muni explained the often vague and deliberately esoteric nature of the *haṭhayo*ga tradition and, in the process, transmitted his personal understanding of *yoga*.[17] His principal disciple, Swami Oṃ Shivatva Muni, continues to share his knowledge of this subject as it relates specifically to the Ardhanārīśvara motif.[18]

What has become reasonably clear from my own intense study and practice within this orally transmitted *yoga* lineage is the humbling realization that the adept practitioner understands more than this scholar can ever hope to. While I collect, classify, and analyze images and texts, the adept *yogin/ī* lives the direct experience daily.[19] Engagement provides, first, the solid experiential and observational grounding necessary to speak as an authority on behalf of the tradition and, second, a primary source from which to understand precisely how Ardhanārīśvara functions as an image in the living tradition of Indian *yoga*. As Swami Oṃ Shivatva has repeatedly reminded me, Ardhanārīśvara is symbolized primarily in *haṭhayo*ga treatises so that the *yogin/ī* can understand his/her stage of *sādhana*. In other words, Ardhanārīśvara is not "a picture." The image is used in *yoga* specifically to encode and explain subtle processes that are going on in the higher stages of *nivṛtti mārga sādhana*.

From this insider perspective, Ardhanārīśvara provides a guiding image or meditational map that assists the professional practitioner understand the dynamics of transformation in his/her own gradual systematic spiritual quest for emancipation (*mokṣa*, *mukti*). The subject-object duality that is stamped in the divided consciousness of every human being is embodied in this image alongside an esoteric guide for overcoming the fragmentation and alienation that human beings feel because of it. Many cultures have developed approaches to this human situation through their use and application of the androgynous motif, and *haṭhayoga*, with its attendant imagery of the divine androgyne Ardhanārīśvara, is just one among many.[20]

In a male-dominated culture it is not surprising that a male-dominated image and interpretations of the image are psychologically projected along with an often one-sided view of the feminine. This, however, is only part of the story. There is no doubt whatsoever that the basic structure of the Śaiva *haṭhayoga* universe erects patternized and parallel concepts modeled on the more conventional, hierarchical male and female paradigms of Indian society. However, the final goal of this formulaic design overtly stresses the attainment of equilibrium or equipoise between the coincidence or complementarity of seemingly polar opposites depicted in the androgynous image of Ardhanārīśvara. Indeed, the adept practitioners with whom I have had the opportunity to study extensively encouraged and supported a feminist critique of the image of Ardhanārīśvara and its attendant male-dominated psychology if it is to be a truly emancipatory paradigm that speaks to and for men and women in a contemporary context. However, since *advaita* metaphysics are in many ways founded on the absorption of the feminine, and upon the negation of her difference, this is not an easy task.

From their perspective, the actual *yoga* practices that lead human beings from bondage (i.e., ignorance, *samsāra*) to freedom are intended for both men and women, even though male anatomy and so on has typically been the traditional psycho-physical model in most *sādhana* treatises. The dual pairs that we see fused together in the homologous metaphysical system symbolized by the image of Ardhanārīśvara are relative to the men and women who methodically and systematically practice *yoga*. By the force and purification of *haṭhayoga* practice, both male and female adepts are propelled to a new level of consciousness in which such things as rigid view regarding sexuality and gender are seemingly transformed or dissolved in the unity of the nameless and formless void. The androgynous figure of Ardhanārīśvara depicts precisely this stage of meditation (*dhyāna, samādhi*) in which the demarcation between divine macrocosm and physical microcosm is not sharply drawn. In fact, it marks a distinct turning point in the spiritual direction of the adept practitioner, leading to deeper and more meaningful states of connectedness, wholeness, and integration. As such, Ardhanārīśvara signals the beginning of *rājayoga* and marks the *yogin/ī's* return to a state of absolute, primordial, undifferentiated consciousness.

In this sense, it is not the image *per se* that is the focal point in this section but rather an analysis of the precise stage of the adept meditator when she/he experiences or embodies the image. This is possible because the image itself functions in *yoga* as a *mudrā*, that is, a condensed sign or an internalized seal of what is potentially possible for the human consciousness to obtain in meditation and an explanation as to why. Ardhanārīśvara, experienced primarily in the *viśuddha* and *ājñā cakras*[21] of the subtle body of the adept *yogin/ī*, embraces two simultaneous aspects of being, that is, ultimate (*advaita*) and conventional (relative, *dvaita*) reality personified as male (Śiva) and female (Śakti), respectively.

In the world of *haṭhayoga*, the body of the *yogin/ī* is conceived of as tripartite, namely, physical body (*sthūla śarīra, apara*), composed of the five elements, earth (*bhū*), water (*jala*), fire (*agni*), air (*vāyu*), and space (*ākāśa*); subtle, astral body (*sūkṣma śarīra, para-apara*) or self (*ātma, jīva*); and subtlemost or supreme body (*para śarīra, brahman*).[22] As mentioned earlier, this threefold human schema similarly corresponds in reverse direction to the unfolding of the triune nature of Śiva in Indian iconography as Parabrahman/Paraśiva, Sadāśiva, and the anthropomorphic figures Maheśvara and Ardhanārīśvara. Thus, in *haṭhayoga*, as in iconography, the gross and subtle bodies are understood as an empirical consequence or a *karmic* effect, that is, a projection (illusion, *māyā*) of the subtlemost body for the ultimate purpose of self-realization, and *sādhana*, in all of its various forms, including *satkarmas* (six purifying actions), *japa* (recitation of *mantra*), *yantra* (diagrams, also *maṇḍalas*), *āsana*, *mudrā* (postures), *bandhas* (locks), *prāṇāyāma* (breathing techniques), *dhyāna* (meditation), and so on, is the primary means of discovering or unveiling the primordial nature of this essential nondual being.[23] It is in this sense that the subtle body of the practitioner manifests as an internal and symbolic expression of Ardhanārīśvara in the penultimate stage of *haṭhayoga*.

The subtlemost body, as this theory suggests, precedes sexual differentiation (splitting). Hence, the goal of the adept *yogin/ī* is the realization of the innate unity and oneness of the threefold permutation of this subtlemost body into *jñāta* (knower), *jñāna* (knowledge), and *jñeya* (known) within his/her own body-mind complex, corresponding to the tripartite scheme of the three bodies and the triarchic unfolding of Paraśiva. This culminating experience or message conveyed by Ardhanārīśvara also is a direct realization of the evoluting (*pravṛtti*) and involuting (*nivṛtti*) creative powers of the deity, by which the practitioner, through *sādhana*, returns to the primal essence (*śūnyatā*) via the very stages implied by cosmic emanation.[24] This suggests that the adept practitioner must overcome identification with the apparent dualistic tendencies of "self" and "other" imprinted on, and deeply sedimented within, conventional human consciousness.

However, at yet a deeper level, the subtlemost body also refers to the *guru* or the innermost mentor who guides the *sādhana* process of the practitioner toward self-realization (*ātma vidyā*). This so-called inner *guru* or subtle force is awakened and mediated through the specific practices of *haṭha* and *rāja yoga*. Although much has been written about the role of the *guru* in Indian tradition, here I am suggesting that the *guru* is ultimately not an actual outward form or a human person, though according to the early stages of *haṭhayoga* practice a human *guru* is vital, but, rather, that *guru* is perhaps better, or more fully, understood as *īśvara* or *nātha* (i.e., lord, *yogevśara, ādinātha*, etc.).[25]

In the subtle body (*sūkṣma śarīra*, etc.) of the practitioner, this is simply one's own self (*ātman, jīva, Śakti*) who awakens the body and mind to the potentiality of the integrity of being as depicted in the image and subtle processes signified by the form and figure of Ardhanārīśvara, once again, bearing in mind that the subtlemost aspect of being realized is in the fourth stage (*turīya*) and the subtlemost *yoga* body (*para*) is *arūpa* (not form), that is, *brahman, Śivatva, śūnyatā*, and so on.

As early as the classical *Upaniṣadic* period of Indian culture, we find the physical universe typically perceived as the *karmic* result of cause and effect, and one's own role and place in society is understood in various ways as the outcome of actions, past, present, and future. Thus an explication of *karma* is essential to any discussion of Ardhanārīśvara. According to Swami Oṃ Shivatva, Ardhanārīśvara depicts the conscious meeting of action (*karma*, evolution) and inaction (*akarma*, involution), or what we would call cause and effect. In *haṭhayoga* tradition, active *kuṇḍalinī* is conceptualized as Śakti (also Mahākālī), whereas dormant, inactive, or static *kuṇḍalinī* is Śiva.[26] The meeting of *karma* (Śakti) and *akarma* (Śiva) in the *viśuddha cakra* occurs in its gross or *sthūla* form. It becomes progressively subtle or *sūkṣma* in the *ājñā cakra*, which leads to the subtlemost or *para* meeting in the *sahasrāra cakra*, at which time the adept practitioner experiences the great dissolution (*mahālaya*) of Śiva *and* Śakti, or *yoga*.

We can discern that from the *viśuddha* to the *sahasrāra* the adept experiences a progressive movement from gross to subtlemost. In other words, advanced stages of *sādhana* actually cause the restraint and dissolution of *karma* and *vāsanā* (desire) in the adept practitioner.[27] As a direct result of the purification and penetration of the *ājñā cakra*, *prāṇa* (*śakti, kuṇḍalinī*) flows upward through the *paścima mārga* (rear middle half[28]) into the *sahasrāra*, and the *yogin/ī* attains sustained or prolonged periods of *unmanā* (no mind or beyond mind). Consequently, in this stage of higher meditation, all practices and manifestations, that is, the effects of *karma*, are uprooted, and they begin to disappear or dissolve. This also implies that differentiation and distinction begin to dissolve, for it is in this stage that Śakti loses her capacity for action and, consequently, separation (HYP 4:24–25; YS 1:2; SS 1:1; also see parallels with the Vajrayāna practice of *Mahāmudrā*).

This, however, refers to an advanced stage of *yoga* that commences, as Kṛpalvānanda explains, only with the onset of *kevala kumbhaka* (retention of breath) in the formative stages of *sabīja samādhi*. Understood in this way, Śakti indicates the evolution (*pravṛtti*) of *karma*, the dormant Śiva (hence, Kālī dances on Śiva's corpse). The involution (*nivṛtti*) or progressive dissolution of *karma* reflects the regressive activity of Śakti, or dominant Śiva. In other words, Śiva as Śakti is active (*karma*). With the return of Śakti to the subtle body of the practitioner between the *ājñā* and *sahasrāra* through *dhyāna* and *samādhi*, Śakti as Śiva becomes dormant or inactive (*akarma*). Ordinarily in this stage Śakti cannot retain any sense of individuality or appearance, having been emancipated from *karma* and *vāsana*.

To reach this stage, *haṭhayoga* texts speak of the awakening of *kuṇḍalinī* as the female serpent located in dormant form at the base of the *mūlādhāra cakra* in the subtle body of each and every human being (HYP 3:97, 101; SS 5:57–62). This female serpent power is homologous in constructions of *haṭhayoga* theory with the cosmic serpents Śesa and Ananta seen wrapped around the right half of Ardhanārīśvara in various iconographic representations (e.g., Fig. 1.6 Bādāmī; White 1996, 218). The successful *yogin/ī* awakens this so-called female serpent power by force (*haṭha*) and through progressive techniques that reverse the natural evoluting order of life, "she" leads the practitioner on a path of inversion or reversal to the highest *yoga* realizations of *samādhi*, *samarasa*, and *laya* (HYP 3:102–05). Consequently, "she" unites with, and is absorbed into, Śiva in the crown of the head (*sahasrāra cakra*). This represents the ascent of Pārvatī, which we will consider in more detail in a later chapter.

What is significant here is that the subtle body of each and every human being, male and female, is essentially androgynous (i.e., Śiva-Śakti) according to *haṭhayoga* theory. That is, men and women are macrocosmic emanations of the primordial androgyne Ardhanārīśvara. The process of *haṭhayoga* entails awakening and uniting the female-identified, action (*karma*, *samsāra*)-oriented energy (*kuṇḍalinī*, Śakti, etc), with the male-identified, static energy (Śiva) in the subtlemost body of the *yogin/ī*.[29] It is not surprising that the imagery and metaphors employed to explain these subtle processes of *haṭhayoga* are cast primarily in male-centered terms. The metaphysical and hierarchical claims of *yoga* certainly became codified in an iconographical and a textual system that eventually absolutized the doctrines of this system in fixed gender terms stemming from patriarchal culture. But the ultimate goal of this spiritual journey, as the *haṭhayoga* texts clearly indicate, lies beyond the path of speech, the object of thought, or hierarchical forms and appearances. The three levels of the body, *sthūla*, *śukṣma* and *para*, coalesce in the final stages of *yogasādhana* and are recognized as singular or nondual by the adept. The seemingly endless stream of *samsāra* that the *yogin/ī* strives to overcome is in actuality only the fixed belief in a separate ego (I, *ahaṃ*).

It is important, I think, to recognize and remember that the embodiment of Ardhanārīśvara in the *sādhana* of the adept signals the incomplete union or the penultimate stage of *sabīja samādhi*. Emancipation from the manifestation of Ardhanārīśvara, or any manifestation for that matter, in the *sahasrāra* or beyond marks complete reintegration (*nirbīja samādhi*) with the primordial void (*śūnyatā, brahman*). In this sense, Ardhanārīśvara signals and correlates with the completion of *haṭhayoga* in *sabīja samādhi* only. For this reason, an examination of the *haṭhayoga* material is crucial. While Śakti and Śiva are totally united in the *sahasrāra* in meditation, there can be no manifestation or form (e.g., *ahaṃkāra*)—there is only *śūnyatā*.[30] In this state, no gender difference remains whatsoever, either masculine or feminine.

Furthermore, in the resorption of cosmic emanation according to *nivṛtti mārga haṭhayo*ga, the basic categories of form, that is, the twenty-four *tattvas* (elements) of Sāṃkhya-Yoga *darśana*, enumerated as *prakṛti, buddhi, ahaṃkāra, manas, pañca buddhīndriyas, pañca karmendriyas, pañca tanmātras*, and *pañca mahābhūtas*, are each absorbed into the preceding subtler form through an arduous process of purification (*śuddhi*), piercing (*vedha*), and inversion (*ulaṭā*), explaining why the *viśuddha cakra* is the limit of *haṭhayoga*.[31] Reaching the *viśuddha* indicates not only the purification of the fifth *cakra* or final locus of the gross or physical elements based upon Sāṃkhya evolutionary theory but the purification of the preceding four *cakras* as well. Once pierced, the purification process proceeds upward into the *ājñā cakra*, marking the entrance to the crown of the head or subtle *tattva* mind and signaling to the adept the beginning of *rājayoga*, or *sabīja samādhi*. Consequently, *haṭhayoga* is understood as a process of dissolution, immobilization, and transmutation, that is, the progressive and systematic assimilation of form (e.g., Ardhanārīśvara) into formlessness (*Śivatva, śūnyatā, brahman*, etc.) in the *sahasrāra*.

We read in the *Haṭhayogapradīpikā* that the absorption of *Śakti/prakṛti* in the elemental forms *citta* and *prāṇa* (and also *bindu*), or *jīva* and *ātma*, in the final stages of *samādhi* is analogous to salt dissolved in water and camphor dissolved in fire (HYP 4:6–7, 58). In order to understand this process, we must remember that the hierarchy of elemental emanates situated in ascending order from lower to higher along the subtle columnar form of the subtle *yoga* body, called Mt. Meru (or *brahmasūtra*, in iconography), recedes one into another, causing the last remaining and subtlemost forms of mind to be gradually reintegrated into the great void (*mahāśūnyatā*). This brings us back once again to the ultimate goal of *yoga*, which is the recognition of pure or primordial consciousness, variously referred to as *brahman, Śivatva, śūnyatā, kaivalya, asaṃprājñāta samādhi*, and so on. This is portrayed in various *yoga* systems through an elaborately constructed system of gendered correspondences, including such seemingly bipolar pairs as *prakṛti* and *puruṣa*, *iḍā* and *piṅgalā*, sun (*sūrya*) and moon (*candra*), *prāṇa* and *apāna*, guru (*nātha*) and disciple (*chela*), inhalation (*pūraka*) and exhalation (*recaka*), left (*vāma*) and right (*dakṣiṇa*), northern and southern, and so on, all based on the conventional, underlying, hierarchical gender paradigm of masculine and feminine. But these are still references to form, or Ardhanārīśvara. In a more extended sense, we also encounter triads in *yoga* tradition insofar as the members of the aforementioned pairs unite to form a third unified field. When the dyadic homologues become unified (emptied of duality), then and only then can Śakti ascend through the medial channel of the subtle body (*suṣumṇā*) to unite (*yoga*) with Śiva and to attain emancipation.[32] As mentioned previously, it is in this sense that the *suṣumṇā* or central channel (middle way) is not a separate *nāḍī* but rather the union of the *iḍā* and *piṅgalā* (GP 1:62; HYP 3.12, 27). This applies equally to all of the above dyads. For example, inhalation and exhalation unite in *kevala kumbhaka*. The united form of each of these pairs reflects the androgynous motif or sign of progressive absorption at the subtle level of *yoga* experience.

Based on Sāṃkhya-Yoga *tattva* theory, the seat of the mind (*citta*) is located in the cerebrum between the two eyebrows in the center of the forehead (*ājñācakra*),[33] and the seats of matter, or the five gross elements (*paṇcamahābhūtas*), of space, air, fire, water, and earth, are located in the five lower *cakras* from the throat (*viśuddha*) to the base of the spine (*mūlādhāra*), respectively. Forming pentads, they correspond to the five senses and five organs of sense (*tanmātras* and *karmendriyas*) signified, for instance, as the five heads of Sadāśiva. Pentadic homologues also can be extended to phonic emanations as well. Return movement commences with the densest of the five gross elements, earth, located in the *mūlādhāra,* using the technology of *haṭhayoga* practice (e.g., *satkarmas, āsana, prāṇāyāma, mudrā, bandha, kumbhaka,* etc.), until Śakti absorbs all of the elements into the subtle body, signaled by the completion of *haṭhayoga* in the *viśuddha cakra* (first five *cakras*), and mind becomes increasingly subtle in the subsequent stage of *ājñā cakra.* This is what is conveyed by the symbol of Ardhanārīśvara in *haṭhayoga.* As we will see, there also are parallels in *nādayoga,* or what Beck (1993) calls "sonic theology."

The *yogin/ī* experiences the ascent of Śakti, according to *haṭhayoga* doctrine, in the physical and subtle body during *sādhana.* As "she" ascends, or as dynamic energy or vibration rises through the body via the *suṣumṇā nāḍī,* "she" purifies and absorbs all that is associated with the five-sense centers and mind, one by one, until they enter into the *laya* state (HYP 4:18–21). In other words, the various senses and their corresponding manifest actions, sense organs, sounds, and so on are purified, restrained, absorbed, and emptied so that Śakti can ascend in *sādhana* along the path of the *suṣumṇā* without distraction or obstruction directly from the *mūlādhāra* to the *sahasrāra cakra.* When Śakti reaches the *viśuddha* and *ājñā cakras,* the primary sites of Ardhanārīśvara, manifestation and vibration become very subtle. Once Śakti enters the domain of Śiva (inaction) in the *sahasrāra*, the *yogin/ī* is liberated from the three *guṇas* (*tamas*, *rajas*, and *sattva*), therefore, no vibratory manifestation (*vṛtti*) on any level whatsoever remains. In simple terms, Śakti loses her power to act (*karma*), and in this sense she is no different from Śiva (*akarma*).

By probing the *cakra* system of *haṭhayoga* further, we can see the theoretical basis of this ascent. Each *cakra* is associated with a presiding deity, element, *bīja* (seed syllable), form, color, sense organ, and so on, depicted in the pericarps of the various lotuses of the subtle *yoga* body (SS 5:56-131). In the *Haṭhayogapradīpikā*, the first *cakra*, the *mūlādhāra*, is associated with the earth element and the sense of smell. The presiding deity is the elephant god Ganeśa, and his vehicle (*vāhana*) is a mouse. The seemingly humorous analogy depicted by the imagery of an elephant boy traveling on a mouse conveys the *haṭhayoga* idea that it is extremely difficult for the practitioner to awaken, purify, harness, and move Śakti through this initial root *cakra*. Once this is accomplished, however, the element and the sense (action) are yoked or restrained. The ascent moves gradually to the second *cakra*, the *svādhisthāna*, and so on, until Śakti moves through all three remaining *cakras* (*manipūra* or navel, *anāhata* or heart, and *viśuddha* or throat) into the *ājñā cakra*, and the process of emptying, unveiling, or yoking of the subtle element of *citta* (mind) begins. It is in this center that the adept *yogin/ī* experiences Ardhanārīśvara as *mudrā* or sealed experience (*mahāmudrā*).

Suspension of respiration (*kevala kumbhaka*)[34] indicates this advanced state. According to Oṃ Shivatva, sustained practices such as *kevala kumbhaka* open the cranial cavity into the upper regions of the *sahasrāra* where *sattva guṇa* is released into, and pervades, the entire consciousness, making it light and pure. By this method of *sahaja* (spontaneous) *sādhana*, gross physical elements are absorbed into subtleness, each dissolving (i.e., purifying), into their immediate cause, and all dissolving into *citta*. Between the *ājñā* and the *sahasrāra* lies the subtle cavity called *brahmarandhra*, into which the upward-faced *suṣumṇā* (*nāḍī*, nerve) reaches. At this stage, Śakti touches the *candra cakra* or moon disc in the middle of the *sahasrāra*, and nectar (*amṛta*, *somarasa*)[35] begins to flow into the *ājñā cakra* (HYP 3:51, 76). The whole body is filled with the blissful secretion of the nectar of immortality (*amṛta*). The energy of Śiva becomes purified *tamas*, or the pure static energy of cessation (*nivṛtti*, *nirodha*). But this is not experienced until the upward-faced *suṣumṇā* is opened, and Śakti is absorbed (*laya*). This is what is meant by *nirbīja samādhi*, the final stage (*aṅga*) of the *yoga* process that does not manifest as *sakala* Ardhanārīśvara, or any other sign or indication for that matter.

This stage of Ardhanārīśvara constitutes the end of the reverse movement of Śakti, wherein sun and moon are converted into the unified triad or final fire called *brahmāgni*. This fire, as Oṃ Shivatva explains, has no flame (*nirvāṇa*), no form (male or female), and no darkness whatsoever. Since the seats of *karma* and *vāsanā* reside in the *citta* (*ājñā cakra*), each gross element absorbs into the next subtler element (i.e., its cause), hence, in this way all cause and effect (*karma*, active *Śakti*) is ultimately dissolved (SS 1:78). *Prāṇa* dissolves into *citta*, since they, like Ardhanārīśvara, are simply two ends of the same pole (HYP 4:24–25). When the adept's stage or experience of Ardhanārīśvara becomes progressively sustained, subtle, and steady, she/he attains perfect knowledge (*jñāna*, *prājñāparamita*), that is, she/he knows the root cause and effect (*karma*) of the universe as *avidyā* or desire. All bipolarisms or dyads, with their relative propensity for hierarchy and opposition, are overcome as the essential subject-object dichotomy dissolves or coalesces in undifferentiated consciousness (*śūnyatā*).

Ardhanārīśvara also signals the restraint or preservation of *bindu*[36] (sexual fluid) according to *haṭha* treatises (HYP 4:28). Even though the poet Bhagīratha is saddened by the anti-erotic nature of Ardhanārīśvara, the *yogin/ī* considers fully attained *brahmācarya* or *ūrdhvaretas* a great achievement.[37] Oṃ Shivatva explains that Ardhanārīśvara is a sign to the practitioner that she/he is ready to dissolve all *karma* (including sexual activity) and attributes (*guṇas*) in the *sahasrāra*. Once again, we see that Ardhanārīśvara announces a level of *sādhana* to the practitioner. As such, it is imperative to understand what is happening inside the *yogin/ī* in this stage.

Here, Oṃ Shivatva's understanding is immensely valuable. He explains that there are two phases of the autonomic nervous system, sympathetic and parasympathetic. According to *yoga* theory, the brain (*sahasrāra*) is not the beginning of all nerves but rather the end, where the sum of all impressions (*samskāras*, *vāsanā*) is stored. Consequently, we find references to the brain as the "thousand-petalled lotus" (*sahasrāra*) in *haṭhayoga* manuals.[38] These so-called petals surround the subtle cavity called *brahmarandhra*. The static power of Śakti relates to the parasympathetic portion of the autonomic nervous system, and the dynamic or katabolic power of Śakti refers to the sympathetic portion of the autonomic nervous system. As humans, we typically cannot control the involuntary actions of the autonomic nervous system, such as heartbeat, breathing, and so on. It functions regularly and unconsciously. When the *yogin/ī*, however, starts to embody or become Ardhanārīśvara through *sādhana*, it is a sign that she/he can actually control aspects of the autonomic system. This is a direct result of prolonged and intense *haṭhayoga* practices such as *satkarmas* (six purifying actions, including *neti, dhauti,* etc.), *prāṇāyāma* (breathing), *mudrā* (advanced *āsana*/postures), *bandha* (locks), *dhyāna* (meditation), *nāda* (e.g., the spontaneous inner sound of *oṃ*), and so on. All of these spontaneous techniques (e.g., *kevala kumbhaka, anāhata nāda*), affect the vibrational system (*Śakti*) and propel the mind of the *yogin/ī* into the *laya* (absorbed, still) process. As a result, the involuntary actions of the body, such as breathing (e.g., *kevala kumbhaka*), are controlled or restrained (*nirodha*) (HYP 4:31; YS 1:2).

Similar to other dyadic correspondences, such as *prāṇa* and *apāna, iḍā* and *piṇgalā*, inhalation (*pūraka*) and exhalation (*recaka*), and so on, the two portions of the nervous system are polarized in *haṭhayoga* as male (*nara/īśvara*) and female (*nārī*). According to *haṭhayoga*, even the tissues of a living body polarize into anabolic and katabolic, that is, some tending to change (evolution, vibration, Śakti) and others to conserve (involution, stasis, Śiva). In advanced stages of *sabīja samādhi*, signaled by Ardhanārīśvara, the *yogin/ī* experiences the stilling of the autonomic nervous system. Here, *iḍā* and *piṇgalā*, the two principal *nāḍīs* or nerve impulses in the subtle *yoga* body, rest in the *ājñā cakra* or the nasociliary extension of the cavernous plexus of the sympathetic nervous system, and they unite or become one in the final, upward-face region of the *suṣumṇā*. In other words, the dynamic (*karma*, active, Śakti) pole and the static (*akarma*, Śiva) pole of ultimate reality merge, or they cease to be polarized.

In this sense, the process of *haṭhayoga* is preparation for the awakening of the sealed experience (*mudrā*) of Ardhanārīśvara in the subtle body of the disciple. Once an advanced practitioner reaches this stage of *sabīja samādhi*, the duality between *guru* (Śiva, *īśvara, nātha*) and disciple (Śakti, Pārvatī, *nārī*) dissolves (Ardhanārīśvara).[39] In the early stages of *haṭhayoga*, the disciple often experiences intense sexual passion during *sādhana*. In many ways, this is precisely why energy is projected as female. *Haṭhayoga* treatises have been written from a male perspective, for primarily a male monastic or celibate community. However, from the *viśuddha* to the *sahasrāra*, desire is theoretically restrained, if not overcome completely, and as *vairāgya* (spontaneous renunciation) intensifies, the meeting of Śiva and Śakti loses its initial and oftentimes powerful sense of physical eroticism. Consequently, once the fear of losing genital fluids is genuinely overcome, the *yoga* process appears to be framed in increasingly egalitarian terms.

As mentioned earlier, Ardhanārīśvara occurs in progressive stages corresponding to the three bodies of the *yogin/ī*. The gross or physical form of passion dissolves into a subtle, inner beatitude, according to Oṃ Shivatva. This marks the beginning of neutrality, or *śūnyatā*. All symptoms or signs of Ardhanārīśvara dissolve, so that there is no gender, no polarity, no form, and no remainder of any kind. Thus the seeming polarity of the subject-object split that we feel as human beings is really an experience of mind (*citta*) only. In the final stage of Ardhanārīśvara, the practitioner reaches the border between *haṭhayoga* and *rājayoga* and enters the last stages of manifestation (or vibration). This stage of *sabīja samādhi* indicates the transformation of the body's entire psycho-physiology. *Nirbīja samādhi,* the fourth and final stage (also referred to as *laya, turīya,* etc.), is actually the end of *sakala* Ardhanārīśvara. After this, the *yogin/ī* enters the stage of *niṣkala* or *avadhūtī,*[40] in which the cessation (*laya, nirodha*) of all fragmentation, duality, or fluctuation (*vṛtti,* desire) of mind (*citta*) is realized (SS 5:158; YS 1:2). From here on, nothing manifests (*mahāmudrā, unmanī, laya, śūnyatā*). The experience is ineffable, beyond time and space. When Śakti reaches the *sahasrāra,* as Oṃ Shivatva shares, the body becomes cold and corpse-like (lifeless) except for the topmost part of the skull which is warm (HYP 4:106). This is where the static (*akarma*) and kinetic (*karma*) aspects of consciousness unite. The downward return of Śakti (life force, *karma*) after the meditation is complete is indicated by the resumption of bodily function, mental process, warmth, vitality, and so on.

Conceptualized as a creative symbol of the power of evolution and involution, but experienced as embodied insight or wisdom, Ardhanārīśvara explains to the *yogin/ī* the complete balance of the human process polarized as differentiation and integration. As direct evidence of the embodied experience of Ardhanārīśvara, the adept *yogin/ī* could spontaneously experience *sambhavī* and *unmanī mudrā,* indicating the restriction of sexual desire and the restraint of the nervous system, as well as *kevala kumbhaka, laya,* and so on. When *yoga* (union) is ultimately realized in *nirbīja samādhi,* there are no remaining manifestations, no male and no female and, consequently, no Ardhanārīśvara. The *yogin/ī,* as Śiva and Śakti, unites within himself/herself in the subtlemost plane. This, says Oṃ Shivatva, is the great truth of Ardhanārīśvara. A feeling of wholeness arises within as if the *yogin/ī* is "alone," echoing the feeling sense of *ātman* in the *Bṛhadāraṇyaka Upaniṣad* (BU 1.4.3, cited in Olivelle 1998), in which there is only the self. Male and female are perceived as different on the physical or phenomenal level only, but in *yoga* they are integrated and homogeneous. According to Oṃ Shivatva, this is the implied secret of *haṭhayoga* (and *tantra*). The absolute stillness and fusion between Śakti and Śiva in the subtlemost body of the *yogin/ī* advance through three stages, beginning with the *viśuddha cakra,* to completion in the *sahasrāra cakra,* where the final dissolution or integration of the two-as-one is realized. Emptiness is possible, precisely because form proceeds from emptiness, that is the encrypted message in Śaiva iconography and the *haṭhayoga* textual tradition. Recognizing this fluid interrelationality between transcendence and materiality removes duality (i.e., *nirvāṇa*).

Ardhanārīśvara and *Nāda-yoga*

The *haṭhayoga* practice of *nāda yoga* pertains directly to our understanding of Ardhanārīśvara. Heilijgers-Seelen (1994) observes that iconographic and geometric expressions of *yantras* and *maṇḍalas* convey "the idea of creative multiplication" (16). They communicate in diagrammatic form the active powers of manifestation at the level of "phenomenal" and "phonic" reality. This creative process, as we have seen, is symbolically portrayed in anthropomorphic terms as male and female, and is represented in the practice of *nāda-yoga* by a phonetic system of *bījas* (seed syllables, sounds) and *mantras*. The Sanskrit alphabet finds correspondence here as well (Hoens 1972, 95; Heilijgers-Seelen 1994, 17). As such, *nāda yoga* expresses the theistic and anthropomorphic iconographic equivalent of Ardhanārīśvara as a cosmological and an emancipatory paradigm in sonic or vibrational terms. The present study of *nāda yoga* involves the practice or process of voiced and unvoiced (*anāhata nāda*) sound, and the two terms, *nāda* and *bindu*, are often coupled in *haṭhayoga* treatises to operate as sonic homologues of Śiva-Śakti (Beck 1993, 81; Padoux 1990; Heilijgers-Seelen 1994, 16–17; Hoens 1970, 95).

Beck (1993) explains that the term *candra-bindu*, found most commonly in the *haṭha* and *tantra yoga* traditions, "refers to the symbolic combination of *nāda* as semicircle (*candra*, or half-moon) with *bindu* as dot" or ँ in its diagrammatic form (82). As we see in iconographic illustrations of the *ājñā* cakra, the *candra bindu* placed above the female *trikoṇa* and *prāṇava* usually stands alongside the representation of the *prāṇava* (auṃ or oṃ) symbol. Beck explains the process in terms of sound:

> The *nāda* sound fades away into the point of *bindu*, which means the nasal point of the *anusvāra*, especially in its position as the dot above the *ardha-mātrā*, half-syllable, or half-moon, within the total three and one-half morae—sometimes four morae—of metrical time in the pronunciation of AUM. Thus, we have the configuration A + U + M + *nāda-bindu* repeated throughout the pertinent traditions. (Beck 1993, 82)

In other words, *bindu* absorbs *nāda*, described in the above passage as an *ardha-mātrā* (half-syllable) or *ardha-candra* (half moon). From this we can ascertain a distinct correlation emerging between the image of

Ardhanārīśvara and the symbol of *ardha-candra*. In *hathayoga* metaphysics, *nāda* represents Śakti, and *bindu* represents Śiva (HYP 4:101).[41] Consequently, *nāda-bindu* represented by the symbol of the *ardha-candra* (half-moon) and *anusvāra* (dot) signify a sonic and an aniconic representation of the anthropomorphic image of Ardhanārīśvara.

To extend this analogy a step farther, a significant passage from Vācaspati's commentary of Patañjali's *Yogasūtras*, the *Tattva Vaiśāradī*, makes the point that the *ardha-mātrā* of the *candra-bindu* is located above

> the sphere of fire, the place of dreamless sleep, the M. Above that is the higher space, the Sound of Brahman itself *[param brahma vyomatmakam nādas turīya-sthanam]*, the fourth state of ultra-consciousness, which the knowers of Brahman call the half-measure (the *ardha-mātrā*). (Vācaspati, cited in Fuerstein 1975, 63)

In this excerpt, Vācaspati indicates that insight during meditation of the fourth stage, or four degrees, of *oṃ* occurs in the *turīya* stage. This is known as *amātrā*, according to the *Maitrī* and *Māṇḍūkya Upaniṣads*, and in *yoga* terminology it is synonymous with *samādhi* or *śūnyatā* (HYP 4:3–4). According to Beck, Śaṅkara, and other *advaita* commentators such as Gauḍapāda, use the concept of *amātrā* to signify the idea of "beyond sound" or "the absence of sound in the *turīya*, or fourth degree" (Beck 1993, 90). In their commentaries, the *amātrā* is identified with *aśabda* (soundlessness), which in turn describes *brahman* or undifferentiated consciousness (bear in mind that the *viśuddha cakra* is closely associated with *śabda*). The letter "M" or the "M" sound that directly precedes the *turīya* stage enables the practitioner to attain *prājñā* through its internalizing vibrational effects. After the "M" sound *nāda* disappears or is absorbed into *bindu*, the fourth state of consciousness, called *turīya-ātman*, is realized. This is designated "the Sound of Brahman," or the "*ardha-mātrā*" (Beck 1993, 91).

Basing our analogy on this premise, Ardhanārīśvara can be identified with the above concept of *ardhamātrā*. The *ardhacandra*, as Padoux (1990) clarifies, corresponds to the *ājñā cakra* in the forehead region (405). Sadāśiva is associated with creation, and this explains why he/she often is figured as half male and half female (45). But there is another stage of final repose or formlessness in which Śakti is absorbed into Śiva, just as *nāda* is absorbed into *bindu*, beyond the *niṣkala-sakala* form of Ardhanārīśvara (or *sabīja samādhi*).

Therefore, to push our analysis farther, Ardhanārīśvara, as a paradigm for *haṭhayoga* attainment, like the sonic theory of *nāda-bindu* that Beck proposes, juxtaposes the dualistic, foundational, philosophical principles of *yoga*, such as *puruṣa-prakṛti*, Śiva-Śakti, *ātman-māyā*, into a single composite image that only then may be said to transcend the duality of its parts. Ardhanārīśvara, like *ardhacandra-bindu,* denotes the union (or emptiness) of masculine and feminine (i.e., Śiva-Śakti). *Nāda-bindu* and Ardhanārīśvara are not separate. They are simply two modalities or representations of the exact same state or condition. Just as *nāda-yoga* describes *nāda* as being absorbed into *bindu* in the fourth stage of *yoga* attainment (i.e., *turīya*), *haṭhayoga* maintains that Śakti is reabsorbed into Śiva in *nirbīja samādhi* in the fourth stage called *turīya*[42] (HYP 4:3–4, 47). In this sense, definite structural subtleties and nuances begin to emerge between these two theories, however, an extended inquiry into the specific theories of *nāda-yoga* would require further research beyond the scope of this book. Nonetheless, a formative structure can be pointed to with regard to the relationship between the unitive experience of *nāda* and *bindu* and the representational metaphysical image of Ardhanārīśvara. In other words, the juxtaposition of Śiva-Śakti in the image of Ardhanārīśvara is identical to the symbolic formation of *ardha-candra* found alongside the *prāṇava* or oṃ sound and other dyadic homologues. Consequently, both *nāda-bindu* and Ardhanārīśvara capture the relative dualistic roots of *haṭhayoga* while at the same time articulate the organic fluidity of the language of *advaita,* a kind of duality-in-union or two-in-one philosophy that ultimately points to neither one nor the other. Second, it is important to point out that *nāda-upāsana* is not completely distinct from *haṭhayoga* but rather is considered a significant stage leading toward *haṭhayoga* attainment (HYP 4:76, 80–101).

If we compare the movement of the *prāṇava* in relation to the subtle physiology of the *yoga* body, we see that the *prāṇava,* also referred to as *mūla-mantra* (root *mantra*) or *nāda-liṅga,* originates in the *mūlādhāra.* According to the *Yogaśikha Upaniṣad,* the *mūla-mantra* (*oṃ*) is made up of Śiva and Śakti (YU 1.168–78, cited in Beck 1993, 94–95). Śakti (like *nāda* and the *oṃkāra*) rises from the *mūlādhāra cakra* along the central axis through the subtle *suṣumṇā nāḍī* to unite with Śiva (*bindu*) in the *ājñā cakra.* The *Haṭhayogapradīpikā* states that the *ājñā cakra,* also known as *śūnya cakra,* is the center where *turīya* begins (HYP 4:110; 4:75). It is here, in the *ājñā cakra,* according to the aniconic representation of the *ardhacandra-bindu,* that Śakti as *nāda* is absorbed into Śiva as *bindu.* This is clearly illustrated in the iconography of the *ājñācakra,* and it is here that *sabīja samādhi* begins.

For this reason, the motif of Ardhanārīśvara, whether in its anthropomorphic form or its alternate sonic manifestation as *ardhacandra-bindu,* is experienced by the *yogin/ī* in the subtle body of the *viśuddha* and *ājñā cakras.* It also is here that *haṭhayoga* is complete, and the final stages of *yoga* (*turīya, rāja, laya,* etc.) begin. The *Haṃsa Upaniṣad* (HU) (employing the word *prāṇa* for Śakti), indicates that by closing the *mūlādhāra*, *prāṇa* moves through the second, third, fourth, fifth, and sixth *cakras*, as if it were the *prāṇava* (HU 3 cited in Duessen 1987, 719). At this stage, *prāṇa* ascends into the second *brahmadvāra* and enters the *sahasrāra cakra* in the crown of the head (HYP 3:47). When Śakti merges with Śiva, pure or *brahman* consciousness is attained, and the final state of *ātman-turīya* is experienced by the *yogin/ī* (HU 9). This is signified throughout *haṭhayoga* treatises by the eternal coalescence and absolute singularity of Śiva and Śakti. The *oṃkāra*, like the dyadic couple figured by the image of Ardhanārīśvara, conveys *haṭhayoga's* essential, nondual conception of the universe, and the human or microcosmic parallel experiences this in the final, absorptive stages of *yoga*.

Conclusion

As we see, there can be no doubt that, understood from within the context of *haṭhayoga*, the individual *yogin/ī* seeks, through the path of *sādhana*, a genuine reconciliation of all apparent dualities signified by the form and figure of Ardhanārīśvara, *yoni-liṅga*, Śiva-Śakti, *nāda-bindu*, and so on as relative aspects of his/her being. In this sense, the image of Ardhanārīśvara, the divine androgyne, does not merely present a synthesis of masculine- and feminine-identified gender traits, as a number of feminist critiques of Western expressions of androgyny have suggested, but rather attempts through the medium of subtle *yoga* iconography and praxis to portray in embodied anthropomorphic terms a fundamental belief in the possibility of personal transcendence, usually understood as the attainment of nondual consciousness (i.e., *brahman*, Śiva-Śakti, Paramaśiva, Śivatva, *śūnyatā*). However, scholarship on and interpretations of images of Ardhanārīśvara in *haṭhayoga* are at times charged with profound ambivalence. The experience of Ardhanārīśvara, on the one hand, collapses the categories of male and female by appearing to subsume or reabsorb the female pole (Śakti, *karma*) into the privileged male pole (Śiva, *akarma*), or what Jean Varenne (1989) calls "the demise of Pārvatī." While, on the other hand, the half-male and half-female motif often is vividly maintained in a fluid, complementary, iconographical tradition in which both halves (male and female) are ultimately dissolved in *turīya* or *laya*.

The coded system articulated in the esoteric language (*sandhyābhāsā*) of *haṭhayoga's* theoretical assumptions at times reproduces relations of domination and male subjectivity by reducing or negating the status of the feminine through less privileged associations (e.g., negative, left, etc.). Nevertheless, *yogis* and *yoginīs* who are profoundly committed to the metaphysics of *haṭhayoga* must work through the esoteric ritual practices (i.e., the body-mind) equally to achieve the tranquility (*sthiti*), peace (*śānti*, *nirodha*), and emancipation (*samādhi* or *yoga*) proposed by the male-identified vision and essentialist philosophy of *advaita* figured by the image of Ardhanārīśvara. Although Ardhanārīśvara is an ambitious vision that attempts to contain and convey in metaphysical terms all that is ultimately possible, it can only capture this ideal if and when the ego of gender, which at times distorts and privileges the male half of the image, has been recognized and named.

In her feminist appropriation of Foucault, Susan Bordo (1989) explains that "the body . . . is a medium of culture" (13). Citing anthropologist Mary Douglas, Bordo explains that the body is "a powerful symbolic form, a surface on which the central rules, hierarchies, and even metaphysical commitments of a culture are inscribed and thus reinforced" (ibid.). Through the ritual performative practices of *haṭhayoga*, canonized icongraphic formulae, gendered homologous structures, and so on, "culture is made body" (ibid.). For this reason, it is necessary to see *haṭhayoga* theory and praxis, which not only valorizes but works primarily through the body, as a part of, and not separate from, a systemic network of patriarchal institutions that oftentimes promote images of male dominance and female subordination (15). If, as Bordo says, "our bodies are trained, shaped, and impressed with the stamp of prevailing historical forms of selfhood, desire, masculinity, [and] femininity," then a feminist analysis of Ardhanārīśvara is imperative and long overdue (ibid.). It can help us understand, name, and hopefully overcome any subtle mechanisms of power and privilege that are deeply sedimented in the androgyne idiom in *haṭhayoga* theory by the subtle symbolizations of body and gender placed there by the projections of a patriarchal culture.

Ardhanārīśvara stands as a cultural paradigm for one of the highest spiritual achievements in human attainment: liberation. As such, this mythic *yogin/ī par excellence* is imaged as both, or half, male and female. This suggests that access to *haṭhayoga* orientation, and its attendant goals (i.e., physical strength, autonomy, wisdom, liberation, immortality, equanimity, and so on), is not gender exclusive but rather open to both men and women. While it is true that the entire *haṭhayoga* tradition is based on the premise that the emancipatory teachings were revealed to Pārvatī by Śiva, and that she herself was an adept practitioner (*tāpasvinī*), as a rule, women have not participated to the same extent in writing the symbolic structures of the *haṭhayoga* tradition, and oftentimes they have been excluded from orthodox male monastic organizations (GS 3:4–5; HYP 4:27; SS 5:1–3; HU1). Nor are women's bodies considered the normative models from which to learn the spiritual exercises and practices of *yoga*. As a rule, *yoginīs* must adapt and adopt male-centered *yoga* theories to their own female anatomy. Even though the exercises are available to both men and women, few if any Indian *haṭhayoga* classics have been written from the perspective of the psycho-physiology of the *yoginī*. The female practitioner must rely upon male anatomy and male-identified experience as the norm. The fixed patterns of male psycho-physiology in *haṭhayoga* theory limit female biology and psychic experience to male specifications. The classical training and patterns of *haṭhayoga* practice are clearly defined by male physiology and, except for two interpolations in the *Haṭhayogapradīpikā* that pertain to the female body do not account for differences between the psycho-physiology of men and women.

Moreover, in traditional *haṭhayoga* treatises, the human female usually is conceived of as a locus of fear for the male practitioner (SS 5:3). A female-centered praxis, which is of growing concern for contemporary women in India and abroad, addressing specific concerns of women, can only come about through the participation of female-identified adepts and scholars in a reconstruction of *yoga* ideology, but "real" women have long been marginalized in the monastic traditions. For this reason, the same conditions of subdued roles and submission that we encounter in social life on the part of the wife, as Frederique Apffel Marglin (1982) observes, find parallel in the often erotic and hierarchical conjugal relationship between Śiva and Pārvatī in the language of *haṭhayoga* (Marglin 1982, 43–44).

A recent study by Miranda Shaw (1994) argues that women have become accomplished practitioners, *gurus* (teachers), and creators of discourse in both the Hindu and Buddhist *tantric* traditions. Perhaps the expressed realization within *tantric* and *haṭha yoga* traditions of the ultimate and fundamental nonduality of reality conceived in symbolic terms as male and female (e.g., Ardhanārīśvara), provides an avenue of accessibility to women. Clearly, women in India have asked fundamental questions of philosophy, and were/are concerned with epistemological and soteriological questions. In the *Upaniṣads*, Maitreyī, the wife of philosopher Yajñavalkya, attained liberation through the practice of *yoga*. Kausalyā, the mother of Rāma, Sulabhā, the daughter of King Pradhān, Madālasā, the wife of King Ṛtvdhvaja, Lallā, the fourteenth-century Kashmirī Shaivite poet-saint, Shāradā Devī, the wife of Ramakrishna Paramahansa, and others also have gained liberation through the practice of *yoga*. This provides evidence that women were at least students, if not teachers or writers, of philosophic discourse. Yet, overall, women have not made contributions comparable to men in the field of *haṭhayoga* praxis. Their duties (*dharma*), as defined typically by traditional societal norms, were prescribed primarily by their roles as wives and mothers (*strīdharma*). In this sense, the interpretive principles of feminist theory are most useful for reclaiming and revisioning the historical agency of women in Indian traditions, and for naming and disrupting possible asymmetrical gender assumptions inherent in the male-identified codified systems of *yoga* when appropriate, in particular, metaphysical claims to sameness through subtle mechanisms of negation and absorption.

Chapter 3

Ardhanārīśvara in Devotional Poetry

Introduction

In this chapter I show that Śaiva *bhakti* poetry provides us with fundamental images of Śiva in the aspect of Ardhanārīśvara. As evidence for this we first look at several poems written by Tamil poet saints. Raju Kalidos (1996) observes that monumental work on the pan-Indian character of Naṭarāja by scholars such as Śivaramamūrti (1974b), neglected to look at the substantive material found in the Tamil *Tēvāram* hymns (Kalidos 1996, 13). For this reason, an examination of Ardhanārīśvara in this genre is necessary. These poems, as we demonstrate here, offer a rich source of what Indira Peterson (1989) calls "poetic iconography," and they are contemporaneous with the temple *mūrtis,* discussed in chapter 1. We then look at the *Ardhanārīnaṭeśvara Stotram,* attributed posthumously to *advaita* philosopher Ādi Śaṅkara, as an instance of the *stotra* tradition that sculpts the half-male and half-female figure of Ardhanārīśvara through the medium of metaphor and simile. Drawing upon Sherry Ortner's (1974) pioneering thesis of universal female subordination, we probe and delineate predominant gender conceptualizations in these images and hymns, and we disclose their relation to what we see as a broader dialectic between nature and culture.

Ardhanārīśvara in Tamil Poetry[1]

A study of the *Tēvāram*[2] indicates that the metaphors used in Tamil *bhakti* (devotional) poetry focus on a range of religious themes from

Indian myth and tradition and evoke the presence of Ardhanārīśvara through the imaginal conventions of poetic iconography in no less than 100 references (Kalidos 1993, 86). We may adduce that due to the Tamil poet-saints' close association with the Śaiva *Āgamas* and *Tantras*, and the spread of theism and temple worship, we find the metaphors and similes used in the hymns in many instances consistent with the canons of Indian sacred art. Peterson tells us that the Tamil Śaiva community was "united by their passionate love for Śiva and his shrines" (Peterson 1989, 12). Consequently, the various diagnostic features found in Śaiva temple *mūrtis* are similarly recalled by the poet-saint and, acting as an intermediary, arouse the presence of the deity in the minds of his/her audience through their own personal ecstatic experiences of the *saguṇa* god/dess.[3]

One image used in both Indian iconography and Tamil poetry to convey the androgynous aspect of Śiva is of a woman's earring on the left ear (see Figure 1.2 in chapter 1).[4] This emblem is one of the most significant in the vast repertoire of Śiva's attributes and immediately evokes the female presence of the androgynous form of the deity on the left side. In the following verse, translated here by Peterson, the female aspect of Ardhanārīśvara is identified by this single ornament. Campantar declares in a mystic vision that he "saw the Lord," and he sings the following:

> He wears a woman's earring on one ear;
> riding on his bull,
> crowned with the pure white crescent moon,
> his body smeared with ash from the burning-ground,
> he is the thief who stole my heart. (Peterson 1989, 15, 246)

Art historian Alice Boner (1962) states that the male earring that Śiva wears on his right side "denotes his Puruṣa-aspect," and the female earring "he" wears on his left side represents "his Śakti-Prakṛti-aspect" (184). In her interpretive response to the diagnostic feature of different earrings, Boner refers to the conventional gender construction that polarizes the male and female halves of the deity into the seemingly dualistic and potentially hierarchically perceived categories of right side masculine/*puruṣa* (spirit) and left side feminine/*prakṛti* (nature). Why? What is it about their dissimilar male and female ear ornaments that identifies them as *prakṛti* and *puruṣa*? Boner does not tell us.[5]

Sherry Ortner (1974), however, provides a possible theoretical perspective from which to frame an analysis of this significant identifying ornamentation and other diagnostic features that represent parallel gender patternization in *bhakti* poetry. Her main hypothesis to explain what she sees as the universal devaluation of women is germane to the images and symbols, such as different earrings, associated with the figure of Ardhanārīśvara. Ortner maintains that the universality of female subordination can no longer be challenged; it can be discerned "everywhere," she writes, "in every known culture" (69).

Without a doubt, this hypothesis of universal subordination based on the dialectic of nature and culture has been the subject of much discussion and criticism.[6] One objection is that the use of such a dichotomy masks a more nuanced historical reading of the actual ways in which these categories are mediated in any particular living society, such as India. For this reason, Ortner recommends that each culture must come to understand its own internal mechanisms of female oppression and the cultural assumptions and social organizations that stress the inferiority of women. Nonetheless, the central postulate that Ortner proposes to explain the overwhelming global subordination of women is, to some extent, useful here, given the subject of our investigation and the dichotomous categories arising from it, such as Śiva-Śakti as *prakṛti-puruṣa*.

Ortner argues that "woman" in every culture

> is being identified with—or, if you will, seems to be a symbol of—something that every culture devalues, something that every culture defines as being of a lower order of existence than itself. Now it seems that there is only one thing that would fit that description, and that is "nature" in the generalized sense. (Ortner 1974, 72)

Furthermore, Ortner claims that

> women are being identified or symbolically associated with nature, as opposed to men, who are identified with culture. Since it is always culture's project to subsume and transcend nature, if women were considered part of nature, then culture would find it "natural" to subordinate, not to say oppress, them. (Ortner 1974, 73)

To avoid charges of oversimplification in her thesis, Ortner clarifies her position to state succinctly that "women are seen 'merely' as being *closer* to nature than men" (Ortner 1974, 73). Men, in turn, are identified with culture. Here Ortner "minimally" defines culture as "the transcendence, by means of systems of thought and technology, of the natural givens of existence" (84). According to this theory, it is culture's constructed duty to assert itself over, control or transcend nature (73).

If, as the title of Ortner's article suggests, female is to male as nature is to culture, then a rationale for the superiority of male (right, *puruṣa*) over female (left, *prakṛti*) is provided in the culturally constructed dialectic between nature and culture. Ortner points to this when she insists that these two realms, nature and culture, are a human (male) construct. In other words, they are both "conceptual categories," and "one can find no boundary out in the actual world between these two states or realms of being" (Ortner 1974, 72). In addition, we must bear in mind, that

> the whole scheme is a construct of culture rather than a fact of nature. Woman is not "in reality" any closer to (or further from) nature than man—both have consciousness, both are mortal. But there are certainly reasons why she appears that way. (Ortner 1974, 87)

In this sense, gender is made.[7] It is historically determined and, therefore, culturally specific.[8] For these reasons, an examination of the gendered diagnostic features used to render images of the androgynous Ardhanārīśvara at the level of *dvaita*, that is, conventional reality, in *bhakti* poetry is critical.

The next poem also contains a reference to different earrings, as well as other significant female identifiers that place a secondary status on the female half. The following poem by Appar[9] extols:

> An earring of bright new gold on one ear;
> a coiled conch shell sways on the other.
> On one side he chants the melodies of the ritual Veda,
> on the other, he gently smiles.
> Matted hair adorned with sweet *konrai* blossoms on one half of his head,
> and a woman's curls on the other, he comes.
> The one is the nature of his form,
> the other, of hers;
> And both are the very essence of his beauty. (Peterson 1989, 105)

In this poem it is clear that although "both" halves "are the very essence of his beauty," the male half "chants the melodies of the ritual Veda," an elite act that was traditionally prohibited to women, while the "other" half "gently smiles."

The silence of Śiva's feminine side, clearly illustrated in the contrasting image of a gentle smile, is similarly echoed in another Tamil hymn by Cuntarar, the last of the three saints of the Tēvāram. To quote:

> The Goddess Gaṅgā, whose waves flow
> over your moon-crowned matted hair,
> is a silent woman. (Peterson 1989, 233)

The reading of textual and iconographic diagnostic features such as these cannot simply be set aside, but rather the dominant male half of the deity must be acknowledged in Indian tradition, because the division between fact and fiction, or metaphor and historical reality, often is ambiguous.[10] Hence, the legitimacy of the symbolic devices used here and elsewhere to render an image of the deity actually becomes plausible at the level of human social reality.[11] Images of the divine androgyne in devotional poetry, as well as iconography, myth, *haṭhayoga*, dance, and so on, give divine sanction for continuous replication of this model in the contemporary sociohistorical realm. In other words, Ardhanārīśvara, as a model of the transcendent, affects "real" people. The use of metaphors, such as the ones mentioned above in which he chants Veda and the other half gently smiles, or Gaṅgā is esteemed as "a silent woman," guarantees or sanctifies the equivalent paradigm at the level of "real" women and men. The male half of Ardhanārīśvara chants Veda in Sanskrit, while the female half smiles. For the most part, she cannot engage equally in the liturgy of elite male *brahmanical* discourse, thus in this metaphor the gap between his privilege and her lack of privilege is even more marked than it first appears. To read the text (e.g., icon, poem, *stotra*, etc.) as simply a metaphor, or as a transcendentalized vision of the divine only, is to ignore or dismiss subtle and complex signs of gender embedded in the formulaic descriptions of the deity by the male elite, as well as any subtle markings of sectarianism.[12]

When we look at the temple *mūrtis* of Ardhanārīśvara, we see that male and female are situated side by side. Similar to iconography, devotional poetry can function as a regulative paradigm for the dominant male ideology, as well as an effective tool for the construction of gender identity in the religious imagination. Such images prescribe or influence norms of behavior for men and women in their daily lives. As stated in the above devotional metaphor, the male half chants Veda, and the other half gently smiles. This corresponds to the majority of pan-Indian temple *mūrtis* of Ardhanārīśvara, from Kashmir to Tamil Nadu, in which the male half of the divine androgyne is placed in a position of authority and privilege simply by being situated on the culturally designated dominant right side.

At the same time, in the course of this chapter, it also has become apparent that Tamil poets invoke Ardhanārīśvara through traditional metaphors and similes that parallel the canonized emblems of Śiva iconography.[13] By employing this type of iconographical imagery in their poetry, Tamil saints render an experience of Śiva that is at once intimate and authentic, as well as congruous with other cultural representations of the deity. They create, as Cutler says, a "verbal icon" in the mind of the audience (Cutler 1987, 112). In the next poem, Cuntarar refers to Ardhanārīśvara as follows:

> Ārūraṉ has described Ōṇakāntaṉṟali's Lord
> who has the poet for his bondservant,
> the bull rider who is manifest as the primal syllable "Aum,"
> and binds the colorful sari with a silken scarf
> over his loincloth. (Peterson 1989, 235)

Here, Cuntarar's reference to a "colorful *sari*" recalls the highly stylized conventions of female dress and symbols of regal feminine beauty in Indian iconography and identifies the aspect of Ardhanārīśvara as the devotee might experience him/her in the Ardhanārīśvara *mūrtis* of Śaiva temples. In order to move the listener closer to a personal experience of *bhakti*, Tamil devotional poetry appeals to the vast and magnificent imagery of each and every aspect of the Śaiva religious themes. The hymns, as Peterson explains, command "absolute faith" in the "text as an instrument of devotion," so that the devotee not only expects to see (*darśan*) but also is moved to see Śivārdhanārīśvara, precisely because of the poetic iconography evoked in the poems (Peterson 1989, 73).[14]

In this sense, the hymns of the Tamil poet-saints provide vital images that record and channel a vision of Ardhanārīśvara in an alternate iconographic style, and their role in the religious life of the Tamil devotee is coterminous with the works of the *śilpins* of Indian sacred art. As Cutler (1987) shows, they are "songs of experience" that transport the hearer through the conventions of poetic device into direct communion with god (12). As such, Cutler claims that "*bhakti* poems and the worship of embodied images of god mutually implicate one another" (112). Thus it is evident that *bhakti* poetry is a powerful medium with transformative potential. However, as long as any recurrent abstract categories that potentially marginalize the female half or entrench outdated stereotypical expressions of "woman" that partake to sculpt the deity literally and/or figuratively go unnamed, an ambivalent message of human emancipation for women and men is all that Ardhanārīśvara can offer.

As Rangaswamy (1958–9) points out, the images of Umāpati and Ardhanārīśvara function in the *Tēvāram* specifically to praise "the devinity (*sic*) of women" in the context of her "holiness" which is associated with "the right kind of domestic life." Rangaswamy states that a woman's worthiness or divinity is contingent upon her "right" relation to motherhood and domestic life. Furthermore, he explains that "contemplation of this image takes a firm hold in the minds of Brahmins" (Rangaswamy 1959: 612).

However, this kind of "right relation" can have ambivalent consequences and is extremely problematic for the concerns of Indian feminism. Spivak's (1988) analysis of Mahasweta Devi's "Stanadayini"

("Breast-Giver") makes this point quite poignantly. Stanadayini and its protagonist Jashoda are parables of Mother India, bonded in struggle against the burden of abuse and slavery felt by women throughout the subcontinent. There is no doubt that the pan-Indian goddess/mother is worshipped and valorized, but her role historically has been to tend the hearth and nurture the sons of patriarchy. These are powerful ideals of womanhood, according to Spivak, which offer constructs not only of human social reality and codes of behavior but have become deeply sedimented structures in the Indian cultural psyche. While constructs of motherhood as a woman's only option entrench women in oppressive, stereotypical expressions, Spivak and others show how this voice can become the agency of subaltern protest.

When we look at the next poem, the androgynous aspect of Ardhanārīśvara is conveyed by his/her half-male and half-female form. In sacred verse, as well as in Indian iconography, this metaphor is paradigmatic and signals one of the constitutive features of Ardhanārīśvara. Campantar says:

> My master who rules over Accirupākkam,
> displays two forms,
> having taken as half of himself
> the soft girl with waist as small as gathered lightning. (Peterson 1989, 105)

The essential diagnostic feature of the half-male and half-female form of Ardhanārīśvara is eluded to in the following passage as well. It reads:

> he who bears the white moon
> on his pure, matted red hair,
> God who is both man and woman. (Peterson 1989, 109)

And, once again, in the following lines by Campantar:

> him who has an old white bull,
> and Umā as half of himself. (Peterson 1989, 108)

The images of Ardhanārīśvara in the above three passages are distinguished by phrases such as "God who is both man and woman," "Umā as half of himself," and "my master" who "displays two forms." This poetic depiction of Śiva as half male and half female is clearly consistent with the bipolar vertical division seen on all anthropomorphic, iconographic counterparts. To elicit a vision of Ardhanārīśvara, references to his/her half-male and half-female body are acknowledged by the Tamil poet-saints, and the fundamental, emblematic features of the canons of Indian iconography are vividly realized through the medium of metaphor and simile. As such, the poetic images that we find in these hymns clearly parallel Śiva's iconographic symbolism through the medium of devotional speech.

The following verse, similar to the three mentioned above, draws the devotee into a vision of Ardhanārīśvara through the simple juxtaposition of Śiva's composite female and male form. To accomplish this, the poet specifies that Śiva shares his body with the Goddess and then draws upon several simple metaphors to evoke the female side of Ardhanārīśvara for his devoted audience. Cuntarar asks:

> When shall I see, to my heart's delight, . . .
> the body like a white lotus that he shares
> with the Goddess with soft young breasts? (Peterson 1989, 106)

Again, he queries in the second verse of the poem:

> When shall I see the majesty of his bull,
> the cluster of *konrai* blossoms on his bright fragrant hair,
> the form he lovingly shares with the Goddess
> who has a slim waist and a smile white as jasmine? (Peterson 1989, 106)

In these verses, traditional emblems of feminine beauty indicate Śiva's female half. These marks, namely, "soft young breasts," "a slim waist," and "a smile white as jasmine," accord with the traditional organization of dual-gender classification that demarcates through body identifiers the female side from the male side. Patterned signifiers such as these are instantly recognizable by the devotee and reveal an image of the divine androgyne.

This is precisely the point. According to Peterson (1989), the metaphors and images of Tamil *bhakti* poetry are "meant to conjure up a precise "icon," a concrete image of Śiva in the hearer's mind" (29). This is achieved by assimilating features of the Sanskrit tradition, such as the *stotra*, epics, myth, and temple iconography, with the indigenous ancient Tamil bard or folk tradition, that is, *caṅkam* poetry classified as *akam* (interior) and *puram* (exterior).[15] In this sense, the Tamil poets, like the *yogin/ī* and *śilpin*, are guided not only by their divine visions and revelations but also by formulaic prescriptions that remember, reenact, and reinforce the metaphors established and preserved by the dominant creators of culture.[16] In this way, a tradition of correspondences or homologous structures is constructed and maintained across time and place. David Gordon White (1996) shows that there are distinct parallel coordinates among the *haṭhayoga*, *siddha*, and *rasāyana* traditions, and to this we can certainly add iconography and *bhakti* poetry. Thus the poems appear completely realistic and authentic as they endeavor to sustain and remember (*smṛti*), rather than to create, a powerful cultural image of the deity in the devotee's mind.

If the poet wants to evoke the aspect of Ardhanārīśvara, she/he visualizes and recalls through poetic convention such stock diagnostic features as "woman's earring," a "slim waist," "both man and woman," a gentle smile, "soft breasts," and so forth. In this way, the Tamil poems provide the hearer with not only a "verbal icon" based on "icongraphic accuracy" but also correct "devotional vision" (Peterson 1989, 29; Cutler 1987, 112). Consequently, the hymns of the Tamil poet-saints, like the temple images themselves, recall an abundance of imagery so to arouse powerful feelings of *bhakti* in the devotee. The poet-saint, similar to the *yogin/ī* and the *śilpin*, functions as the "seeing eye" of tradition, revealing a vision of the deity so powerful as to enable the devotee to see god (*darśana*) for herself/himself (Peterson 1989, 32). Hence, the goal of Tamil *bhakt*i poetry (like *haṭhayoga* and iconography) is to bring the devotee to an experience of god/dess.

However, as we have demonstrated, the male side of the deity is, in some instances, rendered dominant by imprinting recurring metaphors such as left/female, right/male, different earrings (nature/culture), he chants Veda, she smiles, and so forth. These gendered indicators, which are intended to arouse intense feelings of *bhakti*, also influence normative models of human behavior. The recitation and repetition of Śiva's varied manifestations, such as the divine androgyne, *yogi* and ascetic, cosmic dancer, and so on, reenact for the devotee not only the various episodes depicted in Śiva mythology, and how the devotee should see the deity in his/her own inner expression, but also how human behavior is encoded in culture. As Clifford Geertz (1979) claims, symbols are "sources of information," and consequently, they "shape public behavior" (80).[17]

Another important functional dimension of the modality of poetic iconography is that it leads the devotee to an inner apprehension or progressive awareness of his/her own subtle and essential likeness with the deity (e.g., Ardhanārīśvara). The fundamental goal for Śaivites is to attain *mokṣa* by recognizing one's essential self as a "second" Śiva.[18] This involves the self-realization of one's own so-called androgynous nature. The Tamil poet-saints, by utilizing the marks of Śiva's male and female nature, imply an androgynous counterpart in the listener's own essential or subtle being, and by symbolizing Śiva in the canons of Tamil poetry as the lord who is half woman, the poet conveys the normative ideal to the devotee that she/he too is an integral part of the phenomenon of possessing a subtle body or self-nature that is half male and half female. To this end, the priests at the Śiva temple complex in Chidambaram (Tillai) assume the half-male and half-female hairstyle depicted in the poetry and iconography of Ardhanārīśvara as an outward sign of their belief not only in Śiva's male and female divine form but also their own. This androgynous likeness is said to have been exhibited in the lives of several well-known Indian saints, such as Paramahansa Ramakrishna, Paramahansa Yogananda, and Caitanya. Hence, it is paradoxical that the very image that frequently supports the ideal of overturning the norms of male social identification and hierarchy is the one that, at times, reproduces relations of gender inequality. Herein lies one of the many paradoxes inherent in the image.

Metaphor and Ornamentation

The metaphors used in Tamil devotional poetry focus on a range of religious themes from Śaiva myth and tradition. The androgynous aspect of Śiva is just one of at least twenty-five aspects portrayed in the Tamil genre of religious literature. Hymns that evoke an authentic presence of Ardhanārīśvara do so by invoking images that accentuate the female form, primarily through ornamentation, such as a small waist, soft breasts, a lotus-like body, curls of hair, gold earrings, a gentle smile, and so on. This convention of ornamentation focuses the reader on Śiva's female aspect which, as we have pointed out, is the one explicit identifying feature of Ardhanārīśvara. Similar to the *mūrtis*, the hymns are constructed on a pattern of comparison between Śiva's male and female form. The male aspect of Śiva is characterized by such traditional ornamentation as matted hair, ash, crescent moon, third eye, sacred thread, trident, dark throat, snakes, his character as a great ascetic and *yogi*, and so on. This pattern, which borrows its symbols[19] from the canons of Indian myth, *yoga*, and temple iconography, positions the two sides of Śiva in a complementary format that is formulaic in its design. The overall intent or message presented by the image points to the ultimate singularity of divine reality.

The figure of Ardhanārīśvara as part of the iconological tradition of Śaivism reflects a convention of synthesis and acculturation. The composite and so-called syncretic nature of Ardhanārīśvara, as the above hymns demonstrate, is indicated specifically by fluidly juxtaposing standardized emblematic features of the female divine alongside the male. The following lines by Campantar illustrate this pattern quite clearly:

> He shares his form with the Goddess
> whose shoulders curve gracefully like the bamboo. (Peterson 1989, 109)

The *Tēvāram* hymns also describe in vivid detail the mythic narratives, clothing, *āsanas*, *mudrās*, weapons, ornaments, vehicles, and accoutrements of Śivārdhanārīśvara. However, the principal identifying features of this composite image are consistently the markings of the female form. In the above passage, the precise reference to Ardhanārīśvara is found unequivocally in the form of the goddess and her graceful shoulders. In this metaphor, gesturing to the female body, Ardhanārīśvara is recognized instantly. The prominent, poetic, iconographic, diagnostic feature of Ardhanārīśvara is the synthesis of the female form and the various insignia that mark her body, whereas the salient, distinguishing features of Śiva iconography, such as matted hair, dark throat, crescent moon, ash, and so on, are abundantly featured in minute detail in the Tamil hymns; yet when those identifying attributes juxtapose with those of the goddess, Śiva is immediately recognizable as Ardhanārīśvara. In other words, unless the female half of the deity is made explicit, Śiva is figured as singularly male, even though he is, as Śivaramamurti insists, "eternally Ardhanārīśvara" (Śivaramamūrti 1974b, 89).

Even in the broader context of Indian poetry, the image of Ardhanārīśvara is signaled by his/her female features. Daniel Ingalls (1965) has translated various poems from the vast literature of classical Sanskrit court poetry, and several poems included in this work illustrate this point. For example:

> Let the god's delight have been unsurpassed
> that bearing your slender body joined to his,
> he receives, oh Gaurī, your tight embrace;
> still, Śiva's heart must often grieve
> to think your glance cannot by him be seen,
> sweet, loving, innocent, and motionless with love. (Ingalls 1965, 89)

According to Ingalls, this poem plays on the nonerotic aspect of the eternal union of Śiva and Śakti, which evokes a feeling of sadness in the poet Bhagīratha. However, the point that is significant for this particular analysis is that the image of Ardhanārīśvara is immediately recognizable by the female indicator of Gaurī's "slender body joined to his."

Again, in a poem by Manovinoda, the single reference to Śiva's female half signifies Ardhanārīśvara in this poem to Kāmā, the god of love. It reads:

> Lord Śiva, though his foe . . . ,
> still keeps a woman at his side. (Ingalls 1965, 151)

And the following lines, written from the voice of Skanda, Śiva's son, pose a perplexing question to Ganeśa:

When father and when mother became a single body,
what happened, elder brother, to the other halves of each?
Victory to Ganeśa, who explains to the young prince,
The one on earth was born as everyman, the other as everywoman.
(Ingalls 1965, 89)

In all three of the above devotional verses, female indicators are employed to convey visually the image of Śivārdhanārīśvara. The union of Śiva and Śakti in one body is portrayed consistently through the inclusion and juxtaposition of the female form and/or her prescriptive insignia. This imaginal convention of poetic iconography does not in any way contradict the canons of Indian sacred art; indeed, it only serves to reinforce its revealed authenticity. In this sense, the images evoke a vision of the embodied androgyne and are consistent with alternate forms of iconic representation. Even though Peterson maintains that poetic iconography "is governed not by the canons of temple sculpture but by the aesthetic of devotion," as it turns out, the simple images that portray Ardhanārīśvara correspond accurately to the prescriptive codes of temple iconography (Peterson 1989, 96). Moreover, it is the patternized or formulaic female attributes that mark the deity as Ardhanārīśvara in each instance.[20]

We also agree with Peterson that the value of the hymns does not lie in their adherence to the prescriptive conventions of the iconographic repertoire but rather in their power and undeniable ability to evoke *darśan* in the devotee. The iconographical and poetic tradition has acquired a storehouse of conventional images that can be used to arouse or evoke a particular deity. The mood that this particular image of the deity is intended to awaken in the devotee must be compatible with the theolology of Śiva-Śakti. The image of Ardhanārīśvara suggests the ultimate oneness of divine reality. Ardhanārīśvara extols a doctrine of eternal union and the absolute inseparability between Śiva and Śakti. The image also calls our attention to corresponding themes of renunciation, love, *viraha*, *yoga*, and so on, found in the mythology and theology of Śiva and Śakti. These hymns, like their iconographic counterparts, praise the deity and reinforce a conscious relation between the centrality of the image and its philosophical associations in the lives of the poet-saints and their devotees. The poems are transformative insofar as they arouse the impassioned emotion of *bhakti* or the deep absorption of *samādhi*. To this end, these hymns are highly developed and serve their ultimate function as an integral part of the South Indian *bhakti* tradition. The epithets, attributes, qualities, deeds of the deity, and iconographical specificity arranged in the poem or hymn remind the devotee, as Zvelebil (1974) suggests, of memorable themes and events in the deity's mythology (94). As such, they are powerful devices that elicit feelings of intense devotion.

The hymns are also the authentic testimonials of the *darśanas* of the poet-saint and, as such, bear witness to a valuable primary source of Ardhanārīśvara iconography. They capture and convey a personal relationship between the *bhakta* and his/her god/dess. Through the saint's vision of the deity, as depicted in the hymns, one glimpses the image of the god/dess from the perspective of one who has just been to the temple or shrine; yet it is clear that here the intended temple also is the inner heart or *antaḥkaraṇa* (inner mind) of the poet-saint.[21] However, in these hymns to Śivārdhanārīśvara, the goddess with whom Śiva shares half his body has a secondary or "subdued" role, as Peterson says (Peterson 1989, 101). In this sense, there is an inherent contradiction in the image itself as a projection of the teachings of *advaita*. The divine androgyne is an ideal, an image invoked in Indian theology and metaphysics to arouse devotion and absorption, leading the devotee to the ultimate attainment of *yoga* or union. Consequently, Ardhanārīśvara is an icon of liberation and, according to Peterson, should portray a symbol of "perfect love, unity, equality, and completeness" in the *Tēvāram* hymns (101). To illustrate this point, it is interesting that Peterson refers to the tenth-century Chola bronze from the Tiruvenkatu temple—an image that pronounces the dominance of the right-Śiva side by portraying Ardhanārīśvara with three arms (see Figure 1.12 in chapter 1).

The *Ardhanārīnaṭeśvara Stotra* (Hymn to the Lord of Dance Who Is Half Woman)

The *Ardhanārīnaṭeśvara Stotra* is a devotional poem attributed to Ādi Śaṅkara, the principal expounder of the *advaita* school of Indian philosophy. *Stotras*, or hymns of praise, to a particular deity are typically eulogistic in nature and, as Jan Gonda (1977) suggests, trace their roots in uninterrupted continuity from the Vedic age to the present (233). Bruce Long (1983) agrees, and he claims that the invocation of the pantheon of deities through such hymns of praise was "common practice" in the Vedic period (103). For this reason, the *Tēvāram* hymns find their most likely source of inspiration in the Sanskrit *stotra* tradition, in particular, the *Śatarudrīya* (*The Hymn of Praise to the Hundred Rudras*), included in both the *Vajasaneyī Saṃhitā* (*khaṇḍa* 16) of the *Śukla Yajurveda* and the *Yajussaṃhitā*, or *Kṛṣṇayajurveda Taittirīya Saṃhitā*.[22] The *Ardhanārīnaṭeśvara Stotra*, in which the emblems, attributes, and qualities of Śiva-Śivā are praised by its (anonymous) author, is of particular interest here. Overall, it provides an excellent illustration of the *stotra* tradition and the doctrine of *bhedābheda*[23] (unity-in-difference) and is a rich primary source of poetic iconography embellishing our typology of diagnostic features that informs the image of Ardhanārīśvara.

The *stotra* is a simple formulaic device recited or chanted by the worshipper as an integral part of ritual *pūjā* and was sung for me in the *jogīya rāga,* (or, *rāga* of renunciation).[24] It involves a string of simple epithets declaring obeisance to the deity. Below is a transliteration of the *Ardhanārīnaṭeśvara stotra* from the *devanāgarī* script, a translation, and a brief analysis of the hymn.

The Ardhanārīnaṭeśvara *stotra*[25]

1. cāmpeya gaurārdha śarīrakāyai
karpūra gaurārdha śarīrakāya.
dhammillakāyai ca jaṭadharāya
namaḥ Śivāyai ca namaḥ Śivāya.
2. kastūrikā kuṃkumacaricitāyai
citārājaḥpuñja vicarcitāya.
kṛtasmarāyai vikṛtasmarāya
namaḥ Śivāyai ca namaḥ Śivāya.
3. calat kvaṇat kaṅkananpūrāyai
pādābjarājataphaninūpurāya.
hemāṅgadāyai bhujagāṅgadāya
namaḥ Śivāyai ca namaḥ Śivāya.
4. viśālanīlotpalalocanāyai
vikāsipaṅkeruhalocanāya.
samekṣanāyai viṣameksṇāya
namaḥ Śivāyai ca namaḥ Śivāya.
5. mandāramālākalitālakāyai
kapālamālāṅkitakādharāya.
divyāmbarāyai ca digambarāya
namaḥ Śivāyai ca namaḥ Śivāya.
6. ambhodharaśyāmālā kuntalāyai
taḍitprabhātāmrajaṭādharāya
nirīśvarāyai nikileśvarāya
namaḥ Śivāyai ca namaḥ Śivāya.
7. prapañcasṛṣṭyunmukhalāsyakāyai
samastasamhārakatāṇḍavāya
jagdjjananyai jagadekapitre
namaḥ Śivāyai ca namaḥ Śivāya.
8. pradīptaratnojjvalakuṇḍalāyai
sphuranmahāpannagabhūṣ aṇāya
Śivānvitāyai ca Śivanvitāya
namaḥ Śivāyai ca namaḥ Śivāya.

Translation of the *Ardhanārīnaṭeśvara stotra*

1. Her body is fair like the *campā* flower,
   his body is like camphor.
   She has a braided hairstyle ornamented with pearls,
   and he has matted hair.
   I bow to Śivā and I bow to Śiva.
2. Her body is sprinkled with musk-vermillion powder,
   his body is besmeared with a collection of ash from the funeral pyre.
   She has the power of, and he is adverse to, sexual desire.
   I bow to Śivā and I bow to Śiva.
3. From her you hear the movement of tinkling anklets and bracelets,
   his lotus feet have shining anklets of snakes.
   Her body is adorned with golden armlets
   and his body has armlets of snakes.
   I bow to Śivā and I bow to Śiva.
4. Her eyes are like large blue lotuses,
   his eyes are like the red lotus.
   Her eyes are even, his eyes uneven.
   I bow to Śivā and I bow to Śiva
5. She is wearing a garland made from the *mandār* tree in her hair,
   he is wearing a garland of skulls on his neck.
   The fabric she is wearing is divine, he is sky-clad.
   I bow to Śivā and I bow to Śiva.
6. Her hair is dark like the clouds,
   his matted hair is like the luster of lighting.
   She is not Lord, he is Lord of all.
   I bow to Śivā and I bow to Śiva.
7. Her body is dance preparing for the creation of differentiation,
   his is the dance of destruction that destroys everything.
   I bow to Śivā, mother of the universe.
   I bow to Śiva, father of the universe.
8. Her ear ornaments are radiant precious stones giving light,
   his adornments are hissing snakes.
   He is embracing her, and she is embracing him.
   I bow to Śivā and I bow to Śiva.

Analysis of the *stotra*

This hymn attests to the iconographic, mythic, and philosophical tenets of Ardhanārīśvara, which suggest the ideals of *bhedābheda* philosophy. It consists of eight short verses, with nine oblations by the author in the form of the repeated eleven-syllable *mantra* "*namaḥ Śivāyai ca namaḥ Śivāya*" echoed at the end of each verse.[26] This Sanskrit literary genre, says Gonda, follows a "stereotyped prose formula beginning with "homage (*namaḥ*)" that is paid to the god, his manifestations, functions, activities, weapons, abodes, . . . and so on" (Gonda 1979, 75). The sacred five-syllable *mantra* of homage, *namaḥ Śivāya*[27] (referred to as *pañcākṣara-mantra* or *pañcākṣarī*), first appears in the *Śatarudrīya*[28] (Long 1983, 109). A variation on this *mantra* is extended in the *Ardhanārīnaṭeśvara stotra* to explicitly invoke the god and goddess in eleven syllables, or two *pañcākṣara-mantras* joined by the conjunction *ca* (and). Thus the overall tone of these *mantras* appears symmetrical as the author propitiates the female and male halves of the divine androgyne equally by following a rhythmic pattern at the end of each verse that is consistently employed throughout the hymn.

According to convention, the *Ardhanārīnaṭeśvara stotra* describes the physical appearance of the deity and, in this sense, calls to mind Cutler's reference to the *Tēvāram* hymns as "verbal icons" or "embodiments" (Cutler 1987, 112). The first line begins by delineating the bipolar body of Ardhanārīśvara as half female and half male, recalling the *brahmasūtra* (line of demarcation, *axis mundi*) running through the midpoint of the physical body on the temple *mūrtis*. The author draws our attention to the deity's female attributes first, then to his male half. Each unpretentious verse is patterned symmetrically on a similar comparison between Śiva's feminine and masculine form.

In the first line Sivā's complexion is compared to the *campā* flower. *Campā* has a delicate golden hue, whereas camphor (*karpūram*), the metaphor used to convey the shade of Śiva's complexion, is opaque white in color. In the *Śatarudrīya*, the color of Śiva's skin also is white, except for his blue-black throat, which is a reference to the deadly poison (*hālahāla*) that Śiva swallows when the gods churned the primeval ocean to obtain the nectar of immortality (*amṛta*). To save the world from impending threat, Śiva ingests the poison without harm and was marked in Indian mythology by his blue-black throat to commemorate this event. The demarcation of gold and white we see in this verse also corresponds to the exposition of the *viśuddha cakra* in *haṭhayoga*, in which the body of Ardhanārīśvara, located in this *padmacakra*, is described as half golden and half white. In both accounts, the golden-hued left side, suggestive of *hiranyagarbha* (golden womb), refers to Śakti, and the white complexion of Śiva is a result of ash (*bhasma*, *ūrdhvaretas*), and/or camphor used in the *ārti* temple rituals. The *Bṛhan-Nāradīya Purāṇa* gives an unusual reference (2.73.49) to Ardhanārīśvara as half black and half yellow (Agrawala 1966, 122).

One of the most popular attributes of Śiva in iconography is his matted hair (*jaṭa*, *uṣṇīṣa*), as it typically depicts his persona as the great *ūdhvareta* acetic and *yogi*. In sculpture, the matted locks are arranged as a crown adorned with a crescent moon, snakes, and the goddess Gaṅgā flowing from the top.[29] Sivā is described as wearing a *dhamilla*, a traditional braided hairstyle for women usually ornamented with pearls and other precious gems. These dissimilar hairstyles are evoked by the author to demarcate the distinctions between the male and female halves of Ardhanārīnaṭeśvara. At the end of the first verse, and each verse thereafter, the author bows twice, first to Ardhanārīśvara's female side, and then to the male side, and recites the eleven-syllable *mantra "namaḥ Śivāyai ca namaḥ Śivāya,"* offering salutations of praise to the androgynous god and goddess of dance. As part of Indian hymnal literature, the context of this *stotra* is personal devotion to Ardhanārīśvara.

In the second stanza, the fragrance of musk and the vibrancy of vermillion powder identify Śivā. The mark or dot of red vermillion (*kumkum*) indicates her marital status as the wife of Śiva which, as Susan Wadley suggests, is the normative role for an Indian woman and constitutes a necessary requirement for her liberation (Wadley 1975, 158; Wadley 1992). Śivā also is portrayed in this verse as having the power of sexual desire,—an attribute that must be contained through marriage (Wadley 1975, 28; Wadley and Jacobson 1992, White 1996, 219ff). By using imagery associated with the householder stage of life (*gṛhasthāśrama*), conveyed in this verse by the metaphors *kumkum* and *kṛtasmarāyai*, Śivā personifies the creative energy of sexuality (*bhoga, bhogavatī, kuṇḍalinī*) and fertility. Vermillion (*kumkum*) is used as a ritual paste or substance to pay homage and obeisance to the goddess, and it is used in this *stotra* to refer to Śivā's auspiciousness, fecundity, and creativity. According to White (1996), it is precisely this aspect of female fertility that poses such peril for male seed and virility, particularly in the context of the more orthodox monastic and ascetic schools of *yoga* over which Śiva is Lord (218). Accordingly, Śiva turns Pārvatī away because of her "femaleness" (O'Flaherty 1980, 141[30]; Khandelwal 1997, 83).

Śiva is depicted throughout the *stotra* as the *yogi par excellence* who has transcended or sublimated *bhoga* (or *bhogavatī, kuṇḍalinī*) through his internalized and *ūrdhvareta yoga* prowess. This is revealed in the second verse by the image of Śiva as *smasānavāsin*. Consequently, his appearance with his ghoulish body besmeared with ashes (*bhasma*) from the funeral pyre and burning cremation grounds where he sports is the embodiment of the power of dissolution, as he has purified himself of his creative powers through an ashen bath (*bhasma-snāna, ūrdhvaretas*). Like Agni-Soma, Prajāpati, and others in Indian tradition, the symbolic use of ash identifies and attests to Śiva's transcendence through his ability to sublimate desire.

However, it also is important to recall that in iconographic representation, Śiva and Śivā (i.e., Ardhanārīnaṭeśvara) are not two separate deities but rather a two-in-one form (*bhedābheda*). In other words, in union, Ardhanārīnaṭeśvara possesses the power of creation as well as destruction/transformation in one embodied androgynous, anthropomorphic form. Wadley (1991) makes an interesting observation regarding the inclusiveness of Śiva's "power of fertility" when she refers to the Nātha *yogi* lineage of Gorakhnāth as representing Śiva's "offspring" (142). This power or gift of creativity to propogate lineage is possible precisely because Śiva is always half Śivā. In this verse, the spontaneously arising complementarity divinized in the singular form of Ardhanārīnaṭeśvara gestures to the fusion of these two seemingly polar aspects of creation (life and death) as one interpenetrating iconographic symbol of primordial unity.

In the third stanza, the images used to represent the male and female form of Ardhanārīśvara express the coalescence and meeting of *pravṛtti* and *nivṛtti*. To illustrate this, the devotee hears Śivā's adornments, specifically her tinkling anklets and bracelets (*kvaṇat kaṅkana nūpurāyai*), precisely because the female half is portrayed as moving (*calat*), creative, and active (*karma*).[31] Śiva's anklets, on the other hand, just like his body, are decorated with snakes. Here, the association with snakes at Śiva's feet could be in reference to the hooded, coiled snake positioned at the right of Śiva's foot in the dance of the *ānanda-tāṇḍava*.[32]

Symbols in Indian tradition often are multivalent, and they suggest alternative or parallel explanations. According to Śivaramamūrti, the snake symbol was associated with the healer or physician (Śivaramamūrti 1976, 38). Like Śākyamuni Buddha, another epithet of Śiva's is the divine physician, and the disease that Śiva cures in this aspect is *bhava*, that is, the attachment to, or craving for, coming into existence or rebirth (*samsāra*).[33] Śivaramamūrti identifies Śiva's *nāga*-ornaments as the deadly snakes Karkota and Śesa (Śivaramamūrti 1976, 38). Snakes, skulls, ash, and so on also are symbols used frequently in ancient Tamil poetry to indicate Śiva's ultimate transcendence of birth and death (Yocum 1982, 146). When juxtaposed, these two metaphors evoke the dual themes of *pravṛtti* and *nivṛtti*. Śivā, portrayed as the divine energy of *prakṛti*, is associated with *pravṛtti*, whereas Śiva as *puruṣa* is *nivṛtti*.

The two colors of the lotus, blue and red, denote the different sides of Śivā and Śiva in verse five of the *stotra*. Śivā's eyes are the color of the blue lotus (*nīlotpala locanīyai*), whereas Śiva's resembles the red lotus (*paṅke ruha locanīya*). The lotus, according to Yocum, is commonly associated with Śivā in Tamil poetry (Yocum 1982, 126). A look at *haṭhayoga* tradition could provide additional insights about how to best understand this imagery. The color of the *viśuddha cakra*, or the locus of Ardhanārīśvara in *haṭhayoga* theory, is smoky or sky blue. When the practitioner reaches the stage of the *viśuddha cakra*, Oṃ

Shivatva explains that she/he becomes steady and absorbed in meditation on Śiva. Hence, the color of Śivā's eyes reflects her stage of attainment, identified by the color associated with the *cakra* of Ardhanārīśvara.

Śiva's eyes, on the other hand, are the color of the red lotus. His eyes do not convey the balance and symmetry (*samekṣanāyai*) that Śivā's do, but, are uneven (*viṣamekṣanāya*). The goddess is portrayed with two eyes, whereas Śiva has three eyes, usually equated in *haṭhayoga* with the triad moon (*candra*), sun (*sūrya*), and fire (*agni*). This points to a potential power imbalance between the goddess and the god in the *stotra*, since his third eye is typically associated with the divine eye of wisdom (*jñānetra*). As well, Śiva's eyes do not attract; instead, they burn with the color of fire (or the union of sun and moon).

In the next verse, Śivā wears a *mālā* (or garland) in her hair made from the flowers of the *mandār* tree, and the fabric of her royal dress impresses the hymnist as divine or extraordinary. It may be useful here to refer to Hart's (1975) explanation that flowers are important in South Indian society, past and present.[34] Married women, for example, wear flowers in their hair as it represents a sign of fertility (30). Śiva, on the other hand, wears a necklace of skulls around his neck, and he is dressed simply in the four directions (sky-clad, *digambara*). Śivā is fully clothed in the ornaments or emblems of the earth's fertility, whereas Śiva has renounced all materiality; he is clothed only with *ākāśa* (space) or void (*śūnyatā*), thus he is naked (*digambara*).[35] As Marglin (1985) contends, "nudity conveys asceticism," or the detachment of the ascetic from the world (49). In other words, the description of Śiva's state of consciousness, (i.e., *śūnyatā*) is made explicit in his form and appearance by his nakedness.

Similarly, in verse six, Śivā's dark hair resembles the clouds. This simile evokes a stock reference to the rain clouds at the time of the monsoon, the season of anticipated fertility and growth. Śiva's *jaṭā* has the luster of lightning. The *jaṭā* is a hairstyle worn by ascetics and signals the sublimation of sexual energy, and the luster of lightning emanating from it is a specific reference to various forms of Śiva's *yogāgni*, which is depicted as both flame and light. Tamil hymns refer to Śiva's matted hair as fire. Śiva's *yogāgni* (yogic heat) is linked to his sublimation of eros (*kāma*), and generally derives from his third eye. Through the inner heat arrested in meditation, Śiva displays this sign in the *ajña cakra*, and in the crown area of the head as well. Also, in *haṭhayoga* Śiva is the male-sun side, suggesting definite correspondences with the threefold transposition of Agni in the Vedas as fire, sun, and lightning.

In verse seven, creation and destruction, portrayed through images of their different dances, are gendered as feminine and masculine, respectively. Ardhanārīnaṭeśvara, being comprised of Śiva and Śakti, is the cosmic dancer who brings forth both creation (*prakṛti*) and dissolution. Anne Marie Gaston (1982) and Kamil V. Zvelebil (1985) distinguish Śiva's vigorous masculine dance (*tāṇḍava*) from his/her tender feminine dance (*lāsya*).[36] Ardhanārīśvara is "the most literal expression of the interplay of the male (*puruṣa*) and female (Śakti) elements in the cosmic cycle," according to Gaston (Gaston 1982, 139). As in temple iconography, Indian dance delineates the left side as Pārvatī (*lāsya*) and the right side as Śiva (*tāṇḍava*).[37] In the context of live performance, either the costume is differentiated, and a simple handkerchief divides the right and left half of the face of Ardhanārīśvara, or their different natures are portrayed through various *hastas* (hand gestures). When the dancer performs the *lāsya* of Pārvatī, the feminine half of the face is uncovered. For the *tāṇḍava,* or vigorous dance, the Śiva half of the face is visible (Gaston 1982, 139).[38]

As the mother of the universe, Śivā is creative and dances the *lāsya.* As the father, Śiva is responsible for the death and dissolution of *prakṛti* (feminine, nature) through the *tāṇḍava.*[39] From the very beginning of the hymn, the author has utilized various metaphors, such as *ratnojvala* (radiant precious stones), *nīlotpala* (blue lotus), *ambhodhara* (clouds), and so on, to sculpt the female half of Ardhanārīnaṭeśvara through a metaphoric association with the elements (*tattvas*) of the earth and material nature (*prakṛti*). Now, in verse seven, the grand design of creation and destruction to which the hymnist pays obeisance is revealed as the whole of Ardhanārīnaṭeśvara's body. All of the elements, *bhū* (earth), *jala* (water), *agni* (fire), and *ākāśa* (air), have their embodied place.[40] In other words, Ardhanārīnaṭeśvara is presented as both the eternal mother giving birth to *prakṛti* through the *lāsya,* and eternal father into whom creation (*prakṛti*) ultimately dissolves (*puruṣa*). We see a parallel image in the *haṭhayoga* tradition, and numerous metaphors employed in the *stotra,* such as ash, jaṭa, *yogāgni,* snakes, and so forth, convey these implied correspondences.

In the final stanza, Śivā's and Śiva's differences are once again signaled by their ear ornaments. As stated, earrings are used in Śaiva devotional poetry to evoke a vision of Ardhanārīśvara. Śakti wears earrings produced from the wealth of the earth (i.e., precious stones), while Śiva's are the emblems of *yoga* (e.g., snakes). Here a connection between Śivā as creation, nature, or materiality and Śiva as transcendence is conveyed. In other words, the universal cultural dialectic between matter/nature and culture/spirit, articulated earlier by Ortner, is projected in Indian tradition onto the dual-gendered deity Ardhanārīnaṭeśvara.

The hymnist, like Ortner, also makes the significant claim that the boundaries between these two human constructs (i.e., nature and spirit), are not as clearly demarcated as culture would have us believe, in that Śiva is Śakti and Śakti is Śiva; they constitute one inseparable, rhythmic, cosmic dance of coming into being and passing away (i.e., the dance of Ardhanārīnaṭeśvara). The single body of the androgynous divine speaks not only to the interpenetration of these cultural ideals, and their very real human manifestations, but also gestures to the ambivalence and difficulty involved in attempting to separate them. However, if by associating Śakti with lesser-valued roles, tasks, and ideals[41] the male half of the androgyne and his human counterparts are perceived as dominant and superior, then an asymmetrical status is rendered. This is seen most evidently in verse six by the epithets: "she is not lord, he is lord of all." As such, the *stotra* no longer operates as simply a subtle mystification for the notion for divine unity but can indeed be seen as an expression of subtle patriarchal social norms.

To illustrate, Jagadep (1989) investigates the condition of Tamil women in pre-British India only to reveal that the entrenched domination of women was "the norm." As above, men are the so-called "lord of all," particularly in the family, and women observed the rules and codes of behavior deemed proper by male-constituted family law or, as Rangaswamy suggested earlier, icons such as Umāpati and Ardhanārīśvara. Women as mothers are no doubt held in high regard, and often for women this is a significant locus of power and agency. However, for many feminists, the ideal of motherhood also necessitates rigorous rules regarding female chastity, child marriage, restricted remarriage for widows, claims over reproductive rights and, as Jagadep suggests, evidence of matricide (Jagadep 1989; Jeffery 1998; Basu 1998).

Moreover, according to Jagadep, religion can play a substantive role in the systematic subordination of women, for example, in less valued roles, including exclusion from religious initiation, performance of public liturgy, omission as functionaries at ancestral funerary rites, and so forth. This religious status finds its parallel in economic and political life as well in terms of patriarchal, patrilineal lines of inheritance, access to resources, and so on. However, Basu (1998) rightly argues that religion also can provide positive images for women, and can affirm women's membership and sense of belonging in the community (Basu 1998, 9). We will consider this in more detail in chapter 5.

In the final image of the *stotra*, and as a final expression of the doctrine of the ultimate inseparability of *prakṛti* and *puruṣa*, the hymn's closing verse presents Śivā and Śiva in a mutual embrace of reciprocated love.

Conclusions

The poems of the Tamil poet-saints present a well-articulated, highly stylized system of correspondence that is coterminous with the canons of temple iconography, effectively related by their recurring motifs and diagnostic features, based on the pan-Indian history of Śaiva theology in Indian tradition. In this sense, their function is primarily devotional or religious, though it must also be understood that as a descriptive discourse the hymns, in turn, become prescriptive by encoding normative and divinely sanctioned patterns and models of gender and behavior.

It is in this latter sense that the poems, at times, project a secondary or "subdued" role, as Peterson suggests, for the feminine aspect of Śiva, one that is consistent with the laws of the traditional family in *any* patriarchal society. While it appears that the overall and ultimate message of the image is one of unity and equanimity, the subtle markings of feminine convention at times betray this intent. For this reason, we probed some of the possible gender meanings of the diagnostic features found on the half-male, half-female images of Ardhanārīśvara by using, for example, Ortner's thesis of female subordination to explain how such a pattern could come about.

One possible, though often debated, explanation lies in the wider debate between nature and culture/spirit, and the ways in which these concepts are typically gendered in any particular cultural context. As such, an analysis of sacred images that derive from binary metaphysical, ideological, and theological paradigms, such as *prakṛti-puruṣa*, begins to explore the complex issue of gender myth making that is evident in the composite half-male and half-female image examined here. Rather than continue the unquestioned assumption of egalitarianism and symmetry thought to be portrayed in this image of transcendental union, instances of possible male dominance must be acknowledged and named in Indian textual materials, whether they are found in devotional poetry, iconography, mythology, or treatises on praxis. Then, with each new reading of the androgyne in these various cultural institutions, indications that this two-sexed model of humanity has been credited with the discourse of human emancipation can be questioned. As we saw in an earlier chapter, similar gender references are constructed in *yoga* though oftentimes encoded in the esoteric language of metaphysics. In safeguarding the illusion of equality often assumed to be evident in androgynic images, East and West, attempts to articulate aspects that limit women's roles, tasks, and status in society are subverted. Instead, with each new reading and critique of symbolic images conferring normative status on men and women, the hope of emancipation draws ever closer.

Chapter 4

An Indian and a Feminist Perspective of Androgyny

Introduction

In this chapter we consider the image of Ardhanārīśvara, the divine androgyne, in the context of two sustained studies on androgyny. Wendy Doniger's (1980) study looks at the androgyne in India and beyond using the comparative method of phenomenology. Kari Weil (1992) investigates androgyny in Western culture from the perspective of feminist theory. Both of these works have significantly influenced my theories on the image of the divine androgyne Ardhanārīśvara.

I also draw upon the main arguments offered in the debate among Western feminists on the subject of androgyny to situate my analysis of this image. The premise is that through dialogue two disparate theories/traditions of androgyny are able to inform each other and raise some questions about their own use of the symbol. For instance, the debate among Western feminists provides tools, on the one hand, for identifying and deconstructing the male subjectivity of Western androgyne motifs and brings to light subtle, and not so subtle, gender issues privileging male agency in the image's metaphorical and metaphysical binary structures. In other words, a feminist perspective can point out not only the asymmetry of power, authority, and privilege often embedded in the image itself, and commentaries surrounding the image, but also in the message it conveys in the real lives of the women and men to whom it speaks. On the other hand, Ardhanārīśvara in Indian tradition, unlike exclusively male-identified images of god in Western monotheistic religions, presents a gender-inclusive, two-in-one model of god/dess.[1] Along with this, the attained *yogin/ī* provides instructive techniques for understanding and experiencing this image as a metaphor for "self." Nevertheless, it is our contention that as long as images of Ardhanārīśvara, and interpretations surrounding the image, within human history, advantage his/her male half, the motif of an androgynous divine cannot be a truly emancipatory paradigm for women (or men, for that matter).

Wendy Doniger and Androgyny

Perhaps the most exhaustive and provocative treatment of the androgyne motif in Hindu mythology to date is Wendy Doniger's now classic work entitled *Women, Androgynes, and Other Mythical Beasts* (1980).[2] In this study, Doniger considers a myriad of androgynous themes and deities from the vast corpus of *purāṇic* mythology. Although this is not her only book to consider this type of gendered narrative,[3] it is particularly helpful here in order to probe the connection between Ardhanārīśvara and the broader motif of mythic androgyne in Indian tradition and elsewhere. For this reason, we concentrate on two particular aspects of Doniger's work, namely, her comparative taxonomy of androgyny and her significant treatment of Śivārdhanārīśvara in the *purāṇas*.

One of Doniger's substantive contributions in this book is to create a phenomenology of androgynes. She develops a cross-cultural analytical taxonomy to distinguish categories of androgynes found in various religious and cultural traditions. For instance, Doniger distinguishes between "good" and "bad" androgynes, "psychological" and "physical" androgynes, and "vertical" and "horizontal" androgynes.[4] She delineates among "split" androgynes, "two-in-one" androgynes, "fused" androgynes, "pseudo" androgynes, "twin" androgynes, "alternating" androgynes, and "positive" and "negative" androgynes, though this list is certainly not exhaustive. In a more recent study, Doniger (1999) explores Indian and Greek narratives of splitting and doubling which, in some cases, also imply tales of androgyny. From these comparative categories, three patterns emerge that pertain directly to the image of Ardhanārīśvara, namely, the vertical two-in-one androgyne and the fused androgyne, both of whom are considered "good" in Indian tradition.[5]

The anthropomorphic, vertical, two-in-one androgyne used by Doniger to categorize Ardhanārīśvara coincides with the Greek term *hieros gamos*, or "sacred marriage." As Harman (1989) observes in his study of sacred marriage, the term *hieros gamos* (or hierogamy) refers to the mythic metaphor of union between deities. As such, the term functions either as a projection or blueprint for, or paradigm or model of, prescriptive and divinely sanctioned codes of behavior in the human realm.[6] Ardhanārīśvara as a hierogamy of Śiva and Pārvatī simultaneously and vertically joined in a single anthropomorphic male and female body symbolizes the ambiguity of an essentially "positive" and "good," though primarily male-identified, androgynous deity. According to Doniger, it is perceived as "positive" and "good" by its influence on and success in controlling the normative social behavior of women and men.

The two-in-one androgyne referred to by Doniger (and Eliade 1954) also is equated with the *coniunctio oppositorum*[7] in Jungian psychology. According to Jung's (1977) substantial work on Western alchemical traditions and the human individuation process, the components or factors united by the psyche in the *coniunctio*, and in the primary archetypes of Self and Absolute, are typically conceived of as opposites. This so-called union of opposites, which for Jung is the end goal of all human striving, can be achieved by metaphorically reuniting or transcending such dualistic and oppositional pairs as heaven/earth, fire/water, spirit/nature, good/evil, mind/body, light/dark, masculine/feminine, anima/animus, and so on.[8]

Of course, one problem with this kind of binary imagery is that each half in the paired equation eventually is gendered male and female. Rather than espousing an egalitarian archetypal model of Self, the male and female halves of the androgyne/*coniunctio* are related to concepts and abstract designations such as, but certainly not limited to, those mentioned by Jung in an uneven distribution of power. Consequently, Jung's idea of the *coniunctio oppositorum* arouses uncritical, ambivalent associations, and often becomes the repository of inferior cultural constructions associated with the feminine (e.g., dark, evil, nature, body, etc.). Moreover, recent cognitive theories of religion (Boyer 1993; Lawson 1993) claim that binary referential categories such as these do not reflect the way the mind actually conceptualizes mental images and symbols and therefore imply that Jung (or any structuralist descriptions based on binary oppositions) proposes a limited reading of human psychology.

As a choice example of a two-in-one androgyne, Ardhanārīśvara displays aspects of splitting and/or positive chaos (called fusing). One necessary requirement, according to Doniger's schema, is that the mythological androgyne "must split before it can become physically creative" (Doniger 1980, 292). Consequently, we read in various *purāṇic* accounts about the creative function of Ardhanārīśvara, wherein Śiva summons Śakti to create women. Thus the female principle emerges from the two-in-one androgyne for the exclusive purpose of creating womankind (see, e.g., *Liṅga Purāṇa* 1.70.325, 1.41. 7–9, 1.5.2; *Visnu*

Purāṇa 1.7.12–13; *Kūrma Purāṇa* 1.11, 2–13; *Śiva Purāṇa* 2.1.15. 55–56). In other words, for the sake of creation, the androgynous deity distinguishes a female nature, and in this precise moment a splitting occurs. Having fashioned and satisfied the conditions of splitting that Doniger sets out before us, Śakti is then reabsorbed into Śiva's body. That is, Śakti emerges from, and returns to, the male-identified godhead (Śiva).

Handelman and Shulman (1997) reveal an alternate instance of this very same process of androgynic splitting in their account of Śiva's game of dice. In this account, we witness the process of sexual differentiation where the game of dice constitutes the exact moment of division (or splitting) between the Śiva/male and Pārvatī/female aspects of the homogeneous deity for the explicit purpose of human creation. What is interesting about this critical reading is that for Handelman and Shulman, Śiva represents the undifferentiated cosmic whole that transcends the human realm of time and space and, I would imagine, gender. Once the initial impetus or desire to create emerges, Śiva begins to split by becoming the androgyne and he/she eventually proceeds toward total separation.

However, it is important to call attention to the fact that in these myths (and others in the cycle) it is typically the male-identified god (e.g., Śiva) and not the woman/goddess who becomes the divine androgyne. Consequently, an explicit androgynization or femininization of the male-identified deity must occur in order for human creation to take place. Through a process of "creative inversion," in which the male god projects the female aspect and her unique role as child bearer, man/god becomes the "mother" and "father" of all creation. Thus, in Tamil poetry, Śiva is referred to by the dual epithet *ammaiyappar*, meaning mother-father.

In her insightful study of the creation of patriarchy in Western civilization, historian Gerda Lerner (1986) points out that in Judeo-Christian creation myths, Eve is formed from the rib of Adam. This specific event, she argues,

> defines Woman in a very special way as a "natural" part of man, flesh of his flesh, in a relationship which is a peculiar inversion of the only human relationship for which such a statement can be made, namely, the relationship of mother to child. The Man here defines himself as "the mother" of Woman, and through the miracle of divine creativity a human being was created out of his body the way the human mother brings forth life out of her body. (Lerner 1986, 181)

Similar to this account, Indian androgynic creation myths, including Sāṃkhya-Yoga evolutionary theory, also involve a reversal process signaling the centrality of the male-dominated divine hierogamy or principle (e.g., *prakṛti-puruṣa*) in the generation of the universe. As Lerner claims, it could well be that the ideology of patriarchy is being birthed in these myths, and by it the prescriptive laws defining human gender relations are clearly revealed and given divine sanction, thus becoming even more deeply embedded in the cultural psyche.

A process of "creative inversion" also underpins the androgynization of the *yogi* (referred to by Doniger in masculine terms only). Categorized as embodied, psycho-anthropomorphic androgynes who exhibit traits of positive chaos or fusing, the *yogi*, in Doniger's account, offers a model of reintegration and union through the mythology of mysticism and its attendant goal of a return to a homogeneous or an undifferentiated consciousness prior to splitting or separation. Though Doniger gestures to a quality of wholeness and equality in this androgynous form, in her final analysis, the *yogi* (like Ardhanārīśvara) signals a dominant, male-identified androgyne in Indian tradition.

Doniger (1980) and Goldman (1993) turn to Freudian analysis to provide several important clues to explain why culturally perceived positive androgynes are primarily male identified. In myths of gender exchange (such as Iḷa, Bhaṅgāśvana, and Śikhaṇḍin), women (or goddesses) who are transformed into men (or gods) are stereotypically perceived (by men) as dangerous, sexually voracious "phallic women" primarily because they threaten male potency and virility (Doniger 1980, 305; Goldman 1993).[9] In other words, the mythic stereotype of the male-identified woman stands in stark contrast to the normative role of woman as submissive wife and (good) mother and, hence, she is perceived as "dangerous" and "deviant."[10]

A potent example of the male-identified phallic woman in Indian tradition is the female ascetic or *yoginī*. Perceived from a dominant male perspective, she is portrayed as being potentially dangerous, precisely because of the power (*śakti*) she accumulates through intense ascetic practices (*tāpas*), as well as the possible sexual threat she poses to male virility and seed. For this reason, Doniger cites the myths of Pārvatī and Ambā to illustrate the fury of the ascetic, phallic woman. The destructive ("bad") mother, similar to the *yoginī* or ascetic woman, challenges culturally endorsed and deeply internalized prescriptive roles for women as well as for men. Consequently, we see a distinct preference in traditional patriarchal society for "woman" in the contained role of wife and mother rather than the powerful and free *yoginī* or ascetic. To a large extent, Indian tradition explores the valorization of the eternal feminine, but primarily within the context of the feminine counterpart, providing a transformative effect on the male subject and thereby contributing to the achievement of male wholeness. Alternative roles, such as *yoginī* or ascetic, which apply to "real women," typically threaten the status quo.[11]

As a general statement, this is equally valid in Western culture. Adrienne Rich (1976) writes:

> What we did see, for centuries, was the hatred of overt strength in women, the definition of strong independent women as freaks of nature, as unsexed, frigid, castrating, perverted, dangerous; the fear of the maternal woman as "controlling," the preference for dependent, malleable, "feminine" women. (Rich 1976, 45)

Rabbinic folk narratives cast the independent Lilith, for instance, in a negative and marginalized perspective to ensure subdued roles for women, just as Indian tradition portrays its own culturally endorsed mythic roles. We see that oftentimes women had to feign madness or strike out against normative social roles to take up a devotional or an ascetic life. Two examples of this are Mahādevīyakka (Akka Māhādevī), a twelfth-century South Indian woman from Karnataka in love with Śiva, Lord of the Jasmines, and Mīrābāī, a sixteenth-century saint from Rajasthan, in love with Kṛṣṇa. Mahādevīyakka deserted her husband, King Kauśika, to be with her beloved, Lord Śiva. Like Śiva (and the Jaina monks of her husband's religion), she clothed herself only with her long hair as she wandered sky-clad (*digambara*) to Kalyāṇa.[12] Mīrābāī also abandoned her husband to pursue her intense love of Kṛṣṇa. Both examples attest to the restrictive and ambivalent roles for women ascetics in a traditional patriarchal society.

In her comprehensive analysis, Doniger recounts the dynamic evolution of the androgyne in Hindu mythology, and her general discussion of the history of the androgyne is immensely informative. What is clear is that a sacred tradition of dual or androgynous deities dates in some instances as far back as the early Vedic period.[13] The earliest androgynous motif in the *Ṛg Veda* is Dyāvā-Pṛthivī (Sky-Earth), gendered as sky/father and earth/mother. We also see the "alternating androgyne" Indra influencing the development of Śiva mythology (Doniger 1980, 310). Prajāpati, the pregnant male who is perceived as Puruṣa, appears as the primeval being in the *Brāhmaṇas* who desires to create through an act of primordial dismemberment or splitting. Prajāpati functions, like Dyāvā-Prthivī, as both mother and father. This narrative is recast in the *Bṛhadāranyaka Upaniṣad* (1. 4. 3–4 cited in Olivelle 1998, 47) and tells the story of a single androgynous being who divides into two parts giving rise to male and female, and husband (*pati*) and wife (*patnī*). The myth of the androgynous Śiva (i.e., Ardhanārīśvara), is a variant of this cycle, or what Doniger calls "a secondary model" (Doniger 1980, 312) and finds its specific origins in the Śiva-Rudra myth of the *Śvetāśvatara Upaniṣad.*

Accordingly, the principal role of Ardhanārīśvara, like Prajāpati, Dyāvā-Pṛthivī, and other dual deities, is essentially parental (though not sexually procreative). All of the above-mentioned androgynous or dual forms function in a creative or cosmogenic capacity as the primordial parents of human beings. As Doniger (1998) says, these myths are retold precisely "because the community becomes attached to the signifiers, and they become authoritative and historically evocative" (79). More importantly, these early androgynic mythic structures provide the primary prototypes in the eventual promulgation of a system of homologues that builds gradually upon increasing *brahmanical* ritualization, on the one hand, and the culturally constructed system of gender meanings, on the other hand, specifically in the tradition of *tantra* and *haṭha yoga.*

Hindu myth and folk traditions also cast Śiva as a "fusing" androgyne. Doniger observes that out of "passion, gratitude, or some other emotion, Śiva embraced Pārvatī so closely that their bodies fused into one" (Doniger 1980, 314). However, once they have become Ardhanārīśvara, Śiva and Pārvatī are unable to participate in sexual relations or, as Doniger claims, they are "barren." Doniger explains this in Freudian terms as Śiva "forestalling sexual activity with the mother"[14] (ibid.). However, if we apply an alternative interpretive lens, such as *haṭha yoga* theory, we see that Śiva's and Pārvatī's bodies are androgynously paired not as a result of forestalling sexual or erotic love but rather out of a transformed love or *prema*. In the ascetic or spiritual marriage model, the *yogin/ī* remains integrated and touching (i.e., an internalized hierogamy of Ardahnārīśvara), precisely because she/he transforms *kāma* into *prema* through *sādhana*. As such, the living tradition of *yoga* offers an alternative reading of the fusing androgyne in Indian mythology. Nonetheless, as Doniger clearly shows, any *tantric* reading of Ardhanārīśvara as a symbol of *yoga* attainment (i.e., *nivṛtti marga*) requires us to at least acknowledge that when texts speak of a reversal of generative fluids, it usually signifies a reversal of power, and the theory of creative inversion that I mentioned earlier resurfaces. In other words, Doniger claims that by "reversing the flow of the fluids, Tantrism reverses the flow of power" from the female to the male (Doniger 1980, 262).

By extension, in the Indian nuptial ideal of *ardhanārī*, the perfect wife or *pativrata* (like Pārvatī in the myth of Ardhanārīśvara) becomes absorbed into half the man, that is, he does not become absorbed into her. Leslie's (1989) analysis of Tryambaka's *Strīdharmapaddhati* challenges what she refers to as the "much extolled" metaphysical ideal of oneness, which Ardhanārīśvara exemplifies, precisely because "it does not bear close examination on the human level" (2). In Leslie's own words, the "oneness of the married couple means not the merging of two individuals but the self-effacement of one of them," that is, "the wife" (ibid.). This, in Leslie's view, is the practical and all-too-common meaning of "*ardhanārī*." The nineteenth-century Hindu reformer, Rammohun Roy, also identifies the *ardhanārī* ideal as privileging the male half. Roy claims:

> [A]lthough woman is recognized as being "half of her husband," she is in fact treated as "worse than inferior animals," and is made "to do the work of a slave in the house." (Roy, cited in Karlekar 1993, 46–47)

However, scholars such as Sheryl Daniels (1991) and Frederique Marglin (1982) suggest that the image also can evoke positive connotations and has in fact inspired marital arrangements in South India based on an alternate understanding of the complementarity and egalitarian nature of the masculine and feminine aspects of Śivārdhanārī. Although this form of marriage is not the normative model, one plausible interpretation of the embodiment of the divine as gender inclusive makes this marital arrangement possible.

To convey the "lopsidedly male" emphasis of androgyny, Doniger calls our attention to the *Śiva-liṅga*. The *liṅga* is usually accompanied by a *yoni*, the sign of the female principle, and together they signify the unitive nature of the male and female aspects of Śiva, or an aniconic version of the Ardhanārīśvara motif. But the *liṅga* as the cardinal aniconic form of Śiva "functions in mythology as a phallus pure and simple" (Doniger 1980, 317–18). Doniger is aware that even if the *Śiva-liṅga* is viewed as androgynous, it invariably emphasizes the male anthropomorphic form more than his/her female half.

The syncretic aniconic image of the *yoni-liṅga* is a comparatively late design. The earliest *liṅgas*, such as the Guḍimallam *mukhaliṅga* (c. third-second century C.E.), do not appear to have an explicit *pīṭha* design. Actually, it is not until the last stage of development in the seventh–eighth centuries that we see the circular or octagonal design appear (Mitterwallner 1984, 26). Rao calls the yoni *praṇālī* or pedestal in which the *liṅga* is firmly placed a *pīṭha* or *piṇḍikā*, and Banerjea thought that this design feature simply functions as a drain to ensure the flow of water or milk poured by devotees during *pūjā* or *abhiṣeka*. Later iconographical texts such as *Mayamata* provide precise instructions for its proper construction, including the specific use of male stone (*pum-śīla*) for the *liṅga* and female stone (*strī-śīla*) for the *yoni*, gesturing to the intended syncretic union of male and female in a later stage of development (Rao 1968, 102; Banerjea 1956, 169; Mitterwallner 1984). However, we also see that the earliest *liṅgas* rise directly out of the earth, often personified as a female divinity (e.g., Pṛthivī, Bhū). Consequently, even though the *yoni-liṅga* as such is a comparatively late design, it is possible that the conjoined male and female unit was already implied in earlier constructions.

Whether in iconic or aniconic form, the androgyne motif in Indian tradition does not always represent "a symbol of perfect union" (Doniger 1980, 318). For Doniger, the image conveys mostly a sense of "nonequality" and "primary maleness" (331). The primary maleness of the form of the androgyne, as Doniger suggests, "may represent not only the androcentrism of the religious context but also a deeper feeling of imbalance, a male's need to correct his own incompleteness by assimilating to himself the form of the female" (ibid.). For this reason, it will be useful to look at the debate in Western feminist theory on androgyny to explore from a comparative perspective how such an interpretation could come about in another culture as well.

Androgyny and Western Thought

Kari Weil's (1992) insightful study traces the history of the androgyne in Western thought using a feminist theoretical perspective, specifically Luce Irigaray's deconstruction of the patriarchal "dream of symmetry" (Weil 1992, 12; Irigaray 1985b). While she contextualizes her critique in Western philosophical, aesthetic, literary, and historical discourse and focuses primarily on fictionalized representations of the androgyne from nineteenth-century France, Weil's insights into the construction of androgynic mythologies as part of a broader patriarchal structure and ideology offer an instructive comparative model for this examination of the image of the divine androgyne Ardhanārīśvara in Indian tradition. It is this analysis of androgyny that we devote our attention to in this section. Following this, we draw upon a summary of Western feminism's debate on androgyny as a springboard for our own observations on this subject.

According to Weil, the androgyne is typically defined as the union of "male and female," "subject and object," and the "spiritual and material worlds" (Weil 1992, 2). In the Western classical tradition, the androgyne represents an image of oneness and, according to Weil, offers "a vision of man's original primordial nature before a fall from divine unity into alterity and difference" (2, 10). Weil (1992) and Hoeveler (1990) agree that the androgyne reflects a synthesis of "what is objectively known (identified as the masculine) and the unknown Other (identified as feminine) who will make that knowledge complete" (Weil 1992, 2; Hoeveler 1990, 5).[15] However, classical Western representations and cosmologies of this type, that is, ones that postulate an androgynous metaphysical or transcendental ideal, have come under close examination by current poststructuralists and feminist theories because, as Weil observes, they are rooted in structures of binary opposition and are contingent upon hierarchical and dualistic norms (Weil 1992, 11). In other words, Western models of androgyny, as early as the writings of Plato and Ovid, have functioned in Western culture "as a conservative, if not misogynistic ideal" (2). If we actually look at various representations of this figure in Western culture, as Weil (1992) and Hoeveler (1990) show, we cannot help but see that the so-called "givens"of the androgyne are in fact constructions of patriarchal ideology rather than the "results of divine or natural law," as they would have us believe (Weil 1992, 203). This becomes even more apparent when compared to the so-called "givens" of another cultural model, such as the divine androgyne Ardhanārīśvara in Indian religious tradition. The opposition of binarisms reflected in Western mythifications of the androgyne imputes dualistic themes such as body and soul, nature (*prakṛti*) and spirit (*puruṣa*), top (right) and bottom (left), and so on. Western critics of androgyny take exception to the seemingly hierarchical values being polarized by such designations as male/female, culture/nature, heaven/earth, right/left, active/passive, subject/object, which are idealized over and over in the figure of the androgyne (West and East).

Consequently, one significance of androgynic construction is that its formulaic design juxtaposes a constellation of symbolic devices set side by side in one composite image. As such, the vision offered by the androgyne concretizes currents of (patriarchal) culture that potentially generate and sustain complex (and often subtle) blueprints for male hegemony. Hence, the task at hand is a systematic analysis of the sets of symbolic devices being fused or constellated into an androgynous image, and a critique as to why. A deconstruction of the abstract and metaphorical associations merged in the form and figure of androgynic constructions often will expose androcentric idealizations and mystifications of sameness and essentialism and also mask the reality of sexual difference and the various forms of hierarchy that it often engenders.[16]

Irigaray (1985b) and Kristeva (1974) even insist that "woman" as such does not exist. Irigaray (1985) argues that since "the feminine occurs only within models and laws devised by male subjects," there cannot really be "two sexes, but only one" (86). In this sense, Irigaray is aware that conventional representations of "woman" (or "*nārī*") are merely prescriptive products of male culture (and so is the notion of "*īśvara*"). These claims simply remind us once again that wo/man is not born, s/he is made. It is here that an analysis of the image of Ardhanārīśvara, at least from the applied or praxis-oriented perspective of *haṭha yoga*, interjects the dynamic possibility of a probing and destabilizing internal or indigenous critique of identity based on illusory ideas of fixed identity and subjectivity, and it is in this sense, I think, that a contemporary analysis of Ardhanārīśvara offers a critical dimension within Indian and feminist dialogue. Poststructualist feminists' refusal to accept gender constructs as anything but products of the (male) imagination is not irrelevent to the process of higher meditation in the praxis-oriented tradition of *haṭhayoga*. At the same time, an uncritical reading of this tradition will simply repeat normative assumptions and traditional idealizations of "woman" and the "feminine."

Western Feminist Theory and Androgyny

Western academic feminists' responses to the concept of androgyny from its first phase in the 1960s to the present day are worth looking at here. This analysis provides a variety of insights into the early days of feminist theory when discussions of androgyny as a viable two-sexed model of humanity provided a possible alternative to fixed gender identity and were then being considered. Borrowing from Kristeva and Moi, Weil utilizes their three-phase chronological scheme to reflect upon this debate in her study of androgyny in Western tradition.

In the first phase during the early 1970s, the debate over androgyny was integrated into a vision of psychological and sociological equality between men and women, or what we can call "liberal feminism." The significant players who fought for the idea of androgyny during this period were literary critic Carolyn Heilbrun, psychologist June Singer, post–Christian feminist theologian Mary Daly, radical feminist Adrienne Rich, and the legacy left by modern novelist Virginia Woolf, to name only a few. Specific attention to the catalytic ideas postulated by Virginia Woolf on the subject of androgyny and Western feminists' appropriation of them, especially in their early phase, was crucial to the interplay in feminist theory between androgyny and sexual difference. What is significant to point out, however, is that feminist arguments in favor of androgyny, at least in the initial stages of first-wave feminism, were informed and inspired mostly by Western literary models of androgyny, Shakespeare, the British Romantic poets, Virginia Woolf, and so on. One problem that arises from this, is that Western fictional models of androgyny often have appropriated the so-called feminine for their male-identified heroes (this is equally true of Indian images). The symbol of the feminine has been used in Western literature primarily for the purpose of empowering or transforming the male hero/half. The privileged male as subject and/or author absorbed the female and her presence to bring about the androgynization or totalizing consciousness of the male subject. In other words, the instrumental valorization of the feminine has been used primarily for the benefit and elevation of men and male heroes as a way to make their knowledge complete and whole (Hoevelor 1990).

It is interesting that models of androgyny in Western fiction that exalt the feminine (principle) often go "hand in hand with an effacement of women" (Weil 1992, 148).[17] As a Western literary motif, androgyny typically denies the reality of female subjectivity and difference. Consequently, we see that androgyny in Western literature was never intended as an explicit emancipatory paradigm for women, nor as a feminist ideal to eradicate and disrupt distorted gender stereotypes to overcome the oppression of male hierarchy and authority. Rather, it was exalted primarily as a positive goal for men and appropriated by some early feminists until gynocentric feminism criticized its usage as an inadequate and a barren model.

One of the forerunners in favor of androgyny, whose early arguments draw specifically upon Western literary sources, is Carolyn Heilbrun. In *Toward a Recognition of Androgyny* (1973), Heilbrun proclaims that androgyny is "a forward step and a positive goal for women," and she declares implicitly that androgyny promotes a positive role that will lead women from the "prison of gender" (ix, 115). Furthermore, Heilbrun advocates that "the ideal of androgyny must be realized for our very survival" (xx). Heilbrun and others who initially championed the cause envision androgyny as a symbol of human fullness yielding great promise and emancipation and as a nonhierarchical, complementary, social ideal of human becoming that transcends gender stereotypes and inequality. In a later article (1980), Heilbrun continues to advocate androgyny as "a necessary stopping place on the road to feminism," even though she concedes that the history of the androgyne in Western history shows the privileging of the male half (265, 261).

Psychologist Sandra Bem, who devised an "androgynous test" called the Bem Sex-Role Inventory (BSRI), assessed males and females against an extensive range of "traits traditionally considered 'normal' for male and female" (Bem, cited in Eisenstein 1983, 60). Bem's findings (echoing Romantic poet Samuel Taylor Coleridge) indicated that "it was the brightest and most accomplished people . . . who measured as most androgynous" (Bem, cited in Eisenstein 1983, 61). Bem and other advocates of androgyny in the field of psychology, such as Jungian therapist June Singer (1989), thought that the psychological androgynic model offered a viable alternative to gender stereotyping and would separate sex from gender once and for all.

Unlike Bem, Singer (1989) views the androgyne in Jungian or archetypal terms as a model second only to the archetype of the Absolute. For her, the androgyne constitutes a realizable mystic totality of primordial unity and wholeness imaged psychologically as male and female in one human being (6). Interestingly, Singer also includes a discussion of Indian androgynes such as Śiva-Śakti in her work, but her data, informed exclusively by Heinrich Zimmer, Philip Rawson, Gopi Krishna, Agehananda Bharati, Mircea Eliade, and Swami Nikhilananda, not only essentializes male and female but is based largely on a legacy of androcentric scholarship that does not critically consider the male-centeredness of the androgyne motif in Indian tradition.

Overall, these examples of early models of androgyny as a possible psycho-social alternative to sedimented notions of gender identity are problematic for the concerns of contemporary feminism. While Heilbrun (1980) and Rita Gross (1993; 1996) still crusade on behalf of androgyny, Weil argues that Heilbrun's so-called "literary androgyny" essentializes the feminine as a "civilizing force" for the purpose of "perfecting a male subject whose implicit supremacy is never challenged" (Weil 1992, 147). The current trend in Western feminism is to basically dismiss or question to what extent such a model can be useful for feminist concerns, in particular, its applicability to the critical questions of identity, alterity, and difference.

The second phase in the debate on androgyny, like second-wave feminism itself, took a stance of radical separatism by extolling and valorizing the feminine. Led by Mary Daly, Elaine Showalter, Mary Vetterling-Bragen, Adrienne Rich, and others, these so-called radical feminists reacted against earlier notions of androgyny as a viable ideal for women, rejecting it along with equality and even humanism for not promoting positive ideals for women. To illustrate, the substance of Daly's (1978, 1985) response, like Rich's (1976), announces that there are three words that she cannot use again, and one of them is "androgyny." She explains: "Androgyny is a confusing term which I sometimes used in attempting to describe integrity of be-ing" (Daly 1978, xi; Daly 1985, xxiv; Rich 1976, 76). Subsequently, Daly captures the mood of counterarguments directed against androgyny in second-wave feminism. She writes:

> Feminist theorists have gone through frustrating attempts to describe our integrity by such terms as androgyny. Experience proved that this word, which we now recognize as expressing pseudo wholeness in its combination of distorted gender descriptions, failed and betrayed our thought. The deceptive word was a trap, hard to avoid on an earlier stage of the Journey. When we

heard the word echoed back by those who misinterpreted our thought we realized that combining the "halves" offered to consciousness by patriarchal language usually results in portraying something more like a hole than a whole. Thus androgyny is a vacuous term which not only fails to represent richness of be-ing. It also functions as a vacuum that sucks spellbound victims into itself. (Daly 1978, 387)

For Daly, the once-used term *androgyny* now evokes an absurd image akin to taping John Travolta and Farah Fawcett Majors together.

Daly is not alone. Elaine Showalter also was part of a growing new group of female-identified gynocentric scholars concerned with idealizing women's writing and experience. Showalter identifies female experience "primarily with experiences of the body—menstruation, passion, menopause" (Showalter 1977, 294). She rejected the women's movement's appropriation of Virginia Woolf's vision of androgyny, calling it escapism, passive, subjective or, as Weil observes, a "gender-relaxed utopian ideal," an "evasive fantasy," and a model that is simply not positive for women. Her brand of feminist critique may be categorized as "gyno-criticism" (Weil 1992, 149). From this so-called radical feminist, women-identified position, Showalter rejects androgyny "as a form of sexual sublimation" and argues that it is a "myth" that distances the writer from her body, from herself, and from all association with female sexuality (Showalter 1977, 34). Showalter is specifically addressing what she perceives as Woolf's own sublimation of the female body. However, the specificity of this statement lends itself to a more general critique of the figure of the androgyne from the perspective of the female author/subject during the second phase of the feminist critique of androgyny.

Weil reports that in 1973, the Modern Language Association (MLA) held a special forum to reexamine androgyny "from a literary, cultural, and political perspective" (Weil 1992, 151). All but two of the papers presented in the forum concurred that "androgyny is essentially a masculine ideal and one inappropriate for women wishing to advance themselves or to promote the new discipline of women's studies in the academy" (ibid.). With the exception of Heilbrun, and a collaborative paper by Nancy Topping Bazin and Alma Freema, all agreed in principle that the myth of androgyny is not only sexist but also obviously heterosexist. They argued that androgyny focuses on the complementarity of genital differences and promotes the oppressive institution of marriage. Moreover, the conceptualizations of woman contained in this mythic model reflect a repressive and marginal position that offers little to the cause of woman's liberation. Other than the writers mentioned above, all were in accordance that the concept of androgyny is a patriarchal notion that does not promote positive ideals for women (Weil 1992, 151). It was suggested by the majority of presenters that arguments in favor of androgyny are rooted basically in humanist ideals of wholeness. According to Weil, these are the very ideals that have

> constituted the underpinnings of patriarchal ideology. In the tradition of classical aesthetics, as well as in psychoanalytic theory, wholeness has been the privilege of the masculine—woman being defined alternatively as immanence, and hence too close to nature, or as lacking (castrated), a hole instead of a whole. (Weil 1992, 152)

These arguments are clearly reminiscent of Daly and Ortner.

The third phase occurs in French feminism, as it redefines the concept of androgyny. Weil observes: "With its emphasis on the body and on the ever-changing boundaries between sexes and sexualities, a new ideal was constructed that could be called . . . a dream of hermaphroditism" (Weil 1992, 145). It is this "dream of hermaphroditism" or bisexuality that in fact defines the emerging ideals in French feminist thought and provides the most thorough, deconstructive critique of androgyny in the West.

Toril Moi (1985), aligning herself with this third phase of French feminism, proclaims that the categories "male" and "female" are themselves actually false. Moi, like Kristeva and Irigaray, rejects the notion of identity, or as Kristeva writes:

> [T]he very dichotomy man/woman as an opposition between two rival entities may be understood as belonging to "metaphysics." What can "identity," even "sexual identity," mean in a new theoretical and scientific space where the very notion of identity is challenged? (Kristeva 1982, 52)

Indebted to Kristeva's theories of anti-essentialism, Moi challenges the idea stated earlier that gender identities are in fact (god) given.

This chronological scheme shows that the first phase of androgyny was concerned primarily with equality. The second phase promoted real difference which Kristeva, in the third phase, labels essentialism and male humanism (Weil 1992). That is, their gyno-centric arguments simply invert and, therefore, replicate the very part of patriarchal ideology that they seek to deconstruct. In an important, although lengthy, passage, Moi explains that

> the traditional humanism they represent is in effect part of partriarchal ideology. At its center is the seamlessly unified self—either individual or collective—which is commonly called "Man" . . . this integrated self is in fact a phallic self, constructed on the model of the self-contained, powerful phallus. Gloriously autonomous, it banishes from itself all conflict, contradiction, and

> ambiguity. In this humanist ideology the self is the *sole author* of history and of literary text: the humanist creator is potent, phallic, and male—God in relation to his world, the author in relation to his text.... The text is reduced to a passive, "feminine" reflection of an unproblematically "given," "masculine" world of self. (Moi 1985, 8)

Feminist logic such as this is useful in any cross-cultural dialogue extending to the phallic-identified image of Śiva, but it will undoubtedly encounter strong opposition when applied to an examination of the image of Ardhanārīśvara, given the rootedness of essentialist ideas of masculine and feminine in the theological and metaphysical arguments of Ardhanārīśvara in Indian thought. The vision of *advaita* (i.e., nonduality), which is crucial to any understanding of the philosophical underpinnings of the image of Ardhanārīśvara, would be rejected by French feminist theorists such as Kristeva and Irigaray, who challenge and unmask the ideal of androgyny on the basis of its systematic denial of difference and its illusory claims to sameness or oneness. This is due to the deceptive and pejorative vision of woman offered by patriarchal, androgynous mythifications that typically assimilate or absorb the feminine by fusing it into a masculine-identified image of sameness rather than promoting and sustaining authentic alterity and difference.[18]

As I stated at the outset of this discussion, Weil weaves Irigaray's feminist platform into her own ideas on androgyny. Irigaray envisions

> not unity, but separation—not identity, but difference—define the starting point from which the two sexes must approach each other, touch each other." (Irigaray, cited in Weil 1992, 167)

Weil reads Irigaray's utopian vision as providing a "new symmetry" between the sexes, or, "the positivity of difference rather than the complementarity" (Weil 1992, 167). Irigaray proposes a model "chiasmus," or absolute duality (dvaita), when she writes: "What I see as a manifestation of sexual liberation is god made a couple: man and woman and not simply God made man" (Irigaray 1989, 73). In this plan, women and men can both claim equivalence, equality, subjectivity, rights, and divine identity. Here it is essential to point out that Irigaray is working within a Western religious framework that posits what is understood as a primarily "God-made-man view" of creation. It is at this point that the Indian deity Ardhanārīśvara, and his/her implications for Indian society, differs from this Western view in significant ways. In the mythology of Ardhanārīśvara, we encounter a completely different view of creation, one in which God is both male and female, and men and women, echoing their deity, have not only a divine origin but also an essential bisexual identity. Other celebrated dual images of divinity in Indian tradition, such as Viṣṇu and Lakṣmī, Rāma and Sītā, Kṛṣṇa and Rādhā, and so on, reveal the recurring Hindu belief in God made a couple or, more accurately, God as god and goddess. Nevertheless, sexual identity between "real" women and men is still recognizably hierarchical and, whether God is imaged as an androgyne or as a divine couple, the male half of the transcendent dyad is generally dominant.

In her account of nonduality in Vajrayāna Buddhism, Gross (1993) explains that masculine and feminine remain

> interdependent, complementary aspects of the Whole, aspects which cannot be collapsed into monistic unity any more than they can be brought into real opposition. Furthermore, one identifies with and develops *both* elements of the pair, regarding the image as an *upāya* for contemplating how to develop and balance divergent elements of experience.... The mere presence of two elements is not always evidence of dualistic, hierarchical thinking. (Gross 1993, 198)

Gross proclaims that this ideology is vividly articulated by the Tibetan Buddhist image of the sexual couple *yab-yum* (mother-father). In the iconography of *yab-yum,* the male is typically seen facing the worshipper, and the female, facing the male, embraces his waist. While this may come closer to Irigaray's vision of the "new symmety," the difficulty here is that this specific composite image, similar in function to Ardhanārīśvara in Indian thought, though not explicitly an androgyne, represents a subtle and powerful symbolic form that functions nonetheless as the repository of cultural rules, hierarchies, and metaphysical ideas through which prescribed notions of personhood and identity often are juxtaposed. As Gross herself tells us in her explanation of the various cultural motifs associated with, and encoded in, the iconography of the *yab-yum* figure:

> [S]un and moon, vowels and consonants, red and white, ritural bell and sceptre (*vajra* and *dorje*), liquor or meat, all connote, respectively, feminine and masculine. (Gross 1993, 200)

What is critical to this discussion, as Gross points out, is that the left hand in this composite *maithuna* image holds the bell and the right hand holds the scepter. But what Gross does not fully elucidate here is that at times these symbolizations, similar to the two-in-one androgynous motif of Ardhanārīśvara in Indian tradition, or even *yin-yang* theory in Chinese religion and philosophy, reproduce patriarchal relations of domination and advantage by reducing or negating the status of the feminine through subtle and less privileged cultural associations or positions. In Vajrayāna Buddhism, bell and scepter are associated, respectively, with feminine and masculine, and the right side of the body oftentimes holds a position of superior value compared to the left.[19] Moreover, Gross herself confirms that male and female in this "two-in one" symbol do not stand "independent and solid existing in their separateness," which is a necessary condition of Irigaray's new symmetry (Gross 1993, 102). Since this model, in Gross's words, "is of critical importance for understanding the Vajrayāna view of the proper relationship and interactions between both women and men, and between the masculine and feminine principles," it is important here to point out to the reader that in some iconographic representations of *yab-yum* the male is figured with considerably more arms than the female (there are never more arms on the female side). This is a crucial point to bear in mind in any reading of the iconography, given that the number of arms usually denotes power and extraordinary status. Like the image of Ardhanārīśvara, the Tibetan image of *yab-yum* can, at times, be ambivalent on the issue of gender equality.[20]

Irigaray's ethics of sexual difference asks us to redefine equality and difference from a dual perspective that circumscribes two independent and mutually redemptive realms for men and women. In other words, Irigaray urges that the "old dream of symmetry," in which the androgynous ideal participated, must be reconsidered from the perspective of "wonder" and "love." She writes:

> Two angels face one another. . . . They turn toward one another, guarding and calling the divine presence between them. They do not go in one single direction. There are two of them, halted in their paths. Face-to-face, they stand. . . . Coming from opposite directions, to meet one another, they halt the return from sameness to sameness, before any determination or opposition of presence or absence can be made. (Irigaray 1987, 44)

Irigaray's model of new symmetry presents an alternative to the hierarchical and heterosexist logic that is often deeply embedded in androgynic models, East and West. Her notion of symmetry, which neither privileges the male nor erodes the independence and separateness of male and female, is closer to the theoretical ideal that Gross is calling for by using the ideal of androgyny as a "two-sexed model" of humanity in the reconceptualization of Buddhism and the academic study of feminism and religion (Gross 1993, 1996). But given the debate and history sedimented in variations of this cross-cultural paradigm, one can only question its efficacy as such for a feminist reconstruction of religious theories and traditions.

Conclusion

In this chapter we have looked at two perspectives of androgyny. The first situates the image of Ardhanārīśvara within a broader taxonomy of androgyny, while still considering the image within its Indian context. The second draws upon arguments for or against androgyny in Western feminist theory. These two models were chosen because they raise some important questions about each tradition's/theory's own use of the symbol.

As we have demonstrated throughout this chapter, both models question the explicit androcentric nature of the motif and begin to explain and deconstruct the norms of male privilege that often are present in varying cultural expressions of the image and its interpretations. Tracking the debate in Western feminist theory, we can see the arguments in favor of and against androgyny as an alternative model for fixed-gender stereotypes. While this is a constructive theoretical model offering a number of insights, it is concerned primarily with examples deriving from Greek classical thought, Hebrew creation myths, medieval alchemical traditions, Western mysticism, psychotherapy, and fictional literary accounts, and although there may be profound similarities, ultimately, the image of Ardhanārīśvara cannot be understood in isolation from its own cultural context. East-West dialogue provides a rich engagement, and both benefit in conversation with arguments offered by Western feminism.

In this chapter ideas offered by advocates of androgyny have been presented. For instance, it was argued that androgyny provides a psychological and philosophical model for the perfectibility of the human psyche. But those who take exception claim that androgyny is unshakably embedded in patriarchal metanarratives that displace the writer from her text (i.e., body). Western feminists are generally unfamiliar with the subtleties of Eastern *yoga* theories. In chapter 2 we showed that medieval *haṭhayoga* treatises illustrate not only the centrality of the model of androgyny as an ideal for spiritual attainment, and its normativity within that tradition, but also its recognition and valorization of the necessity of the integration of the body-mind-spirit complex as symbolized by the image of Ardhanārīśvara. For this reason, an understanding of the implications of *haṭhayoga* is fundamental to any Indian work on this motif. Through *sādhana, haṭhayoga* provides not only a pragmatic path by which to achieve or test the so-called goal of androgyny but, as we discussed in chapter 2, it offers insight into an esoteric and a psycho-experiential rather than a simply theoretical and propositional understanding of the androgyne as a possible ideal for human liberation. However, this praxis-oriented tradition is still steeped in androcentric models and pejorative attitudes, hence, the question of the efficacy of such models of androgyny still remains to be seen.

Doniger argues that the *tantric* tradition is hierarchical in its appropriation of the eternal feminine. The *yogic* model while espousing a doctrine of nonduality actually relies upon and fosters dualistic and androcentric presuppositions of reality and therefore cannot provide a model of androgyny that is ultimately liberating for both men and women. As medieval *haṭhayoga* treatises show, to attain this androgynic state of consciousness a reversal or an annihilation of so-called normal functioning modes of human behavior is required. These behaviors often are equated to the feminine in Indian thought (i.e., *prakṛti*) and would therefore be inconsistent with feminist emanicpatory goals and aspirations, even though it is the symbolic feminine that is metaphorically being liberated.

In the end, in Indian *haṭhayoga,* there is no radical difference between the human and the divine realms at the level of ultimate reality. This is why a feminist analysis is so important: if the divine realm favors the "symoblic" male over the "symbolic" female, the human realm will also. But, as we have stressed, feminist theory could benefit from Indian philosophy's living application and experiential understanding of androgyny: *haṭhayoga* as a system of philosophy is inextricably linked to the body and experience in significant ways and therefore offers an image of androgyny that, according to the *haṭhayoga* tradition, is humanly attainable through instruction and practice if its practitioners can transcend patriarchal prejudice.

Chapter 5

Śakti and Pārvatī: A New Interpretation

Enlightenment is creative.

—*Herbert Guenther,* The Life and Teaching of Naropa

This chapter proposes a new reading and interpretation of the relationship between Śiva and Śakti/Pārvatī. In many ways, their symbolic union in the form and figure of Ardhanārīśvara presupposes a fusion of the mutuality and oneness of the universal and the particular, or the transcendence and immanence of divine reality, and the kind of archetypal symbols or paradigmatic models being defined and fused in this unfolding motif influences the psycho-social dimensions of human life and the development of human consciousness. Since most expressions of Ardhanārīśvara are projections of the male psyche, we can ascertain quite a lot about men's attitudes toward the feminine sacred in Indian tradition and the cultural norms of gender ideology, although we find little data by women about their own self-understanding of this image. Nonetheless, the expressions that we do find provide cultural models that have, to a large extent, been internalized as influential norms of social behavior for men and women.

For the most part, we have seen that the stereotypical orthodox category "woman" (*nārī*) in Indian culture describes an idealized role of wife and mother of sons (RV X.85.44-55) that is homologous in many ways with the sacred image of Śakti/Pārvatī in her role as primordial mother in the cosmogonic pair.[1] Presented as the left half of her husband (*ardhanārī*), Pārvatī/Śakti, as the spouse-goddess, often is subdued and contained in this two-in-one image by the secondary status assigned to it via the subtle markings of culture.

We also have seen that to a large extent *brahmanical* tradition explores the valorization of the eternal feminine in her role as goddess, consort, and mother, and as the active energy (*Śakti, kuṇḍalinī, bhagavatī*) and propelling power behind the *yogic* process of self-actualization, though primarily with the provision that the feminine counterpart instrumentally provides a transformative and totalizing effect on the family, the male psyche and, in a more modern context, the nation-state.[2] The alternative of women becoming men is depicted as "dangerous" or "deviant"[3] and, therefore, often is portrayed in mythology as a curse that men fear. Androgynous ideations are, according to Doniger, a creation of male consciousness to explain in part precisely those fears of human sexuality and symbolic associations of male impotence, bisexuality, and/or homosexual desire.[4]

A more useful, I think, way to understand the symbolic image of Śivārdhanārīśvara, the divine androgyne, is as an encoded cultural motif to explain the question of human origins and the culturally specific processes of psychological individuation that attempt to regain the stasis of undifferentiated or pure consciousness in terms specific to the male-identified view of *yoga*. In her Lacanian reading of androgyny in British romantic poetry, Hoeveler claims that "woman" was consistently presented "as 'Other' to man—idealized mother, a second self, a submerged double, an inspirational muse or mentor, or a demonic femme fatale" (Hoeveler 1990, 2). In this sense, a reified concept of "woman" is portrayed as a complement to "man" for the intended purpose of "aiding and abetting" his rise to becoming whole, or a "second Śiva," through various homologous significations such as *kuṇḍalinī, Śakti,* and *prakṛti*. The androgyne motif places the male and female in a relationship of perfect symmetry and balance, but upon closer reflection, this seems most often true from a male-identified perspective and, therefore, it betrays its own internal logic and integrity.

There are two significant themes being considered here. One theme addresses the cosmogonic implications of a dual or an androgynous creator, and the second theme is concerned with human processes of reimaging oneself as deity (*svarūpa*), essentially Ardhanārīśvara, the androgynous god/dess. The *Bṛhadāraṇyaka Upaniṣad* (1.4.1–4 cited in Olivelle 1998, 47), which introduces the idea of an androgynous being that splits for the sake of creation, also contains the philosophical principle that by knowing *ātman* (*eka*), one knows *brahman*. Recast in a distinctly Śaiva or theistic context, this process of mystic androgynization utilizes, at one level, the gendered frames of reference "Śiva" and "Śakti" in the image of Ardhanārīśvara to represent the human (male) process of self-realization (*ātma vidyā*) between *ātman* and the impersonal *nirguṇa brahman*.

In both dimensions, the universe at its divine macrocosmic and human microcosmic levels is perceived as essentially androgynous. Human beings embody this sacred, androgynous model, particularly in the aspect of the *ahaṃkāra* (*a-haṃ*, I, ego). Consequently, the first and last syllables of the Sanskrit alphabet, signified by "*a*" (vowels) and "*haṃ*" (consonants), are identified as male and female, or Śiva and Śakti. Again, this kind of corresponding, phonetic universe is closely associated with the vast system of homologues, discussed in chapter 2. What is important here is the idea that the human being, as well as the cosmos, is ultimately identified with Ardhanārīśvara. As such, humanity is linked and ultimately propelled to act in accordance with the unfolding and evolving rhythms of the original, divine, androgynous body. This process is seen as analogous to the movement of Śakti/Pārvatī (*prakṛti*). In a metaphysical sense, she is portrayed as the active agent/pole in the universal evolutionary and involutionary processes.[5]

Feminists also are clear to point out that the androgyne motif in Western culture reveals a long history that traces its expression in kabbalistic Judaism, gnostic writings, medieval alchemy, Platonic and neoplatonic writings, Jungian psychology, and numerous literary sources, including Shakespeare, Woolf, and others. So, too, Doniger calls the androgyne motif a "universal symbol" as she probes its pervasive presence in Indian, Greek, Native American, African, and Australian culture. In Indian tradition, evidence of the motif of androgyny can be traced back as early as Dyāvā-Pṛthivī, Prajāpati, and other dual deities in the Ṛg Veda. In light of this, one is tempted to ask why this bipolar motif is central in so many diverse cultures.

The mythology of the androgyne in Indian tradition, as we have shown throughout, offers an explanation of human creation,[6] as well as a programmatic, albeit a subtle and an esoteric, guide to mystical knowledge, reintegration, and enlightenment. Alongside this, the androgyne motif emerges as a powerful psycho-social symbol providing political, ideologic, and formulaic gender prescriptions for men and women in human history. Thus it is not surprising that the time has come to provide a feminist reading that examines and illuminates gender issues on many levels in this ambivalent, androgynous image *par excellence*. For, as Hoeveler shows us in Western fiction, "[T]he androgynous fantasy demanded that woman be essentially different from man and therefore a complementary force, but sexual differences institutionalized as gender roles have always been culturally understood as ideologies that justify inequality" (Hoeveler 1990, 5–6). Indeed, it is this very justification of inequality that is being challenged and along with it its fundamental claim to emancipatory potential. Moreover, normative, male-identified readings and interpetations of the divine androgyne also are being challenged. Only when female-identified correspondences are named and/or liberated from even the subtlest implication of lesser valued-cultural designations can sacred androgynous motifs and dualistic metaphors point to a fully authentic paradigm of human emancipation.

Presently, as an expression or a construct of orthodox patriarchal discourse, the feminine side (*nārī*) of the androgyne motif is created to honor and serve the gods, the male half, or *īśvara*.[7] Indeed, it is through her *seva* (service) that "woman" is redeemed (Brown 1974, 196; Jamieson 1996, 253). When contained in the androgynous form, the eternal feminine acts, according to Hoeveler, as a mirror. Hence, Pārvatī, like her Western sisters, holds the emblematic *darpaṇa* in her left hand (see Figure 5.1). With this diagnostic feature, she reflects the male aspect or hero (*puruṣa, yogi*) on his path to self-discovery.

However, in our reading, we see that her own spiritual journey is being charted as she rises from *nārī* to goddess.[8] As divine agent, Pārvatī/Śakti transforms not only each of the devotees she empowers, but as *nārī* and as *tāpasvinī*, she wins her own freedom and liberation through a rigorous, demanding, and one-pointed struggle. In this sense, Pārvatī is a powerful heroine. That is, she is an active and autonomous agent struggling against enforced idealizations of femininity within her own culturally defined process of emancipation. As such, she represents a crucial mediating figure, not only between different realms, as Jamieson (1996) suggests, but also within each embodied human devotee.

As a social and political image the androgyne reflects the Indian domestic ideal of *ardhanārī*. Husband and wife, modeled on the mythic narrative of Śiva and Pārvatī, are united in one symbolic body as an explication of the broader, more pervasive orthodox ideology of Indian marriage and family values. Together the two stand united as a socially manifest "unit" or embodiment of the divine androgynous creator on earth (*ardhanārī*). As an adjunct, the female is portrayed as the left half of the male body and is denied what Irigaray envisions as an independent role of her own. To be certain, the male counterpart also is defined (and/or confined) by this normative marital social arrangement. However, the secondary status of the female in marriage, and not the male, was confirmed by traditional Hindu law, which in many instances posits "woman" as property of her male family (i.e, father, son, husband) and, as such, is dependent upon and subject to them for her economic well-being at various stages of her life.[9] Furthermore, as Amartya Sen (1992) explains, systematic gender differentials such as these (in *any* society) disparage the female in parallel social and economic arrangements, such as early childhood treatment, mortality rates, crude ratio of women to men, intra-household division of labor, access to resources, and admission to positions of public leadership and policy development. Other, more abstract avenues of inequality and inequivalency, such as the "freedom to achieve" and the "capacity to function," also are affected by entrenched gender differentials. While these issues are certainly not unique to India, Sen does apply these vectors to the specific ethical question of unjust conditions based on gender arrangements in contemporary social structures that include, but are certainly not limited to, South Asia.[10]

This so-called secondary position or status, as feminist studies now show, is itself the product of male psychology or patriarchal discourse that has therefore projected onto the female an entrenched cultural stereotype of passivity, inferiority, weakness, and silence. There are, however, potent countervailing instances of female agency that contradict these monolithic orthodox images of female weakness, and the mythology of Pārvatī, read in this light, can provide such a model.[11] However, it is still at an early stage. Reminiscent of Leslie's earlier comments, Kondos (1996) recently announced that the husband in Indian marriage is still "the preeminent person of the pair and is to be ceded a structural *carte blanche*, for in this particular relationship he can do no wrong" (Kondos 1986, 192).

When applied to our study of *haṭhayoga*, we see that it is precisely because of a woman's innate femaleness (i.e., her sexuality) that most orthodox *brahmanical* sources on renunciation and monastic *yoga* treatises claim that "woman" impedes the progress of asceticism (SS 5,3). We typically encounter that the *haṭhayoga* system of cultural homologues converges on or shares the basic assumptions of gender that are operative at various levels of culture. In other words, the image complements the dominant familial structures of Indian culture. Consequently, gender relations are affirmed over and over again in and by the image.[12] However, it is important to bear in mind, as Menski (1992) shows, that issues of equality as we know them today (i.e., between women and men or between men and men) were certainly not a concern for men and women in ancient or medieval times: this is a distinctly modern notion (Menski 1992, 51). Nevertheless, such images remain blueprints for contemporary society and, as such, they affect our present understanding of, and interest in, gender construction.

Based on this, can we affirm that the motivation or inspiration of Ardhanārīśvara in Indian tradition is essentially or wholly religious? Certainly it expresses deeply held traditional beliefs expressed in gendered terms pertaining to the attainment of enlightened or undifferentiated consciousness and provides "secrets" or insights into a psycho-spiritual path leading the adept to a state of primordial union prior to splitting or separation. Given this, it is certainly not surprising that cultural modalities, including iconography, mythology, medicine, music, poetry, and spiritual praxis, are refracted through and continually reinforce this divine motif via parallel structures and homologues.

In her sustained reading of Western romantic poets, Hoeveler shows us that "the androgynous ideal is a quintessentially artificial concept that on one level expresses the fantasy of sexual unity as a denial of death" (Hoeveler 1990, 16). No doubt, in Indian tradition the dream of unity and immortality is equally anticipated in the mythology of the divine androgyne. As Doniger says, duality represents death. Hence, the union of male and female, as represented by the symbolic form and figure of Ardhanārīśvara in *haṭhayoga,* reflects the quest for immortality and oneness through the attainment of a divine body, and the emphasis on the living traditions of *rasayāna* and *haṭhayoga* extends the very real application and possibility of this ideal far beyond the level of fantasy and fiction raised by Hoeveler and Western romantic poets.

For Hoeveler and Weil, who look primarily at Western literary, feminist, and psychoanalytic sources, the androgynous mythic motif is simply an "artificial concept," an "ideological construct," "a child's dream," and an "infantile conception" for a "lost psychic harmony" (Hoeveler 1990, 17–19, 129). Rather, for the embodied *yogin/ī* or *siddha,* it is a living tradition, a realizable goal, and a dynamic symbol leading potentially to a higher state of enlightened or pure consciousness that can certainly be attained with proper guidance and under supporting circumstances and conditions. Consequently, the mythology, iconographic symbols, technologies of praxis, and so on express a subtle system of human healing, becoming, and transformation rather than simply the poetic, fictive, or artificial reality that Hoeveler and Weil see characterized in Western narratives of androgyny. Ideally, it begins with the underlying, divinely sanctioned presupposition that each and every human being is "essentially" androgynous (i.e., "one"), enjoined by a corresponding metaphysical and theological support system embracing the bisexual nature of ultimate reality as Ardhanārīśvara or Śiva-Śakti. What has perhaps been sadly lost in this metaphysical postulation is the genuine celebration of women and the feminine at the level of *dvaita* or phenomenal reality. In the service of this ideal, compassionate adepts must therefore scrutinize the concrete conditions of inequality and injustice.

What remains disheartening is the conclusive reading that Hoeveler, based on Lacan, embraces. That is, in Western literary and psychoanalytic readings of the androgyne, the "self can never transform itself—can never unify with the nonself—because a part can never grasp the whole" (Hoeveler 1990, 23). Hence, in the end, Lacan repudiates the idea of reintegration (20–21). As Hoeveler claims, the androgynous may be an ideal that speaks on the surface of love, unity, social balance, and reconciliation of the sexes, but it finally speaks in a stronger voice of conflict and tension about the irreconcilable divisions between man and women, mind and matter, Culture and Nature. (Hoeveler 1990, 23)

While at present this seems an all too plausible interpretation of the social, economic, and political implications of androgynous motifs, East and West, the prospect of a lived spiritual tradition and corresponding praxis arising from Indian *yoga* traditions carries at least the hope in the possibility that a genuine and an authentic *saṇgha* (community) of practitioners can realize, and perhaps have realized, the emancipatory (and to some extent, egalitarian) ideal tradition cast in this two-in-one image. Nonetheless, it is hard to simply dismiss Hoeveler's observations that the British Romantics "cannibalistically consumed these females characters, shaped them into ideal alter egos, and most of the time destroyed them by the conclusion of the poem," because we find *yoga* traditions gesturing to a similar idea of the male hero/*yogin* who absorbs or purifies the feminine/*prakṛti* only to eliminate her in the final stage of *laya*. However, I think it is important to bear in mind that it is not necessarily the annihilation of Pārvatī being implied in the final stages of involution or *laya*, though at times it certainly seems so, but rather the human consciousness awakening to the already existent mutuality and oneness of Śiva and Śakti, represented as form and formlessness in the *āgama* tradition.

There is no doubt that in the tradition of *haṭhayoga* the union of male and female is at once symbolic and metaphysical. This involves a system of polarized and decidedly heterosexual homologues that are integrated to find the so-called male and female identified hierogamy within. In the West, Jung employed the symbol of the Uroboros, or the tail-eating serpent, as a metaphor for the Western alchemical tradition. This is transferred in *haṭhayoga* to Śakti and *kuṇḍalinī*, the woman-identified serpent through whom perfect union is achieved primarily by the male *yogin*.

There is a marked ambivalence, however, as the *haṭhayoga* tradition also clearly affirms that the transmission of oral teachings proceeds directly from Śiva (Ādinātha, Yogeśvara) to Pārvatī. For instance, in the *Śiva Saṃhitā*, Śiva transmits the teachings of *haṭhayoga* to Pārvatī and essentially "witnesses" her ascent through the various stages of *sādhana* until she becomes adept. In this sense, it seems plausible and possible that a crucial evidential precedent for female agency and participation in *haṭhayoga* traditions is being laid out. Indeed, as recent studies (Shaw 1994; Khandelwal 1997; Goudriaan 1981) show, the highly gendered systems of *sannyasa* and *yoga* include women.

Haṭhayoga traditions usually propagate the oral spiritual teachings on the path to enlightenment through a dialogue between Śiva and Pārvatī. This primeval discourse, as Goudriaan suggests, in turn reflects the prototypical relationship between *guru* and disciple, and it ensures the proper transmission of the tradition in a continuous and an unbroken line down through the lineage. For example, Matsyendranāth of the Nātha *yoga* tradition overheard Śiva transmitting the teachings of *haṭhayoga* to Pārvatī. This helps explain the role of founder in the tradition (Goudriaan 1979, 17).

Another way of understanding this structured dialogical device using the subtle imagery of Ardhanārīśvara is through the extended meaning of *guru* as inner mentor (or *bla-ma* in Tibetan Buddhism, as I explained in an earlier chapter). Understood in this way, Ardhanārīśvara offers an embodied metaphor for the *guru* (*īśvara*)-disciple (*sisya/nārī*) relationship cast in a single body, as the two mutually arising and simultaneous aspects of self (*īśvara-nārī, a-haṃ, prakṛti-puruṣa,* Śiva-Śakti). With this understanding in mind, it is plausible to argue that the tradition of *haṭhayoga* could therefore be accessible to each and every human being, as authentic "offspring" of the primordial parents (*purvaje pitara*). When we look for evidence we see that there are a substantial number of women who have not been excluded from the spiritual traditions of *yoga, tantra,* and *bhakti* and who participate in varying roles from initiates to saints to *gurus* (Shaw 1994; Goudriaan 1979, 30; Khandelwal 1997; Coburn 1988, 36). Still, Goudriaan (1979) and Spivak (1999), unlike Shaw (1994) and Khandelwal (1997), maintain that although the role of the feminine sacred is elevated at the level of the transcendental (*advaita*), the role of "real" women in these traditions (*dvaita*) is nevertheless perceived as socially subordinate.

While this subject is in itself a vastly important one that deserves attention, here we are concerned primarily with the image and associations of Ardhanārīśvara. As such, the Pārvatī-Śakti half of Ardhanārīśvara offers the ideal of a mediating figure in *haṭhayoga* tradition. For instance, she is the active aspect of the divine pair that compassionately moves the aspirant, male and female, to enlightenment. Whether these perceptions derive from men or a predominantly male monastic community, the inherent message is one of mediation, agency, and transformative or compassionate action. Here we have a textual and living tradition that casts the mythic feminine Śakti/Pārvatī in terms of a divine heroine or *tāpasvinī,* affecting not only her own freedom and liberation but also the freedom of all of her devotees. It is in her paradigmatic role as Śakti that Pārvatī mediates and wins liberation for herself and others. For this reason, it is important to look more closely at the concept of "Śakti" in Indian tradition, and at the role of Pārvatī as *tāpasvinī.*

Pārvatī As *Tāpasvinī*

Here we address Pārvatī's practice of *tāpas* (austerity) as a prerequisite for her union with Śiva and the implications of this narrative for contemporary insights into her mythology as a source of agency and empowerment. In the mythological narratives of the *purāṇas,* we see Pārvatī cast, for example, in the role of virginal daughter, beautiful bride/wife, mother, and *tāpasvinī.* Through this latter aspect, Pārvatī is connected to Śiva as Ardhanārīśvara. *Yoga* praxis is the internalized ritual equivalent of sacrifice and constitutes a life of *tāpas,* which culminates in the attainment of divine body. As such, Pārvatī (Śakti) is the *yoginī/tāpasvinī par excellence.* As a rule, the only necessary requisites for the path are access to teachings, a *guru,* and one-pointed dedication to the practices. As we have seen, Śiva (as a *guru*) outlines the systematic and often esoteric points of praxis inwardly to Pārvatī (as a disciple) in the textual tradition of *haṭhayoga.* As a *yoginī,* Pārvatī performs her austerities (*tāpas*) dutifully, such as subjecting herself to strict penance, eating tree bark, standing on one foot, and so on, to win or unite with her beloved Śiva. In this way, she fulfills all three requisites. Her ascetic disciplines address the progressive development or ascent through body, speech, and mind and lead her via preparatory and purificatory practices to the higher attainments of *yoga* realization. Once the preparatory practices are duly accomplished, and through *tāpas* her *karma* (the active pole) is dissolved, Pārvatī as a model disciple is drawn into deeper and more subtle forms of meditation, leading penultimately to the merging of Pārvatī and Śiva in the form and figure of Ardhanārīśvara.

In this model, active engagement through asceticism or *tāpas* is advocated as the cultural prerequisite for union with Śiva. Pārvatī takes form as a human disciple (*nārī*), dresses in the clothes of an ascetic and with matted hair (*jaṭa*) and modest diet (*mitahara*) remains in one-pointed *tāpas* to win her beloved Śiva. Pārvatī knows that to effect a union with Śiva, who is now mourning the loss of Satī through his own life of renunciation and meditation, and to actively save the world from the impending curse of the demon Tāraka, she must perform *tāpas.* The god Kāma and his wife Rātī are sent to Śiva to inform him of the future fate of the world if Tāraka is not defeated by Śiva's son and to convince Śiva that he must marry Pārvatī.

Śiva is informed by the *devas* of Pārvatī's *tāpas,* and he appears before her as a *brahmacāri* (celibate monk) speaking of Śiva's wrathful nature to test her resolve and commitment. Pārvatī, however, is steadfast, and Śiva is duly convinced of her one-pointed determination and devotion. He appears to her as himself and agrees to marry her. Her *tāpas* won for her the self-chosen husband, Śiva. After the birth of their son, Skandha, Tāraka is destroyed. Two other postmarital narratives continue the mythological theme of Pārvatī's *tāpas* and reinforce her agency as *tāpasvinī*.[13]

By insisting on the practice of *tāpas*, Pārvatī actively subverts the normative mode of behavior for women (*stridharma*), albeit advocating that *yoga* is a higher form of love than sexuality. In this way, Pārvatī is the model *yoginī par excellence*. Following from this, the image of Ardhanārīśvara affirms an ideal asexual coupling consistent with the highest teachings of monastic *yoga* traditions and therefore does not display the externalized tensions of erotic pairing that we see, for instance, in *tantra mithuna* images. Together, Pārvatī and Śiva face the devotee, rather than the female facing the male only (as we see, for example, in Tibetan images of *yab-yum*). By the androgynous juxtaposition of Śiva and Śakti in one form, the gender associations become a potentially powerful source of cultural information. In this narrative, Pārvatī is not an object of sexual desire (whereas in the *Ardhanārīnaṭeśvara stotra,* Śivā is), but rather she is portrayed as a heroine who earns her rightful status at the side of Śiva. The only other deity of whom this can be said is Viṣṇu in the image of Hari-Hara (see Figure 17.1).

Śakti

Not surprisingly, the development of the term *śakti*[14] in Vedic Brāhmaṇas literature finds its earliest application construed with cosmogonic union. Prajāpati and Indra create through their respective Śaktis, Vāc/Śacī and Indrānī. In the *Śvetāśvatara Upaniṣad* (4.1, cited in Olivelle 1998, 423), we find a more speculative or abstract usage of the term *śakti* in which the one supreme god creates the manifest world by his power (*śakti*). These Vedic references, according to Pintchman (1997), albeit scant and somewhat muted, provide a basis for later developments in Indian metaphysics in which Śakti comes to be associated with a female divine consort who couples with the male divinity for creation (e.g., Ardhanārīśvara), and/or is conceived as the immanent creative power of the undifferentiated divine or absolute (*brahman*) that facilitates all universal action and transformation (Pintchman 1997, 101). These notions are developed further in the schools of Indian philosophy (*darśanas*), as Pintchman suggests, and by the sixth or seventh century, Mīmāṃsā and Vaiśeṣika literature equates Śakti with an "unseen power" (*adṛṣṭa*) or a "potency" that possesses cosmogonic ability (101–02). It is not until the *purāṇas, āgamas, saṃhitās,* and *tantras* that Śakti develops into a fully articulated conception of cosmogonic and cosmological significance. While an in-depth analysis of the development of the term *śakti* in this context is well beyond the scope of this book, some of the various strands of this concept are relevant to our particular study of Ardhanārīśvara and are included here for this reason. We refer in particular to Śakti's elevated status as goddess (e.g., as Pārvatī), the proliferation of feminine symbolism through homologous relations with micro-macrocosmic processes, and Śakti's cosmogonic and cosmological significance.

As we mentioned in an earlier chapter, *haṭhayoga* perceives the absolute as ultimately singular, though conventionally polarized into female and male aspects. The female active pole is Śakti, and the inactive male pole is Śiva. Together they are inseparable, like moon and moonlight, heat and fire, and milk and sweetness. Śakti, as the active pole, is responsible for the energization or oscillation of the phenomenal universe. Through her power, in union with a male divine (in this case, Śiva), human beings are created and sustained. In Śaiva schools Śiva is supreme, and Śakti (as Pārvatī, Durgā, Gaurī, Kālī, etc.) appears subordinate to him. However, in Śakta schools, we find the reverse—the goddess is above the male god. Thus there are alternative signs and configurations of divine female power deriving from sectarian ideologies.

The development of Śakti reaches its height in the sixth century with the *Devī-Māhātmya*, a hymn to the great goddess contained in the *Mārkaṇḍeya Purāṇa* (c. fifth–sixth century). While an analysis of the great goddess extolled in this *purāṇa* would be extending our examination of Ardhanārīśvara in divergent ways, clearly Devī, as the great feminine divine, assumes ultimacy in this theological narrative, and her status and identity are at times equivalent to Śakti-Pārvatī.[15] It is evident that her autonomous and supreme role places power on the female side. Her male counterpart, Śiva, is clearly given the reverse subdued and subservient position, contiguous with the orthodox image of Śakti in the Śaiva image of Ardhanārīśvara that we have been examining.

As we have seen, in Śaiva *purāṇic* images of Ardhanārīśvara, Śakti is one with Śiva but also is his left-hand subordinate. Śakti is absorbed into, and emanates from, him as an essential and integral part of the inverted male-identified cosmogonic and cosmological pair. From this sectarian perspective, Śakti creates precisely because she is portrayed as his active aspect, rather than out of any independent or autonomous agency of her own. Śakti is simply the consort of, and power behind, the male divine (*śaktimat*) in this mythic narrative, and her creative function, as we have shown, is homologized with the female divine as well as other female-identified correspondences that we have already identified as far back as the early Vedas. Bear in mind that although the goddess in Indian worship is both significant and diverse, Ardhanārīśvara, inclusive of the form of female divinity, is an orthodox expression that does not convey overt heterodox implications.

Similarly, in *haṭhayoga* and *tantra* tradition, the status of Śakti is elevated. That is, female divinities such as Śakti borrow from and essentially reinterpret basic elements and patterns already inherent in Indian tradition. Jacobsen (1996) makes this point in his analysis of the female aspect of the divine in *tantra* and Sāṃkhya-Yoga. In Śaiva *purāṇas*, the notion of divine male and female complementarity pertains to the inseparability and singularity of the divine pair as long as they are united (*advaita*). However, their basic natures when separate (*dvaita*) are distinct and at times one of a different status (e.g., *īśvara* and *nārī*). As such, Śiva and Śakti are, in a sense, sectarian and theistic reformulations of other dual pairs (e.g., *prakṛti-puruṣa*, *māyā-brahman*, *agni-soma*, and so on). The evolution of manifest reality proceeds from *prakṛti* (recast as Śakti), according to the basic Sāṃkhyan *tattva* theory. Puruṣa (recast as Śiva) is simply "witness" to this active creative process and represents the static presence into whom Prakṛti-Śakti is absorbed or takes rest at the time of cosmic dissolution (*nivṛtti*, *pralaya*, *śūnyatā*). Most accounts of creation, and praxis-oriented theories, simply elaborate upon or reinterpret this elemental Sāṃkhyan philosophy.

In the *Kūrma*, *Viṣṇu*, *Mārkaṇḍeya*, and *Padma purāṇas*, Brahmā is incensed that his mind-born sons are static, that is, they do not reproduce. Out of this anger Rudra emerges as Ardhanārīśvara. As dual, or half male and female, Brahmā demands that Rudra divide for the sake of progeny. This he does. From this basic mythic narrative account of creation, we can see that Brahmā acts as a catalyst for Śiva-Rudra's creative emanation as the androgynous Ardhanārīśvara. As we have already shown, as early as the *Śvetāśvatara Upaniṣad* (SU 4.3 cited in Olivelle 1998, 425), Śiva-Rudra is represented as an ambivalent deity. At times, it also is clear that Brahmā himself is androgynous and can produce a female form, Śatarūpā, from half of his body, similar to Śiva-Rudra. Also, the *Vāyu Purāṇa* identifies the female side as half of Rudra. In this instance, she divides herself further into black and white. As such, she manifests as Lakṣmī, Sarasvatī, Umā, Gaurī, and Pārvatī, as well as the dark, ferocious, Kālī, and so on, but she also is collectively referred to as Mahādevī, the great goddess.

The *Kūrma Purāṇa* elaborates on this account of creation (KP 1:11, 2–13). While practicing *tāpas* (austerities), Rudra issues from the mouth of Brahmā. Bearing *triśūla* and three eyes, Rudra appears as half male and half female (i.e., *ardhanārī*). Subsequently, Brahmā demands that Rudra split. The male half divides into eleven parts, or *rudras*. The female half, Īśanī, splits into black and white *śaktis* and, henceforth, the female counterparts of Maheśvara are variously called Pārvatī, Maheśvarī, Śivā, and so on. In such accounts of creation, Śakti and

Śiva are one, though the narrative considers him *śaktimat*, that is, possessor of power (KP 1:11, 42). Ultimately inseparable from one another, these Śaktis are clearly diverse in their manifestations and attributes. The *Kūrma Purāṇa* adds that although Śakti sometimes appears subordinate, in essence, she is thought to be eternally one with Śiva. Only *yogins*, through the practice of self-realization, know the truth of their ultimate identity (KP 1:11, 43).

The tendency in the *purāṇas* to equate the creative power of the divine, designated by the term *śakti* (*māyā, prakṛti*), with the goddess is prevalent, regardless of sectarian affiliation. However, within the Śakta tradition, Devī is identified as the source of all manifestation, male and female. In this school, she is cast in varying degrees as being superior to the trinity of male-identified gods, Brahmā, Viṣṇu, and Śiva (Pintchman 1997). As such, Śakti as a supreme being is beyond attributes (*nirguṇa*) and abides in *turīya* as the fourth state of consciousness (*Devī-Bhāgavata Purāṇa,* cited in Pintchman 1997, 180). What is interesting for us about this viewpoint is that in this account the primary relationship with the male consort is reversed. In other words, Śakti is ultimately superior to Śiva. Even the three gods are subordinate to their female Śaktis (Mahālakṣmī, Sarasvatī, and Mahākālī) in this version (ibid.). In this context, the goddess exists as the supreme *nirguṇa brahman* (Pintchman 1997; Coburn 1991; Brown 1990).

Although an examination of the great goddess is somewhat peripheral to our study of Ardhanārīśvara, of particular significance is the essential theology of Mahādevī, expounded in various *purāṇas,* which describes Śakti as the active pole of *nirguṇa brahman* and, in the *Devī Bhāgavata Purāṇa* (12.12.13), it is *her* body that splits in half (cited in Coburn 1991, 2, 27). In other words, *she* is the androgynous divine (though it must be made clear that this does not represent an image of Ardhanārīśvara). The sacred literature of the Great Goddess presents her as creator, preserver, and destroyer of the universe, as well as the eternal source of compassion necessary to take those beings suffering in *samsāra* to liberation. She appears in ferocious or wrathful form (Kālī), as well as benign (Pārvatī). In the Śakta tradition, Devī is subject to none. This stands in stark contrast to epithets of Śiva and Śakti in the sectarian Ardhanārīnaṭesvara *stotram,* in which Śiva is heralded as "the lord of all," while "she is not lord."

Even so, Coburn (1991) shows that Śakta schools still maintain "a degree of codependency and complementarity" between Śiva and Śakti. He writes: "They stress to greater or lesser degree her supremacy, although her effective authority may be limited to a somewhat circumscribed realm" (22). She may act aggressively with her children or dominate opponents, but with Śiva she is an "obedient" and "submissive" wife, thereby reflecting and fostering normative Hindu social values (ibid.).

The implications of goddess worship in India present a complex problem. Of particular interest to this study is the idea of accessibility and empowerment. In Śakta schools, as Pintchman points out, orthodox Brahmanical tradition is challenged by non-Brahmanical trends (Pintchman 1997, 192). So, too, *bhakti* traditions present an alternative to hierarchical, Sanskrit-based, male-dominated, caste-oriented Brahmanical thought (Chakravarti 1999; Roy 1999). Both suggest wider accessibility and acceptance, particularly for women, though as we have seen, it is not always easy for women to renounce social life and challenge or extend normative models.

It is equally clear that the popularity of goddess worship in all of its pan-Indian forms, although great, is not the privileged domain of women, nor have women been the apparent creators of this tradition. Certainly it is evident that worship of the divine feminine in various forms has been one of the most enduring of religious expressions. Evidence of goddess religion in India has its possible origins in the Indus Valley civilization. Archaeological data, including terracotta figurines, seals, and ring stones, suggests an association with female fertility deities. Moreover, the lack of male-identified objects at these ancient sites implies that these objects were not worshipped side by side but rather independently. Indeed, the merging of divine male and female principles into one iconic or aniconic form (e.g., *yoni-liṅga* or Ardhanārīśvara), through the cultural mechanism of acculturation appears to be a later development.

Aryan immigrants to North India worshipped a pantheon of male and female deities through their Sanskrit Ṛg Vedic hymns. However, generally it is acknowledged that male deities held the primary positions of power, and female deities held subordinate and secondary roles. Over time, the worship of the goddess was gradually and progressively assimilated into the Aryan worldview, through aligning or pairing non-Vedic and Vedic female deities. This synthesis developed into the so-called "Hindu tradition" (Doniger 1982, 130; Erndl 1993, 19; Coburn 1991, 40; Hawley 1994, 1–2).

Erndl (1993), Dehejia (1999), Spivak (1999), and others claim, though here we are not in complete agreement, that the goddess tradition is not a particularly empowering one for women, as it does not directly affect, or impact on, the elevation of the status of women, nor has it been part of the indigenous feminist agenda. Yet in our estimation, there is a connection.[16] We have argued, for instance, that in the Śaiva tradition, influenced as it was by the worship of Śakti, women were accorded a degree of respect and autonomy to practice as saints, *bhakti*-poets, and *yoginīs* (see Gupta et al. 1992, 195; Shaw 1994; Khandelwal

1997; Chakravati 1999; Tharu and Lalita 1991). As well, it is reasonable to suggest, as Roy indeed does, that mythological narratives at times provide a way to relay norms of human sexual identity (Roy 1999, 36). However, this is not to imply that any one reading stands as universal or monolithic but rather that a complex range of possible interpretations must be tracked and a broad spectrum of expressions of female identity explored, as there are clearly diverse, contradictory, and conflicting systems of belief and practice available. For instance, Gold (1994) observes that among Rajasthani women, devotional songs provide evidence that women enjoy the same things as the goddesses they sing about (Gold 1992, 27). Indeed, women emulate the dress, jewelery, makeup, and so on portrayed on the iconographic images of Pārvatī, Sītā, and other so-called spouse-goddesses.

Religion is not always oppressive for women. It can in fact be empowering, though this does not necessarily mean or imply "feminist." For Basu (1998) and Jeffery (1998), and Shaheed (1998) speaking for the Muslim women in Pakistan, aspects of women's religiosity, including the cultural system of religious symbols, promote a sense of "belonging," "community," and engagement, that often "integrates" and "legitimates" women in public and communal space (Basu 1998, 9). On a recent field trip to the Cammuṇḍā-devī temple in Himachal Pradesh, women and men gathered together in public space to glimpse the deity and to mutually partake of her power. Basu and Jeffery explore precisely this potentially empowering relationship in contemporary India and argue that the rise of communalism has in fact heightened women's public participation and their association with religious symbols. Indeed, the cemented relationality between religion, gender, and politics provides an ideological basis from which to assess the domestic and political applications and implications of religious imagery such as Ardhanārīśvara.

However, from a feminist perspective, it remains that such a discourse is still cast in predominantly gendered terms, with "woman" as "wife" and "mother." The goddess/spouse idea is still being valorized, if not idealized. Consequently, the image of woman (and/or spouse goddess, *nārī*) in a divinely sanctioned role of "domesticity and conjugal submission" is, according to Sarkar (1998), very much alive and part of the contemporary Indian religious and communal lens. Sarkar shows that the popularity of the rhetoric of right-wing nationalist Hindu groups, such as the Rashtra Sevika Samiti (RSS), drawing on Sarvakar's ideology of Hindutva, clearly attests to this (Sarkar 1998, 93).[17]

However, perhaps we have moved too far afield and need to bring our discussion back to the implications that this contemporary communal rhetoric could have on the image of Ardhanārīśvara. What this confirms, first of all, is the ongoing socially and politically contextualized use of religious imagery and the modeling effects it has, and indeed hopes to have, on society. Gender is made, as feminism has shown us, and symbols are blueprints for society. That is, they are time-bound, culturally conceived products of the human imagination rather than primordial and god given, as any static image of Ardhanārīśvara would have us believe. Claims to the natural origins of divine identity based on orthodox models that privilege, whether through class, caste, race, or gender, are necessarily being replaced with a growing awareness of the socially and culturally constructed nature of such a discourse, demonstrated here, for example, by examining the historical and cultural development of the Ardhanārīśvara motif. Nonetheless, religious images can be powerful symbols for men and women (even if they are not feminist), and it is not surprising to see from a feminist perspective that there are indeed pervasive parallels at all levels of culture.

However, ambivalent messages are given. We see that female images, such as Pārvatī, are worshipped and adored not only because of their great acts of *seva*, but also their defiance in the face of social norms. Menā, Pārvatī's mother, advises her to cease her pursuit of Śiva, but she is not moved and thus pursues Śiva despite familial resistance and possible repudiation. In the *Kūrma Purāṇa*, Pārvatī gives spiritual counsel to her father, and in an earlier incarnation as Satī she vigorously protests her father's disregard of Śiva by not inviting him to his celebration. We also have looked at the story of Pārvatī as *tāpasvinī*. These instances are just several examples that evoke powerful and multifaceted images of Pārvatī as a faithful and dutiful wife, a strong and loving daughter, a wise counselor, a *yoginī*, and so on. In Śakta tradition, Devī holds the dominant position and even divides her body into male and female. This legitimates the symbolic avenues of female agency and power available to women within the context of Indian culture.

To support this ambivalent casting of female divinity, we find several iconographic instances in which the female diagnostic identifiers found on Ardhanārīśvara are reversed. There is evidence in the writings of the well-known saint and visionary Renuka Ananda that in the seventeenth century, sustained grants of up to 24,000 rupees were donated by local dynasties in Maharashtra to install and maintain a temple to a female counterpart to Ardhanārīśvara, known as Ai Ādi Puruṣa. In the Jalaris fishing caste on the coastal villages of Andhra Pradesh, stories are told about Ādi Śakti, mother of the universe, providing a countervailing image of Ādi Nāth (Nuckolls 1997, 357). The most impressive illustrations for our purpose, however, are those by Raju Kalidos (1993), Krishnamurthi and Ramachandran (1964), Kandasamy (1994), and Adiceam (1967), who examine several rare images from the early Chola period (c. tenth century C.E.) at the Aiyarappar Temple at Tiruvaiyāṟu, Vasisthesvara temple at Karandai, Vedapurīśvara temple at Tiruvēdikkuḍi (see Figure 5.1), and Tirumalapati, in which the female breast appears only on the right side. Kalidos

Figure 5.1 Ardhanārī. Vedopusīśvara Temple, Thanjavur District, Tiruveḍikuḍi, Madras, ninth cenntury. Courtesy of the American Institute of Indian Studies, Gurgaon, India.

refers to this image as a deviation, suggesting that the normative, canonical model is male-right, female-left. Nonetheless, we can see from these examples that there are alternative expressions that reflect the perceived power of the dominant female divine. This reversed version not only accommodates Śiva but also suggests to Kalidos that in South India "the early stage of the Ardhanārī cult seems to have had its base in Devī, the Feminine principle, and not Īśvara, the Masculine principle" (Kalidos 1993, 69).

The theory that Kalidos asserts is that through the process of Sanskritization, Devī-identified images are syncretized over time with Śiva (for instance, as Ardhanārīśvara). This was an effective mechanism of acculturation and social fusion, whereby matrifocal elements are assimilated into the mythology of *brahmin* gods as wife and consort (Kosambi 1981, 170).[18] Kalidos argues that the fifth-century, pre-Pallava story of the one-breasted goddess of Tamil folk origin, found in the Tamil epic *Cilappatikāram* (also known as *Cilampu*), authored by Iḷaṅkōvaṭikal (Iḷaṇkō), was transformed precisely through this type of overlay into an image of Śiva during the medieval period.

South Indian iconographical digests, such as *Śrītatvanidhi, Agastyasakalādhikāra, Kāṣyapaśilpaśāstra,* and others,[19] indicate that the dominant or normative form of Ardhanārīśvara is bipolar, male/right female/left, with two, four, or six arms.[20] It is interesting to point out, however, that the celebrated Chola image (figured in chapter 1) represents Ardhanārīśvara with three arms, placing the emphasis of power on the right-male side. Other iconographical features mentioned in these treatises typically include diagnostic features from our typology, such as half third eye on the right side, differentiated earrings, and right hands holding *paraśu, taṅka,* and *abhaya mudrā* and left hands holding *nīlotpala* and *varada mudrā*. Of course, the left side is distinguished by the female breast. Clothing and adornments reflect the male and female sides of the deity, including tiger skin on the right and silken cloth on the left. Of particular interest is the coloration of the left and right sides. The left side is green, and the right is coral, however, we rarely see this feature in practice, though in all other respects this description follows traditional lines of iconographic demarcation.

In the *Cilappatikāram* we find the story of a female human-goddess who cuts off her left breast. There also are vague references in the *Narriṇai* to an androgynous deity with one breast, called *aṇaṅku*.[21] These references provided by Kalidos indicate that the heroine goddess, Pattinidevī (goddess of chastity), or Kaṇṇaki, either "lost a breast," "cut short the beautiful breast," or "unscrewed the nipple" and used it in a moment of anger against perceived injustice to set fire to the city of Madurai. This "breast" seems to be the source of her power.

She is portrayed in the story as human, fully female, and a paragon of chastity (*karpu*).[22] It is her chastity in fact that lifts her to the status of goddess, since chastity is the female equivalent of asceticism.[23] The image is reinforced in yet another Tamil epic called *Manimekalai*.

We begin to see the elevating social imperative toward female chastity in this tale, as well as the attendant malevolent aspect of feminine power suggested by her furious act of burning Madurai. Consequently, there is a marked ambivalence in the imagery of a right-breasted deity. We ascertain from this tale that, like *tapas*, female chastity has the power to change the status of an ordinary woman from human to divine. Right-breasted images of Ardhanārī also attest to the fact that in South India an institution of worshipping or performing *pūja* to such sanctified images clearly became a religious practice. Temples were erected to her, tales of her exploits were recorded, statues of her were carved in stone, and regular festivals celebrated her mythology.[24]

However, the association of left-right in Indian tradition still conveys inferior-superior status. As Kalidos shows, the left-hand position usually is associated with "something low," "not worthy of being accorded a commendable status of equality," "weakness," "frailty," "baseness and degradation" (Kalidos 1994, 287). In this sense, the removal of the left breast indicates the removal of the inferior female aspect, leaving behind, as Kalidos states, a "folk goddess of the god-man type" that is on par with Mahādevī in her wrathful and ferocious aspect as Mahiṣāsuramardinī, Cāmmuṇḍā, and Kālī (Kalidos 1993, 279–80). Consequently, it is the malevolent aspect or strength of the goddess that is being sacralized in this image. Moreover, the description given by Iḷaṅkō resonates with the male-identified iconographic features of Ardhanārīśvara, such as crescent moon, matted hair, *tanka* in right hand, lotus in left hand, and so on, culminating with the reversal of female form indicated by the female breast on the right.

Ardhanārī in the *Cilappatikāram* is the chaste, one-breasted goddess. She counters the orthodox iconographic tradition of Ardhanārīśvara, in which the feminine is on the left. Another important aspect to bear in mind is that this South Indian folk image first appears somewhere between the second century B.C.E. and the second century C.E.[25] Hence, it falls close to the earliest North Indian Kuṣāṇa images, in which Ardhanārīśvara portrays the breast consistently on the left side. The later South Indian folk image of Maturapati portrays the left side as female and the right side as male, whereas the earlier *Cilappatikāram* casts the reverse perspective. Kalidos observes that the interaction of Ardhanārī and Ardhanārīśvara occurs about the same time in South India, providing evidence of the effective process of Sanskritization and sycretization. From this perspective, Mīnākṣī-Sundareśvara, where

Mīnākṣī refers to Pārvatī, also could provide a similar reading of reversed or female-identified androgyny.[26]

One explanation for Iḷaṅkō's point of view derives, according to Kalidos, from his birthplace in Kerala, which is oriented toward matrilineal and matrifocal social formation. Moreover, he suggests that Dravidian roots contribute to the tale. This could well be a factor behind the reversed Ardhanārī theme in South Indian tradition. However, when this female-identified Devī-Ardhanārī image comes into contact with the dominant *brahmanical* model of Ardhanārīśvara, a process of assimilation and acculturation occurs, and right-male left-female usurps the seemingly non-normative expression. In South Indian art, according to Kalidos, "not less than twenty-seven" examples of Ardhanārīśvara have been found in caves and temples bearing evidence to the transition from Tamil folk image to Sanskritic tradition, and/or her domestication (Kalidos 1993, 92). Of the images considered, the Karandai one is extremely rare insofar as the image has three arms, two on the left and one on the right, along with the single breast (Krishnamurthi and Ramachandran 1964, 74).

To conclude, Kalidos raises as an essential point with regard to the emergence or birth of the masculine from the feminine. In the Bādāmī cave temple specimen of Ardhanārīśvara (see Figure 6.1), the presence of a full-bodied female figure, referred to as "*devī*," stands directly to the left of Pārvatī. This suggests to Kalidos that the dual form, and/or male half, originates from Devī. In addition, the juxtaposition of another syncretic form (i.e., Hari-Hara) with the Ardhanārīśvara form (see Figure 17.1) reinforces this idea. In other words, these iconic representations and their strategic placements suggest the emergence of the masculine from the feminine and, as such, elevate Devī in a way that has not been heretofore acknowledged. The cave sites of Tirupparaṅkuṉṟam provide a rare instance in which Ardhanārī is installed in the *garbhagṛha*, and they also attest to this alternate interpretation (Kalidos 1993, 94–95). In other words, Kalidos is trying to show a more broadly conceived relationship between male and female. That is, the *liṅga-yoni* represents in aniconic form the essential oneness of male and female principles and, like *haṭhayoga* treatises, admits to their cosmological and cosmogonic inseparability and interdependence. The root (*mūla*) of the *liṅga*, as we see, is the *yoni*, or female-identified *pīṭha*. However, prior to the installation of the *liṅga* in the *yoni*, *sthānu* was rooted in the ground or earth, or what could be referred to as another form of female-identified divinity (e.g., Pṛthivī, Bhū). Consequently, even though we have shown that the *yoni-liṅga* is a comparatively late design, it is possible that the conjoined male and female unit was already implied in earlier constructions of the motif, and along with it the idea of male arising from female, as Kalidos suggests.

Evidence of a female-identified Ardhanārī image affirms the ambivalence in the androgynous construction of deity. Although the normative (i.e, dominant), Aryan model portrays the androgynous Ardhanārīśvara in prescribed ways, clearly there are alternative expressions that emphasize and distinguish the power of the feminine. This is pointed to, once again, by essential female diagnostic indicators, specifically the female breast and its strategic placement on the form and figure of the image to indicate the location of power and privilege. We must bear in mind, however, that when the image is right-side-female, the overall image of the deity is conveyed by diagnostic features reminiscent of Śiva and includes a malevolent aspect.

Conclusion

Ardhanārīśvara is clearly the expression of male orthodox discourse. However, this fact does not dismiss or eradicate the role of Pārvatī/Śakti, which constitutes no less than half of Śiva's body. In other words, the image is as much female as it is male. We see her body idealized by the norms of sacred iconographic convention, though we do not hear her voice, for like Gaṅgā, she is portrayed as the "silent woman." Nita Kumar (1994) shows how the voice of resistance or subalternity rises out of the many stories of silent women by focusing on normative models and reclaiming them for women's agency in non-normative ways. In this same way, we have shown how Pārvatī uses the roles of female behavior assigned to her by culture to win her liberation and to find freedom. It is in this sense that Pārvatī/Śakti displays enormous emancipatory potential and disrupts or realigns the symbol of Ardhanārīśvara in new and empowering ways. Pārvatī shows herself to be the active agent of the universe, fashioning her own narrative within constructed social norms. Clearly, her story can be told or interpreted as a voice of resistance, reason, freedom, and strength, as well as silence, obedience, and collusion. Herein lies the ambivalent or paradoxical message. Indeed, it is precisely by claiming the designated roles and realigning them for her own struggle that Pārvatī chooses and uses her power. Pārvatī is not recast as an active agent; as Śakti she has always been in this assigned role of energy, creativity, and strength. One interpretation understands it to be inferior (the "left"-hand side), while another simultaneously exhibits her role as empowering (the "right"-hand side). In the end, both are products of the human imagination, the theistic equivalent, or *pratimā,* of a reality that Indian culture claims points beyond itself.

Notes

Chapter 1

1. Variously referred to in Indian literature as Gaurīśvara, Pārvatī-Parameśvara, Śiva-Śakti, Śiva-Śivā, Ardhanārīnaṭeśvara, and Ardhanaṭeśvara.

2. In the *Śvetāśvatara Upaniṣad,* the term *mūrti* indicates a material form arising from its subtler form, or *liṅga* (Srinivasan 1990, 110). D. C. Bhattacaryya (1987) understands the term *mūrti* specifically as a physical form or body intended for worship or meditation. The term *pratimā* conveys the idea of a physical image, that is, a *mūrti* infused with the presence or life force (*prāṇa*) of the deity. Although often used synonymously, *pratimā* actually refers to a transformed or living *mūrti.* Srinivasan (1997) uses the term *rūpa* in the sense of manifestation or "concrete, outer form" (26), and Harsha V. Dehejia (1997) elaborates to include the idea of an "aesthetic form" that alone enables transcendence. It is in this sense that the terms *rūpa* and *mūrti* are used throughout this study of Ardhanārīśvara. For more details on this subject, see D. C. Bhattacaryya (1987); Doris Meth Srinivasan (1997); Harsha V. Dehejia (1997).

3. For details, see Rao (1968, 361–26); Srinivasan (1990, 108).

4. As Doniger (1994) says, it is the chicken and egg scenario. In other words, "the icon and the myth beget one another," creating a "relationship of mutual parentage" (289). As far as we know in the case of Ardhanārīśvara, image precedes text.

5. See also Krishna Kumar (1975). Here Kumar reiterates Srinivasan's observation that the Maheśamūrti is "the fully manifested form of Paraśiva" (105).

6. The term *kalā* (part) often is used in Indian iconography to describe the number of limbs, body parts, and characteristics of a particular deity. Hence, when the term *niṣkala* is applied to *brahman* or a theistic equivalent such as Paraśiva, it indicates that there are no body parts or characteristics of any kind whatsoever, hence, no form (*arūpa*). The term *sakala* refers to its iconic or aniconic counterform (*rūpa).*

7. See John Mosteller (1987, 1988) for a detailed analysis of specific measuring techniques applied to early Indian images, particularly the anatomical

central axis (*brahmasūtra*) used as a generative point for the images of structural division and formation.

8. I have not found this feature mentioned in the canons of Indian iconography, or their commentaries.

9. Shukla (1996) explains that the crown-like shape of the *karaṇḍa* is common to most gods and goddesses but suggestive of subordinate or inferior status compared, for example, to the *jaṭāmakuṭa* of Śiva (152).

10. The term *hasta* denotes *mudrā* in the *Nāṭyaśāstras*. To convey Ardhanārīśvara through *mudrā* in the Eastern regions of the Seraikella Chhau dance tradition, the performer holds the right hand in *kapittha hasta* (above the head to indicate Gaṅgā), and the left moves in *alapadma*. In the *Bharata Nāṭyaśāstra* tradition, the dancer gestures to the bipolar body of the deity by employing *mṛgaśīrṣa hasta* and delineates the female half and male half by *mukula* (or *kaṭakāmukha*) and *śikhara hasta*, respectively (Gaston 1982, 140). These are the most common dance poses identifying the deity as Ardhanārīśvara. For a comprehensive reading on the relationship between Śiva, dance, and Indian iconography, see Gaston (1982) and Zvelebil (1985).

11. The term *atibhaṅga* refers to an exaggerated *tribhaṅga*, which enhances the three curves or bends in the torso. This posture also has implications in the traditions of *haṭhayoga*. See the discussion in chapter 2 on *tribandha*.

12. *Abhedābhinnā prakṛtiḥ puruṣena.*

13. *Śilpaśāstras* refer to the three traditions of image making (*pratimā*), painting (*citra*), and architecture (*vāstu*). For a comprehensive study of the *śilpa* tradition in India, see P. N. Bose (1978).

14. As early as 1956, the great Indian historian D. D. Kosambi argued that, on the one hand, the *śilpa* tradition should not be used as "a mechanistic device to label religious images," but on the other hand, the texts are not irrelevant either. Kosambi wrote: "The traditional Sanskrit books on architecture and iconography are contradicted by the specimens actually found." See, Kosambi (1981).

15. Shukla (1996), Kramrisch (1959), and more recent studies by Srinivasan (1997) and Maxwell (1989) insist that the *śīlpins* themselves, as a group, are, or at least were, initiated into a strict and rigorous discipline of artistic practice requiring knowledge of dance, music, singing, and adherence to the rules of *yoga*. However, there are varying opinions regarding this subject. For example, P. N. Bose (1978) argues that the *śilpins* were not bound by strict rules and regulations. In fact, he claims that they did not even have a scriptural tradition to follow. For Bose and Dagens, the *śilpaśāstras* appear to be later works signalling decline or deviation.

16. Kramrisch explains that the artist must be trained in the rules of painting (*citra*), as well as dance, music, *yoga*, and so on, to properly understand the art of image making. See Kramrisch (1924).

17. The temple design is patterned on an esoteric *tantric* or *haṭha yoga* understanding of the human body that concretizes the central ideas of that tradition in structural form (e.g., the *śikhara* is the place where the two poles, Śiva and Śakti, symbolized by the two *nāḍīs*, *iḍā* and *piṅgalā*, and two breaths, *prāṇa* and *apāna*, meet via their ascent through the central axis (*suṣumnā*) at the top of the spire). The *haṭhayoga* ideas introduced here will be considered in

more detail in a later chapter. For more details on temple construction, see Mahāpātra (1994).

18. Mathurā Museum No 43:2520. It also is interesting to note that first-stage *liṅgas* generally do not have an altar (e.g., Guḍimallam *liṅga* c. third–second century B.C.E.). It is not until the Kuṣāṇa period (c. first century C.E.) that the *praṇālī* is introduced for the purpose of *abhiṣeka*. Mitterwallner (1984) argues that it is not until the seventh–eighth centuries that the association of union between Śiva and Umā is explicitly identified by the *pītha*. However, the Kuṣāṇa images discussed here indicate the representation of Ardhanārīśvara and the association of Śiva and Śakti prior to this. See Mitterwallner (1984).

19. Srinivasan (1997) refers to the second figure as Kṛṣṇa-Vasudeva (58).

20. Srinivasan identifies this *mudrā* as *vyāvṛtta* (Srinivasan 1997, 19).

21. The *ūrdhvaretas* feature harkens back to the *Bṛhadāraṇyaka Upaniṣad* (BU 11.4.5), which claims that *retas* represents one's sexuality and *ūrdhvaretas* refers to chastity or one who has restrained or drawn up one's sexual energy (seed) through *tapas* or *samyama* (also see chapter 2 on *haṭhayoga*). As well, the lion skin noted by Srinivasan on the right side of the image is specific to Kuṣāṇa and pre-Kuṣāṇa Śiva iconography, though we also see it again on later painted images.

22. Williams (1987) places the Agroha piece slightly before the Gupta period as it displays some features similar to that phase of Indian art, such as the contours of the *liṅga* (301). She also indicates that the red sandstone used in this particular piece derives from the Sikri quarries of Mathurā, though the image itself was found at Agroha in Hariyana (299).

23. Banerjea's system of classification claims, and rightly so, that the "iconic motif of Ardhanārīśvara evolved at a fairly early period, long before explanatory myths came to be fabricated" (Banerjea 1956, 553).

24. From a total of 541 Śaiva images analyzed by Kalidos twenty-two (or 4 percent) were images located at cave and temple sites, such as Elephanta, Ellora, Mahākūṭa, Bādāmī, Paṭṭadakkal, Aihole, Alampūr, and Māmallapuram. See Kandasamy (1994, 491).

25. See Krishnamurthi and Ramachandran (1964).

26. A similar composition (not shown here) is found at Kānchipuram, Chengalpattu District, Śiva Śri Kailasanāda Temple. There are several variations that warrant mentioning, such as three arms, seated on an *āsana* made from Nandin, and the single left arm playing the *vīnā*. Other seated images of Ardhanārīśvara (not shown here), such as the central *murtī* at the Ardhanārī Temple in Mandi, Himachal Pradesh, also display unusual features. This Pahari-style, sixteenth-century stone image displays several significant features not usually indicated in other illustrations. There are four primary characteristics to which I am referring. First, the image is shown seated in *siddhāsana*, that is, the top right foot is pressed against the *ūrdhvareta linga*. Second, the mount is a conjoint dual-headed image of a bull and lion, the respective vehicles of the male and female deities. Third, in front of the deity there also stands an aniconic representation of a *yoni-liṅga*. Fourth, the male side of the deity is identified by a necklace made of *kapālas* (skulls). A half moustache and *jaṭāmakuṭa* characterize the male half of this four-armed image, although when I recently revisited the temple it was difficult to discern the moustache on the

left side. The upper right hand holds a small drum, and the upper left hand holds an *akṣamālā*. The entire body of the deity, rather than just the right male side, is smeared with ash. During *pūjā*, the body is covered in cloths demarcating the bipolar nature of the deity. Overall, this image appears to elicit a male appearance, even though it is clearly a representation of a well-balanced image of Ardhanārīśvara. I would attribute this to an inability to clearly discern a large left breast (illustrated in Singh 1968).

27. Kandasamy (1994) says that Ardhanārīśvara was "a coveted theme" for the Chola dynasty. By the tenth century C.E., Ardhanārīśvara was becoming a significant image in the Tamil Śaivite pantheon (492, 493).

28. Kalidos (1993) and Kandasamy (1994) agree that in assigning three arms to the right/Śiva side the form privileges its male half, and by placing the goddess on the left, she is assigned an inferior status (Kalidos 1993, 73). Srinivasan (1997) also confirms that arms are closely related to "lordship," "sovereignty," and "supra-normal action." In this sense, three-armed images of Ardhanārīśvara could well attest to the emblematic marks of dynastic rulership aligning itself with nonconventional physical prowess on the right male side and the markings of conventional biology on the female left side (22).

29. See Marglin (1985, 1989, 1982), who speaks of Ardhanārīśvara in terms often found in secondary sources such as "half man, half woman," an image that transcends hierarchy and conveys equal status, and so on (Marglin 1985a, 52; 1989, 216; 1982, 300). While this may be the perceived ideal that this image is gesturing to, subtle mechanisms of privileging, such as additional arms on the right/male side, need to be identified and addressed.

30. An alternative reading of the dot, worth mentioning by Kalidos (1989), is that it signifies divine energy (*bindu*) and attests to the eternal presence of the "Universal Mother," who is the "center which is everywhere." *Bindu* also refers to the life essence retained in the process of *yogic* involution and, in this context, it is understood as implying male and/or female substances/fluids, respectively. Both of these references signal a more egalitarian reading of the male and female deities and will be considered again in chapters 2 and 5. It also explains the forehead markings on Figure 1.8 from Orissa. See Kalidos (1989), 115–43.

31. See Deva (1984) for more details on Śiva iconography in Nepal.

32. For two recent articles on the standardization of sacred images in modern Indian poster art, see Smith (1997) and Inglis (1997).

33. Syncretic images of Pārvatī and Lakṣmi also are evident in Indian art, though their iconography has not been given much consideration. See Bhattacharyya (1980).

34. One of the defining characteristics of early Vedic literature, as Gonda (1975) shows, is the recurrence of ambivalent dual deities (*dvidevtya*). Although Gonda examines Vedic deities whose names are primarily formed in dual compound terms (*devata dvandvas*), such as Agni-Soma or Mitrā-Varuṇa, the theoretical analysis he offers is significant when applied to our overall theme of Ardhanāriśvara and syncretic iconography. Gonda says that Mitrā and Varuṇa constitute "an intimately connected couple, as a (two-sided) unity, as acting cojointly (7). Furthermore, Dyāvā-Pṛthivī, the dual deity combining the

spacial domains of heaven and earth, respectively, provides a kind of "prototype" for the classification of dual deities that could well precede the Vedic period. This "prototype"parallels relations of "man and wife" *(sic)*, and the marriage of heaven and earth proceeds from this paradigmatic human basis. Consequently, we see that dual deities are normative in early Vedic thought and affect what Gonda refers to as the "pair system," that is, a system of functional and complementary correspondences that is impressed upon the religious and linguistic imagination as a "fundamental unit" or a two-in-one figure (17).

35. Similarly, the *Laws of Manu* state splitting his body into two, with one half he became the man, with the other half the woman. See Buhler (1993).

36. See R. C. Agrawala (1970) for a discussion of the iconographical features and specimens in the collection. Also see Gouriswar Bhattacharyya (1987) for his examination of Hari-Hara images from South Bihar.

37. Or, *yo'ham sa tvam*. See *Viṣṇu Purāṇa* 5:33, 47–48. Iconographical texts such as the *Matsya Purāṇa*, *Viṣṇudharmottara*, *Śilparatna*, *Aparājita*, and so on furnish succinct formulaic descriptions of the different attributes depicted on Hari-Hara images, but what is of importance here is that the right/Śiva side of the deity is consistent with descriptive images of Ardhanārīśvara.

38. Viṣṇu's subordinate positioning also is evident in the *Tēvāram*, the hymns of the Nāyaṉārs. On composite images such as Trimūrti, Viṣṇu is generally situated in the center, but there are examples of Śiva on the left in the *vāmācara* position. For more details, see Kalidos (1994, 281).

39. Brenda Beck (1973) shows that South Asian society was radically divided into "right" and "left" between the period 1000–1900 C.E. This classification was used to designate certain occupations as well as social groups and religious sects. In many ways, Beck indicates that such a nomenclature still persists today (391ff).

40. The positioning of Viṣṇu is complex and involves not only the so-called denigration of Viṣṇu by placing him in the female position but also his feminization as a *mohinī*. Kalidos (1994) refers to this story as an argument against attempts to suggest that Hindu tradition was free of such practices.

Chapter 2

1. For excellent studies on the history, philosophy, and lore of the Nātha *yogi sampradaya*, see: White (1996); A. K. Banerjea (1961); Goudriaan (1981); Briggs (1989), Das Gupta (1976); Elaide (1969); Gold (1992); Gonda (1977).

2. *Śivasya abhyantare Śaktih Sakter abhyantare Śivah. Antaram naiva jānīyat candra-candrikāyor iva* (Banerjea 1961, 63). Gorakhnāth also describes the nonduality of Śiva and Śakti as *dīpaśikhā* and *dīpāloka*.

3. See *YS* 2:23, *svasvāmiśaktyoh svarūpopalabdhihetuh saṃyogah*.

4. Typically, *yoga darśana* and *haṭhayoga* recognize two stages of *samādhi*, that is, *sabīja* and *nirbīja* (also referred to by Patanjali as *saṃprajñāta* and *asaṃprajñāta*). The term itself derives from the Sanskrit verbal root *dhā*, meaning "to put, place, or hold," and the prefix *saṃ*, meaning "together." Hence,

we can render the meanings "union" or "absorption" for *sabīja samādhi*. Whicher (2000), following Eliade (1969), translates *sabija samādhi* as "ecstasy" and *nirbija samādhi* as "enstasy." For more details on the etymology of these terms and their broader implications, see Whicher (2000, 181–84), and Eliade (1969, 77).

5. For a recent study of the subject of pure consciousness, in light of arguments put forth by Steven Katz (1983) on the mediated nature of mystical experience, see Robert Forman (1998).

6. In her analysis of the *mukhaliṅga*, Srinivasan (1997) explains that if the face of Ardhanārīśvara "is counterpoised with the Yogin *mukha*, the resultant pair could allude to the means for attaining Rudra-Śiva and thereby salvation" (58). In other words, Srinivasan is pairing the *yogin/ī* with Ardhanārīśvara as a means to attain liberation.

7. See Eliade (1969, 207).

8. For example, Heilijgers-Seelen (1994) discusses the *cakra* system in various Śakta *tantric* traditions, in particular the cult of Kubjika. Here Kaviraj (1968) is referring specifically to the centers of spiritual energy as articulated by the Goraksapanthis.

9. See White's (1996) comprehensive study on the correspondences between Indian *siddha* tradition, alchemy, and *haṭhayoga*.

10. For example, descriptions of *vajrolī mudrā* instruct the adept to draw or suck the discharged *bindu* back into the sexual organ or rub it on the body (HYP 3:84-86, 96).

11. See White (1996) for further details of these manifestations and Goldberg (2001a).

12. This is significant. In Indian mythology, the theriomorphic representation of Agni (god of fire) is the androgynous bull-cow, that is, a half-male and half-female form. Agni is identified with Śiva and the bull-cow with his/her androgynous nature (Kramrisch 1988, 200).

13. It is interesting to note that according to the Tibetan *siddha* Naropa, this center controls and regulates body temperature or heat or fire *(agni)*.

14. Ibid.

15. Swami Kṛpalvānanda comments that *cakras* are referred to as *padma* or *kamala* because they open and close like a lotus flower. When the *nāḍis* are full of impurities, the *cakras* are contracted, and when free of impurities, they expand or open (Kṛpalvānanda 1995, 65).

16. There are a number of interesting points about the word *ahaṃkāra* (ego). For example, the *mantra* received in the Milarepa *sādhana* is *ahaṃ mahā sukham* (I am the great happiness). In this sense, *a-haṃ* comprises the first and last letters of the Sanskrit alphabet, and since the throat *cakra* is connected with sound and communication, this seems relevant. As well, the course of unfolding is precisely the *ahaṃ* (I) which becomes subtler and subtler from this *cakra* forward. Indeed, in the *cakra* system of Naropa, the throat is turned upward and is presided over by Amitabha ("Upwards Moving One"). Also, as I indicate further on, *ahaṃ* signifies Śiva-Śakti. For more details see Guenther (1993, 56). Also see Goldberg (2001b) for an in-depth analysis of *buddhi* and Pārvatī's *darpaṇa*.

17. Goudriaan explains that oral commentary in many cases was the only way to explain such treatises (Goudriaan 1981, 9). Elsewhere he argues that "without oral explanation" many passages in *tantric* texts will "remain un-

clear." For this reason, he suggests that exposition by contemporary *gurus,* and and their commentaries on older texts is indispensable if used with caution (Gupta, Hoens,, and Goudriaan 1972, 3–4). Indeed, *haṭhayoga* sources are not self-explanatory, and the oral commentarial tradition is deemed more authoritative by recognized masters of the tradition than the printed word or written manuscript.

18. In this particular lineage, which traces its heritage through Swami Kṛpalvānanda to Lord Lakulish (2c. B.C.E.), *prāṇa sādhana* or *praṇopāsana* is regarded as the highest form of practice. *Prāṇa sādhana* is a form of *nivṛtti yoga* in which the practitioner awakens *prāṇa Śakti* and surrenders to it completely and wholeheartedly. It is a difficult path requiring total renunciation (*vairāgya*), but its rewards are sung about in every Indian treatise on *yoga.* Inwardly directed, their quest requires the dedication of the entire self, its wholeness, and its authenticity. As paradigms of their path, they have shared their personal understanding of the spiritual essence of the human being as depicted in the Indian symbol of Ardhanārīśvara strictly through the transmission of oral tradition. Swami Vinit Muni died in 1996 at age fifty-eight at Kṛpalu Muni Mandal Ashram, in Pransali, Junagadh District, Gujarat, where his disciple, Swami Oṃ Shivatva, still resides.

19. As White also explains, "wet" experience is clearly privileged over "dry" speculation (White 1996, 33). Goudriaan also recognizes the "great importance" that living adepts play in the oral transmission of tradition and their contribution to scholarly understanding of *tantric* doctrine (Goudriaan 1981, 12).

20. See Doniger (1980).

21. Oṃ Shivatva explains that the *viśuddha* and *ājñā cakras* are not separate in themselves. The *ājñā* is in the upper region of the throat, and the two centers are always connected. The throat *cakra* rules over sixteen centers (this explains the sixteen *bīja* syllables on the *padma yantra*), which includes the tongue, base of the nose, and eyebrows. The *sahasrāra,* however, is totally separate.

22. The *Gheraṇḍa Saṃhitā* also refers to three levels of *dhāraṇā,* namely, gross (*sthūla*), subtle (*sūksma*), and luminous (*jyoti, tejas*). The latter is a visualization exercise on inner light in the form of a flame or an *agni* (GS 6:1, 16–17).

23. As David Gordon White says, "[I]t is also an anthropic universe, seemingly created for human realization" (White 1996, 143).

24. Consequently, the three aspects of worship, namely, body (*kāya*), speech (*vāc*), and mind (*citta*), correspond to this tripartite description as well. The *mūrti* is *rupakāya* or *nirmāṇakāya,* or the *sthūla* body of the deity, and is the phenomenal or physical aspect of being. *Vāc,* as depicted in hymns and *bhakti* poetry, aligns with the speech body, and *haṭha* and *rāja yoga,* in their ultimate goal of dissolution of *citta vṛtti,* (1965, 229–83) correspond to mind.

25. For example, see Gonda (1965, 229–83); White (1984); Tulpule (1984, 104–27); *Śiva Saṃhitā* (3:10–15). White offers an interesting translation of the term *dīkṣā* as "habilitation" with specific reference to rendering the sacrificer's body fit for divine communion. In this sense, *dīkṣā* is not so much an initiation between human *guru* and disciple, but rather a purificatory act to prepare the human body for initiation, or communion (White 1996, 270). This follows more closely the meaning of *guru* given by Guenther (1993), in which he

discusses the relationship between *guru* and the Tibetan Buddhist notion of *bla-ma*, translated as "innermost mentor" (23). According to Kabīr, the real *guru* is the hidden nature or soul (*ātman*). Rāmdās also indicates that the true *guru* is the "hidden form" of *ātman* or *ātmadeva* (Tulpule 1984, 109).

26. See Jacobsen (1996). In this article, Jacobsen clarifies the obvious, that the female pole in Hindu *tantra* is the dynamic pole responsible for the manifestation of the universe. However, he also argues that the Sāṃkhya-Yoga concept of *prakṛti* does not necessarily imply a feminine identification. Hence, he claims that the *tantric* bipolarism of male and female is simply a reinterpretation of earlier Hindu thought.

27. Kaviraj (1968) claims that "it is the action of *vāyu* or *vāsanā* on the sensory mechanism of organic existence which projects before it a world of illusion" (118). Hence, the control of *vāyu* (*prāṇa*) through the practice of *yoga* erodes delusional projections, such as duality, separateness, and so on. Buddhists were equally aware of the connection between *tanha* and mind in the perpetuation of *samsāra*.

28. White (1996) translates *paścima* as "western." He cites Mark Dyczkowski's readings as "subsequent," "back," and "latter" (255). I am using the term *paścima* as applied by Swami Kṛpalvānanda in the sense of "rear," as opposed to *pūrva* (front). This is not to imply "secrecy," as White suggests, but simply to follow the path of the *suṣumṇā* up the rear or back of the spinal column.

29. Guenther (1993) refers to Saraha's *Rig-pa-rang-shar* (447), which states that in the complementary symbolic union of man and woman "the male stands for the operational," including such aspects as "vibrations," "oscillations," and "rhythms." The female in this context stands for "appreciation," "insight," and "intuition." Guenther also compares this to Plato's dualism, in which male refers to the "rational" and female to the "intuitive," "emotional," and "aesthetic" (Guenther 1993, 60). Thus we see further examples of the constructed nature of symbolic gender associations. However, I think the underlying implications here are that the adept is liberated from *karma*.

30. According to the *Haṭhayogapradīpikā*, *śūnyatā* is synonymous with *samādhi*, *rāja yoga*, *turīya*, *laya*, *jīvan mukti*, *turīya*, and *sahaja* (HYP 4:3-4).

31. According to White (1996) the alchemical and *haṭhayoga* techniques are constituted by "four phases: purification, immobilization, reversal, and transformation." These phases are clearly described in *haṭhayoga* treatises and establish significant sequential developments in *yogic* transformation. White also shows how Āyurveda (Indian medical system) adapted Sāṃkhya *tattva* theory. For more details, see White (1996, 185).

32. Goudriaan explains that one of the general characteristics of *tantra* is the realization of the "bipolar, bisexual divinity within one's own body" through *sādhana* (Goudriaan 1981, 1). Hoens (1970) discusses numerous instances of triads and pentads in *yoga*. For more details, see Hoens (1970, 95ff).

33. The *Haṭhayogapradīpikā* also refers to this center as *rudra granthi* and the seat of Śiva (HYP 4:47). The *brahmā granthi* is located in the *mūlādhāra* cakra, and *viṣṇu granthi* is in the *anāhata*.

34. *Kevala kumbhaka* refers to arrested in breathing and out breathing. In his treatment of *mūrcchana*, White (1996) defines *kumbhaka* as "potlike" diaphrag-

matic breath retention." He also describes *anuloma viloma* (alternate nostril breathing) and *bhastrika* (bellows or vase breathing technique). In *haṭhayoga* treatises, *kevala kumbhaka* is considered the "supreme"*prāṇāyāma* (HYP 2:74; GS 5:95–96). This state also is experienced in the fourth *jhāna* in Buddhist meditation, which is characterized by arrested breath (i.e., no in or out breath). For more details on breathing techniques and their effects see, for instance, Drakpa (1996, 150ff). Also see Wayman and Wayman (1976).

35. As early as the *Ṛg Veda*, *soma* has been eulogized as the divine nectar of immortality.

36. The *Gorakṣa Saṃhitā* explains that *bindu* is of two types, that is, white (male, *śukra*) and red (female, *rajas*) in color (Briggs 1989, 298–99).

37. This is signified on North Indian Ardhanārīśvara images by the *ūrdhvareta* diagnostic feature. See, for example, Figure 1.3.

38. S. G. Tulpule (1984) refers to the "subliminal consciousness" according to the Upanisadic term *samvit* as a storehouse of conscious impressions (148). In Yogācara Buddhism, we find a similar concept, that is, the *alaya vijñāna*.

39. As I discuss in chapter 5, this is implied in the transmission of *haṭhayoga* by Śiva to Pārvatī. It also is suggested in the famous verse by Kabīr. He says: "When I was, Hari was not, now Hari is, and I am no more; All darkness vanishes when I found the lamp within my heart" (Vaudeville 1997, 178). Vaudeville suggests that the word "lamp" used here refers to the mystical experience given by *satguru*, and *satguru* refers to "innermost mentor."

40. It is interesting to note that the term *avadhuta* is used in Vajrayāna Buddhism to identify the *suṣumṇā*, or central channel. Also, in *haṭhayoga*, the *suṣumṇā* is considered the central nerve of the autonomic nervous system.

41. An alternative to this is *bindu* denotes Śiva, *bīja* denotes Śakti, and their union denotes *nāda*. In this way, *yogis* and *yoginīs* perceive the union of Śiva and Śakti in every sound. In some schools of *tantra*, the *viṣarga* denotes the union of Śiva and Śakti. See Padoux (1990) for more details.

42. In Kashmir Saivism, for instance, *turīya* defines a contemplative state that is "complete" and "integral" (Dyczkowski 1989, 109). In this state of transcendental awareness, Śiva and Śakti are described as essentially one and beyond distinction. This is the ideal of *samarasa*, in which immanence and transcendence coalesce.

Chapter 3

1. My purpose in this chapter is to see how Ardhanārīśvara has been cast in devotional poetry rather than to provide a detailed exposition on this genre of Indian literature. To do this, I simply look at poems that render this particular aspect explicit. For detailed studies of Śaiva *bhakti* poetry, see Peterson (1989); Rangaswamy (1958–1959); Cutler (1987); Hart (1975); Kalidos (1996).

2. The Tēvāram is a collection of 8,469 hymns or 798 *patikams* (groups of ten or eleven) composed by Campantar, Appar, and Cuntarar, who lived in the Tamil-speaking areas of South India during the sixth to eighth centuries C.E. It constitutes the first seven sections of the Tirumuṟai. Of particular interest to

this study is the point that the Pallava and Chola dynasties became royal patrons of the Tamil bhakti poet-saints and recorded their visions in endowed temples and shrines throughout the region. This includes significant images of Ardhanārīśvara.

3. For a detailed discussion of the rhetorical poetics of the Tamil saints, and the triangular pattern of communication involving god, saint, and devotee (audience), see Cutler (1987).

4. For more details, see Peterson (1989, 30).

5. Boner explains that it is "not the aim" of her book "to enter into discussions on particular points of doctrine, but only to show, what different aspects an image like this can reveal to the contemplative mind" (Boner 1962, 184). Although she acknowleges the ambivalence and multivocality of symbols such as ear ornamentation, she nonetheless saturates her formulation in traditional interpretation (i.e., male is *puruṣa* and female is *prakṛti*), without effectively questioning the gendered nature of such constructionist discourse.

6. Two notable sustained efforts to test Ortner's thesis of the universality of female subordination are Peggy Reeves Sanday's *Female Power and Male Dominance* (1981) and Nicole-Claude Mathieu's "Man-Culture and Woman-Nature?" (1978). In these works, they describe counter instances that would challenge Ortner's thesis. Even though they challenge Ortner's claim that female subordination can be discerned "in every known culture," it does not diminish the value of Ortner's theory as an account of some cultures, in this case, aspects of Indian culture and the hegemonic interests at play in the representations of gender. Also see Ortner (1996).

7. However, according to Ortner's most recent work, she also recognizes that there are moments when such constructions also are resisted, enacted, and negotiated by active agents (Ortner 1996, 1). This will be discussed in more detail in chapter 5.

8. Here Ortner is following the idea set forth by Simone de Beauvoir, that "one is not born a woman, one is made a woman." As evidence of this, Hart (1975) says that in ancient Tamil folk tradition "woman" also can be aligned with culture, and man with nature. But in this context it is still the lesser-valued designation that is associated with woman. Hence, we see these categories are constructed, and shifting categories collapse cultural stereotypes, though they often maintain male dominance. For more details, see Hart (1975, 110–12).

9. It also should be noted that Ardhanārīśvara is mentioned in the majority of his hymns.

10. See Spivak (1988).

11. See, for example, Sheryl B. Daniels' (1991) "Marriage in Tamil Culture: The Problem of Conflicting 'Models' " and Frederique Apffel Marglin's (1982), "Types of Sexual Union and Their Implicit Meanings."

12. See Spivak (1988).

13. For more details, see Kalidos (1993), "The Twain-Face of Ardhanārī."

14. Indira V. Peterson (1989) writes: "The poets of the Tamil hymns seek to help their fellow devotees to see (*kāṇ-*) Śiva, to approach him (*naṇṇu-, nāṭu-, aṇuku-, cēr-*), and to melt in love for him (*uruku, neku- nekku-, kaci*). Their description of Śiva focuses on visual images and the act of seeing. Vision

(Sanskrit *darśana*) is of paramount importance in establishing intimate contact or communion with the divine in Hinduism and finds its fullest expression in the traditions of image and temple worship, which are fundamental contexts of *bhakti* in Tamil Śaivism" (Peterson, 32). Also see Dianna Eck's (1985) *Darśan: Seeing the Divine Image in India.*

15. For a more detailed discussion of this tradition, see Peterson (1989, 25); Cutler (1987, 32-33, 66); Hart (1975, 7).

16. Subramania, cited in Peterson (1989, 91).

17. This echoes Marx's view that "ideas become a material force when they grip the masses" (Spivak 1988: xvi). Even Rangaswamy shows that the intent of contemplation on Ardhanārīśvara is to fix in the mind the right relation between male and female to protect the society from the degeneration of the Kālī *yuga* (Rangaswamy 1958–1959, 612).

18. For example, see Richard H. Davis' (1991) chapter, "Becoming a Śiva," in *Ritual in an Oscillating Universe.*

19. Susan Wadley (1992), in her article "Śakti," argues that there is "no intrinsic relationship between a symbol and that which it symbolizes—symbols are arbitrary. The connection between a particular stone and a given deity is imposed by man" (2). This is equally true with regard to the symbolic constructions of the image of Ardhanārīśvara in these hymns.

20. It is in this sense that the image of the androgynous Ardhanārīśvara is androcentric. Androcentrism is simply the assumption that the male is the norm; if the female is identified at all, she must be specified independently from this assumed male norm. The image of Ardhanārīśvara is identified specifically by the image's female indicators. The god, that is Śiva, is generally perceived as male, and the aspects that bring out his androgynous nature need to be identified as female, thus assuming the Śaiva understanding that male is the norm and female is the exception. So, too, the female indicators that are conveyed at times mark the female/left side as less privileged.

21. Cutler (1987) says that the poet also "addresses" or "speaks to" "his own heart" in these hymns (25).

22. For further discussion on this point, see Peterson (1989, 26); Long (1983); Śivaramamūrti (1976).

23. For an account of *bhedābheda* philosophy see, for example, P. N. Srinivasachari's "Bhedābheda School of Vedānta" and Radha Govinda Nath's "The Acintya-Bhedābheda School" in *The Cultural Heritage of India* (1953)

24. This hymn was sung for me in New Delhi by Indian musicologist Dr. Bharat Gupt.

25. This transliteration is based on a popular edition of the *Ardhanārīnaṭeśvara stotra,* acquired outside of the Ardhanārī Temple in Mandi, Himacal Pradesh, India.

26. Appar compares the mantra *namaḥ Śivāya* to the Vedas and their six *aṅgas* as precious jewels.

27. This *mantra,* composed of the five syllables *na, ma, si, va,* and *ya,* expresses the total surrender of the *bhakta* to Śiva. The syllables, according to Rangaswamy, mean the following: "Si, the Lord; Va, His Grace, Ya, the Soul; Na, the Divine power of illusion and Ma, the Mala or impurities" (Rangaswamy 1958–1959, 1119). Accordingly, when *mala* (impurity) dissolves, the *bhakta*

recognizes their complete oneness with Śiva. Is there an implied connection being made here by Rangaswamy between Śakti and *mala*?

28. It is interesting to note, as Long indeed does, that the essential nature of Rudra is "bi-polar and ambivalent," or, as Śivaramamurti says, he "assumes all conceivable forms"(Long 1983, 111; Śivaramamūrti 1976, 3). Hence, this *viśvarūpa* aspect forms the basis for all later *viśvarūpa* descriptions, for instance, Kṛṣṇa in the *Bhagavadgītā* (6:7), and so on.

29. This is a reference to the pan-Indian myth in which Śiva saves the world from destruction by subduing Gaṅgā in his matted locks. We also saw another explanation for this iconographic motif in chapter 1.

30. Doniger writes: "This girl with her magnificent buttocks must not come near me. I insist upon this. Wise men know that a woman is the very form of Enchantment, especially a young woman, the destruction of ascetics. I am an ascetic, a yogi, so what need have I of a woman? An ascetic must never have contact with women" (O'Flaherty 1980, 141).

31. Marglin (1985a) informs us that the *devadāsī* raises her anklets and bangles so that she will not make a sound when she approaches "Bālabhadra clandestinely," who at this time is associated with "Śiva the ascetic." Here, her meeting is "illicit" (50). However, in this *stotra*, we find nothing "illicit" in Śivā's presentation; consequently, we hear the tinkling of her anklets.

32. There is mention of this aspect in the Tamil classic *Cilappatikāram*, by Iḷaṅkō. In this epic, a brahmin boy performs the *kotticcetam* (or dance of Ardhanārīśvara) before the king and queen. In spite of this precedent, dancing images of Ardhanārīśvara in sculpture are surprisingly rare in Tamil Nadu. They are prominent only in the eastern region of Orissa and also in Nepal. However, the dance of Ardhanārīśvara is still quite popular and is performed in live theater throughout India. See Danielou (1955, 182); Gaston (1982); Zvelebil (1984, 44).

33. Although this is beyond the scope of this book, an interesting comparison is raised here between Śiva's ability to heal the thirst for being (*tanha bhava*) and Śakyamuni Buddha's.

34. Hart claims that flowers are not evident in Vedic literature, thus it seems plausible to extrapolate that the use of flowers as offerings in *puja* derives from Dravidian origin (Hart 1975, 30).

35. In a paper by Linda Epp (1992) on the Dalit struggle during the Chandraguti incident, we see traditional and normative values of female modesty clearly being defined by the heated response to female nude worship.

36. Zvelebil categorizes the seven dances of Śiva and suggests that it is "possible, even plausible, that the seven dances of Śiva represent the ascent of *kuṇḍalini sakti* from the *mūlādharacakra* up to the *sahaśrara cakra* (Zvelebil 1985, 4–5). The *lāya*, however, is not included in this list. Also see Bose (1991).

37. It is interesting to note that the Sanskrit term *tāla* referring to the technique of rhythmic timing, is derived by joining the first syllable of *tāṇḍava* and *lāya*.

38. Gaston indicates that the dancer must gesture through hand and body movements the left and right sides of the body. For example, in a pictorial reference, she shows that the "left hand opens from *mukula* to *alapadma* under the left breast, symbolizing Pārvatī. The phallic nature of Śiva is suggested by

the right hand in *śikhara hasta* encircling the left (still in *alapadma*)" For pictures, see Gaston (1982, 141, plates 68a-c).

39. The *stotra* is reminiscent of David Kinsley's description of the androgynous image of Viṣṇu and Lakṣmi. Citing the *Viṣṇnu Purāṇa* (1.8.15), Kinsley writes that Viṣṇnu is "speech and Lakṣmi is meaning; he is understanding, she is intellect; he is the support of the earth; she is a creeping vine, he is the tree to which she clings; he is one with all males; and she is one with all females; he is love, and she is pleasure" (Kinsley 1986, 29).

40. Yocum points out passages from the *Tiruvacakam* in which Śiva is shown to "abide in the five elements," though at times the list is "expanded to eight, adding the sun, the moon, and life" (Yocum 1982, 150). Manikkavacakar sings: "Him who is the five elements/the senses and their objects/every distinct thing/ and yet Himself the great one without distinction" (Yocum 1982, 151–52).

41. Ortner suggests that woman is seen as closer to nature because of her so-called natural procreative and reproductive abilities. Like most feminists, however, Ortner rejects theories of biological determinism which argue that the male of the species is "genetically" superior/dominant, and that women's physiology must somehow consign her to a life of reproduction and child care (Ortner 1974, 73–83).

Chapter 4

1. Christian feminist theologians, such as Elizabeth Schussler Fiorenza and Rosemary Radford Ruether, protest the exclusive masculine symbolism to proclaim the vision of God. They argue that rendering the image of God as male provides the justification for the oppression, exploitation, and marginalization of women. Some Christian feminists have proposed that the gender inclusiveness of God/dess, a termed used by Ruether, offers a first step in the struggle against the exclusion and devaluation of women in the Church. However, the image of the god/dess Ardhanārīśvara offers evidence as to how a two-sexed model of the transcendent can potentially function in patriarchal culture to entrench gender hierarchy, as well as to promote a more egalitarian vision. The underpinnings of patriarchy are rooted deeply in religious systems, East and West, and feminist scholarship, as Fiorenza cautions, "must reject all religious texts and traditions that contribute to 'our unfreedom' " (Fiorenza 1984, xvi). Also Ruether (1983, 1992).

2. As I have pointed out, there are few accounts of Ardhanārīśvara in current scholarship on Indian tradition. One significant discussion of Ardhanārīśvara can be found in Kramrisch (1988). In chapter 8 of her study, Kramrisch provides a summary of the mythology of Ardhanārīśvara in the *purāṇas*. Both Doniger's and Kramrisch's accounts of Ardhanārīśvara are part of larger works on Śiva.

3. See also Doniger (1973, 1998, 1999).

4. Typically, anthropomorphic forms of Ardhanārīśvara are vertical androgynes. It is plausible that the *yoni-liṅga* could be classified as a type of horizontal aniconic form.

5. Doniger uses the term *good* in the sense of successfully fusing two opposites in one symbolic representation. See Doniger (1980, 284).

6. See Harman (1989, 5).

7. See, for example, Doniger (1973); Eliade (1969); Jung (1977).

8. See, for example, Eliade (1969, 108); Dyczkowski (1989, 99); Weil (1992, 72); Jung (1977, 3).

9. See Doniger (1980, 305). See also Goldman (1993).

10. Freud explains that the original narcissism is defined by an attachment to the mother who acts as a mirror to the child and provides the child's earliest experiences of self-identity. This is a significant point, as the female half of Ardhanārīśvara often is depicted holding a mirror. See Kakar (1989).

11. See Harlan and Courtright (1995). Harlan's essay on Mīrā is particularly illuminating in its discussion of the ambivalence that contemporary women admit to regarding her life.

12. For details, see Schouten (1995) and Ramaswamy (1997).

13. (BU 1.4.3). Similarly, the *Laws of Manu* state *dvidha krtvatmano deham ardhena puruso'bhavat ardhena nārī* (splitting his body into two, with one half he became the man, with the other half the woman (Manu 1.32).

14. In a recent book on the Devī, Gayatri Spivak (1999) includes a photo of a young boy in West Bengal who is gazing at several images of a *devī*-in-progress. The heads of the images have not been installed. She reflects on the use of Freud's essay on "Fetishism" in this context to explain the gaze. To this, she adds, "But that is another 'culture' " (Spivak 1999, 191).

15. This appears to be equally true of the Indian model Ardhanārīśvara although, as we have seen, the demarcation between what is objectively known (masculine) and the unknown other (feminine) in Western models of androgyny oftentimes is reversed in the Indian model of Ardhanārīśvara. In Kashmir Saivism, for instance, we see *puruṣa* portrayed as the subjective manifestation and *prakṛti* as the objective manifestation of Śiva (Singh 1968, xxvi). In this system, *prakti* (i.e., what is objectively known or is made manifest) is assigned a feminine gender, though "she" is considered an object of the male subject and therefore still necessary to make knowledge (*jñāna*) complete.

16. See Papa (1994).

17. See Irigaray (1985a) for an interesting perspective on this.

18. As a matter of interest only, Weil concludes her analysis of the feminist response to androgyny with a short discussion on cyborgs, and Donna Haraway is at the forefront of her critique. Haraway constructs the paradoxical cyborg in a manner that, like the androgyne, transcends the boundaries of self and sexual identity. However, that is where the resemblance ends. The cyborg, unlike the androgyne, is animal and human, or animal and machine, and it is situated in a category that Haraway calls "post-gender" (Weil 1990, 161). For an insightful critique of Haraway, see Hewitt (1993).

19. For discussions of left and right in South Asian culture, see Needham (1973).

20. For more details on the subject of feminism and Tibetan Buddhism, see Klein (1995); (1985) and Shaw (1994).

Chapter 5

1. Roy (1999) calls attention to the idea that early Indian brahmanical literature saw the cultural means of copulation such as rituals, *mantras*, and so on as superior to the physical means of copulation (20). As such, sexual fluids (e.g., menstrual blood), are seen as polluting. This culminates in the male initiation ceremony, *upanayana*, which is conceived of as a second birth into masculine society and is considered more prestigious than the boy's natural birth. Rabuzzi (1994) also makes this argument, claiming that the *upanayana* ceremony negates the original birth from the mother (131). See Roy (1999) and Rabuzzi (1994).

2. Amrita Basu and Ritu Menon state that in India woman as mother represents the nation or motherland, whereas man and father represent the state. Patriarchal control is exercised by the paternalistic male rulers of the state to offer "protection to 'its' women and children on the assumption that they cannot protect themselves." According to Basu, the price of this protection is "control over women's sexuality" (Basu 1998, 6; Menon 1998, 17).

3. For more details on this topic see Ramaswamy (1997).

4. Brown (1974) claims that the mythic androgynous motif is associated with incest. For instance, early androgynous indications of Prajāpati convey a father and daughter relationship, in which he attempts to seduce her, hence, the female half runs from her father in fear of incest. Brown also finds evidence of this in the Rādhā-Kṛṣṇa relationship in the *Brahmavaivarta Purāṇa* (Brown 1974, 170–71).

5. An illustration of this is the Śiva cave temple at Amarnath, Kashmir. Housed inside the right-hand corner of the cave is a naturally arising *svāyambhu liṅga* made from an ice glacier. The interesting feature of this particular *liṅga* is that it wanes and waxes in accordance with the lunar cycles associated with Śakti. Under the full-moon skies in August 1989, I set out on a rigorous trek to visit this holy pilgrimage site to see the androgynous *liṅga* at its fullest.

6. Brown (1974) confirms, once again, that the Indian worldview acknowledges "sexual duality as a primary ontological feature of the universe." In this context, "Man and woman are a macrocosmic manifestation of the primordial androgyne" (171–72).

7. Stephanie Jamieson's (1996) analysis of the role of woman/wife in ancient India indicates that even though there are countervailing narratives that contradict normative patterns of female inferiority and weakness, for the most part, maidens in orthodox texts are treated as a "commodity," an "exchange token," a "breeding machine," a "son-producing object," and so on. It is in the roles of wives and mothers of sons that women are seen as "auspicious" and begin to become active subjects (Jamieson 1996, 208, 210, 253).

8. Doniger (1982) refers to Pārvatī as "the quintessence of the lowly mortal woman worshipping the lofty male god" in the form of the phallus. Indeed, for Doniger, the juxtaposition of her "mortal/immortal status" is precisely the "focal point of transition between male-dominated and female-dominated hierogamies." What Doniger points out is that in order to win her position as consort of Śiva, Pārvatī must change or lighten her "color" by purifying her

wrathful and ferocious black Kālī aspect. As Pārvatī she is subordinate to Śiva. Only in her role as Devī does she become supreme. See Doniger (1982).

9. Marriage marks the most important stage of life in most known societies for a woman. In Indian tradition, this life-cycle event was celebrated as a Vedic sacrament considered the equivalent of the *upanayana* ceremony for boys. As such, it announces a new life for a woman in which she serves her husband, just as the *brahmacāri* serves God and guru (Roy 1999; Marglin 1985, 43; Manu 2:67). However, Roy cautions us to explore the range of sexual unions available to women and to deconstruct the notion of matrimony as a monolithic institution. Legally, the joint family is constituted by the male line, and property and so on is passed on from father to son (s). Women do not, as a rule, claim property or inheritance rights. For more details on the legal and economic implications of women's status within the ideology of the family in India see Kapur and Cossman (1996) and Basu (1999).

10. For more details, see Sen (1992).

11. For further reading on marriage, see two recent studies by Jamieson (1996) Roy (1999).

12. The subject of marriage is a complex one. For excellent studies that probe the role of women in marriage, see Harman (1989); Tambs-Lyche (1999); Leslie (1992); Harlan and Courtright (1995); Marglin (1982); O'Flaherty (1982).

13. See, for example, *Matsya Purāṇa* (154.1); *Śiva Purāṇa* (22.29-51); Joshi (1998).

14. For more in-depth studies of the Śakta cult in India see, for example, Pushpendra Kumar (1974); Bhattacharyya (1996); Goudriaan (1981).

15. See Brown (1974, 1990).

16. For example, the use of the name Kālī for the Indian feminist press, Kālī for Women in Delhi, suggests a relationship. Also see the varied essays in Basu (1998) for a discussion of this relationship.

17. Bear in mind that the Rashtra Sevika Samita (RSS) is the counterpart of the male Rashtyria Swayamsevak Sangh. According to Sarkar, the political ideation of "woman" as a result of colonial hegemony and the rise of Hindu nationalism have scripted a proverbial image of "woman" as keeper of hearth and home, morally superior (particularly to women of other communities), and the pride of Hindu religion. However, such an image, as Sarkar shows, rests on the argument that the Hindu woman/wife "accepted scriptural rule out of her own free will and out of love and commitment to the greater glory of the community, for which she had embraced the pain of widowhood, child marriage, and a nonconsensual, indissoluble union—a union severely monogamous for herself" (Sarkar 1998, 93). Thus, as Sarkar shows, her "political status" is a "direct result of her domestic and conjugal submission" (ibid.). This is similar to the moral rhetoric of Rangaswamy that we saw earlier with the image of Ardhanārīśvara, but recast in political and communal terms. See also two recent articles by Bacchetta (1996, 126–67) and Kapur and Cossman (1995, 82–120).

18. More specifically, Kosambi writes: "Matriarchal elements had been won over by identifying the mother goddess with the 'wife' of some male god, e.g., Durgā-Pārvatī (who might herself bear many local names such as Tukāi or Kālabāi)" (Kosambi 1981, 170).

19. For more details, see Adiceam (1967). She surveys twenty-five South Indian sources of Ardhanārīśvara.

20. See Kalidos (1993); Adiceam (1967); Kandasamy (1994).

21. *Aṇaṅku* is a multivalent term that does not refer only to expressions of femaleness. It could be applied to men, animals, and so on that display sexual or asexual behavior.

22. For more details on female chastity in South Indian Caṅkam literature, see Hart (1999, 229–53).

23. See Kalidos (1993, 76); Roy (1999, 32); Hart (1975, 1999).

24. The *Kampam Rāmāyaṇa* portrays Sītā as the chaste wife. For this reason, she is beyond the grasp of Ravana (Roy 1999, 32).

25. Kandasamy (1994) places its date of origin somewhat later, between the fourth–fifth century C.E. This, of course, makes a difference to its time line being coeval with the Kuṣāṇa images of Ardhanārīśvara.

26. For additional details on the mythology of Mīnākṣī, see, for example, Harman (1989).

Bibliography

Adiceam, Marguerite E. 1967. "Les Images de Śiva dans L'Inde du Sud, VI. Ardhanārīśvara." *Arts Asiatique* XIX:8:143–64.

Agrawala, R. C. 1970. "Hari-Hara in the National Museum, New Delhi." in *East and West* 20:3:348–354.

Agrawala, Vasudeva, S. 1966. *Śiva Mahādeva: The Great God*. Varanasi: Veda Academy.

Aranya, Swami Hariharananda. 1983. *Yoga Philosophy of Patañjali: Containing His Yoga Aphorisms with Vyāsa's Commentary*. Sanskrit. English translation by P. N. Mukerji. Albany: State University of New York Press.

Ardhanārīnaṭeśvara Stotra. 1976. Sanskrit. Varansi: Chowahamba Orientalia.

Avalon, Arthur (Sir John Woodroffe). 1972. *Tantra of the Great Liberation (Mahānirvaṇa Tantra)*. 1913. Reprint, New York: Dover.

Bacchetta, Paola. 1996. "Hindu Nationalist Women and Ideologues: The 'Sangh,' the 'Samiti' and Their Differential Concepts of the Hindu Nation." Pp. 126–167 in *Embodied Violence: Communalising women's Sexuality in South Asia*, ed. Kumar Jayawardena and Malathi de Alwis. New Delhi: Kali for Women.

Banerjea, A. K. 1961. *Philosophy of Goraknāth*. Gorakpur: Gorakpur University.

Banerjea, J. N. 1956. *The Development of Hindu Iconography*. Calcutta: University of Calcutta.

Basu, Amrita. 1998a. "Appropriating Gender." Pp. 3–14 in *Appropriating Gender: Women's Activism and Politicized Religion in South Asia*, ed. Patricia Jeffery and Amrita Basu. New York: Routledge.

———. 1998b. "Hindu Women's Activism in India and the Questions It Raises" Pp. 167–84 in *Appropriating Gender: Women's Activism and Politicized Religion in South Asia*, ed. Patricia Jeffery and Amrita Basu. New York: Routledge.

Basu, Srimati. 1999. *She Comes to Take Her Rights: Indian Women, Property, and Propriety*. Albany: State University of New York Press.

Beck, Brenda. 1973. "The Right-Left Division of South Indian Society." Pp. 391–426 in *Right and Left: Essays on Dual Symbolic Classification*, ed. Rodney Needham. Chicago: Chicago University Press.

Beck, Guy L. 1993. *Sonic Theology: Hinduism and Sacred Sound*. Columbia: University of South Carolina Press.

Bhattacharyya, Gouriswar. 1987. "The God Pradyumneśvara and Two Interesting Hari-Hara Figures from South Bihar." *East and West*. 37:1–4:297–307.

Bhattacharyya, Dipak Chandra. 1991. *Pratimālakṣaṇa of the Viṣṇudharmottara*. New Delhi: Harman Publishing.

———. 1987. "Of Mūrti and Pratimā." Pp. 43–47 in *Rūpāñjali: In Memory of O. C. Gangoly*, ed. K. K. Ganguli and S. S. Biswas. Calcutta: Gangoly Memorial Society.

———. 1980. *Iconology of Composite Images*. Delhi: Munshiram Manoharlal.

Bhattacharyya, Haridas, ed. 1953. The Cultural Heritage of India, vol. III. Calcutta: Romakrishna Mission, 447.

Bhattacharyya, Narendra Nath. 1996. *History of the Śakta Religion*. 1974. Reprint, New Delhi: Munshiram Manoharlal Publishers.

Boner Alice 1962. *Principles of Composition in Hindu Sculpture*. Leiden: E. J. Brill.

Bordo, Susan. 1989. "The Body and the Reproduction of Femininity: A Feminist Appropriation of Foucault." Pp. 13–33 in *Gender/Body/Knowledge: Feminist Reconstructions of Being and Knowing*, ed. Susan R. Bordo and Alison M. Jaggar. New Brunswick, N.J.: Rutgers.

Bose, M. 1991. *Movement and Mimesis*. Netherlands: Klawer Academic Publishers.

Bose, Phanindra Nath. 1978. *Principles of Indian Śilpaśāstra: With the Text of Mayaśāstra*. Sanskrit and English. Delhi: Bharatiya Publishing.

Boyer, Pascal. 1993. "Pseudo-Natural Kinds." Pp. 4–47 in *Cognitive Aspects of Religious Symbolism*, edited by Pascal Boyer. Cambridge: Cambridge University Press.

Briggs, G. W. 1989. *Goraknāth and the Kānphaṭā Yogīs*. 1938. Reprint, Calcutta: Motilal Banarsidass.

Brown, Cheever Mackenzie. 1998. *The Devī Gītā, The Song of the Goddess: A Translation, Annotation, and Commentary*. Albany: State University of New York Press.

———. 1990. *The Triumph of the Goddess: The Canonical Models and Theological Visions of the Devī Bhagavata Purāṇa*. Albany: State University of New York Press.

———. 1974. *God As Mother: A Feminine Theology in India*. Hartford: Claude Stark & Co.

Buhler, G. 1993. *The Laws of Manu*. 1886. Reprint, Delhi: Motilal Banarsidass.

Buhnemann, Gudrun, and Musashi Tachikawa. 1990. *Hindu Deities Illustrated according to the Pratiṣṭhālakṣaṇasārasamuccaya*. Tokyo: Center for East Asian Cultural Studies.

Bumiller, Elisabeth. 1990. *May You Be the Mother of a Hundred Sons: A Journey among the Women of India*. New York: Random House.

Chakravarti, Mahadev. 1986. *The Concept of Rudra-Śiva through the Ages*. Delhi: Motilal Banarsidass.

Chakravarti, Uma. 1999. "Beyond the Altekarian Paradigm: Towards a New Understanding of Gender Relations in Early Indian History." Pp. 49–71 in *Women In Early Indian Societies*, ed. Kumkum Roy. New Delhi: Manohar.

———. 1989. "The World of the Bhaktin in South Indian Traditions—The Body and Beyond." Pp. 299–326 in *Women in Early Indian Societies*, ed. K. Roy. New Delhi: Manohar.

Chandra, Pramod. 1985. *The Sculpture of India*. Washington, D.C.: National Gallery of Art.

Chaudhuri, Ajana. 1992. "The Proto-Śiva Seal from Mohenjo-daro: A New Interpretation." *Journal of the Asiatic Society* XXXIV:1–2:19–32.

Coburn, Thomas. 1991. *Encountering the Goddess: A Translation of the Devī-Mahātmya and a Study of its Interpretation*. Albany: State University of New York Press.

———. 1988. *The Devī-Mahātmya. The Crystallization of the Goddess Tradition*. 1984. Reprint, Delhi: Motilal Banarsidass.

Collins, Charles Dillard. 1988. *The Iconography and Ritual of Śiva at Elephanta*. Albany: State University of New York Press.

Cutler, Norman. 1987. *Songs of Experience: The Poetics of Tamil Devotion*. Bloomington: Indiana University Press.

Dagens, Bruno. 1989. "Iconography in Śaivāgamas: Description or Prescription?" Pp. 151–154 in *Shastric Traditions in Indian Arts*, vol. 1, ed. Anna Libera Dahmen-Dallapiccola. Stuttgart: Steiner Verlag Wiesbaden.

———. 1985. *Mayamata: An Indian Treatise on Housing, Architecture, and Iconography*. Translated by B. Dagens. New Delhi: Sitaram Bhartia Institute of Scientific Research.

Dahmen-Dallapiccola, Anna Libera. ed. 1989. *Shastric Tradition in Indian Arts*. Stuttgart: Steiner Verlag Weisbaden.

Daly, Mary. 1985. *Beyond God the Father: Toward a Philosophy of Women's Liberation*. Boston: Beacon Press.

Daly, Mary. 1978. *Gyn/Ecology: The Metaethics of Radical Feminism*. Boston: Beacon Press.

Danielou, Alain. 1955. *Yoga: The Method of Reintegration*. New York: University Books.

Daniels, S. B. 1991. "Marriage in Tamil Culture: The Problem of Conflicting 'Models.' " Pp. 63–91 in *The Powers of Tamil Women*, ed. Susan S. Wadley. 1980. Reprint, Delhi: Manohar.

Das Gupta, Shashibhusan. 1976. *Obscure Religious Cults*. Reprint, Calcutta: Firma. 1946.

Davis, Richard H. 1991. *Ritual in an Oscillating Universe*. Princeton, N.J.: Princeton University Press.

de Beauvoir, Simone. 1974. *The Second Sex*. Translated and edited by H. M. Parshley. New York: Vintage Books.

Dehejia, Harsha V. 1997. *Pārvatīdarpaṇa: An Exposition of Kāśmir Śaivism through the Images of Śiva and Pārvatī*. Delhi: Motilal Banarsidass.

Dehejia, Vidya. 1999. "Encountering Devī." Pp. 13–35 in *Devī the Great Goddess: Female Divinity in South Asian Art*, ed. V. Dehejia. Washington, D.C.: Arthur Sackler Gallery, Smithsonian Institute.

———. 1997. "Issues of Spectatorship and Representation." Pp. 1–21 in *Representing the Body: Gender Issues in Indian Art*, ed. V. Dehejia. New Delhi: Kālī for Women.

Deva, Krishna. 1984. "Śaivite Images and Iconography in Nepal." Pp. 82–91 in *Discourses on Śiva: Proceedings of a Symposium on the Nature of Religious Imagery*, ed. Michael W. Meister. Philadelphia: University of Pennsylvania Press.

Dhyansky, Yan Y. 1987. "The Indus Valley Origin of a Yoga Practice." *Artibus Asiae* 48:89–108.

Doniger, Wendy (see Wendy Doniger O'Flaherty). 1999. *Splitting the Difference*. Chicago: University of Chicago Press.

———. 1998. *The Implied Spider: Politics and Theology in Myth*. New York: Columbia University Press.

Drakpa, Tshongkhapa Lobzang. 1996. *Tsongkhapa'a Six Yogas of Naropa*. Translated by Glenn H. Mullin. Ithaca, N.Y.: Snow Lion.

Duessen, Paul. 1987. *Sixty Upaniṣads of the Veda*. Translated by V. M. Bedekar and G. B. Palsule. 1897. Reprint, Delhi: Motilal Banarsidass.

Dyczkowski, Mark S. G. 1989. *Doctrine of Vibration*. Delhi: Motilal Banarsidass.

Eck, Diana. 1985. *Darśan: Seeing the Divine Image in India*. Chambersburg: Anima.

Eisentstein, Hester. 1983. *Contemporary Feminist Thought*. Boston: G. K. Hall.

Eliade, Mircea. 1969. *Yoga: Immortality and Freedom*. Translated by Willard R. Trask. Princeton, N.J.: Princeton University Press.

———. 1954. *The Two and the One*. Translated by J. M. Cohen. London: Harvill Press.

Epp, Linda. 1992. "Dalit Struggle, Nude Worship, and the 'Chandraguti Incident.' " *Sociological Bulletin* 41:1-2, (March–September): 145–68.

Erndl, Kathleen M. 1993. *Victory to the Mother: The Hindu Goddess of Northwest India in Myth, Ritual, and Symbol*. New York: Oxford University Press.

Feuerstein, Georg. 1975. *Textbook of Yoga*. London: Ryder.

Fiorenza, Elizabeth Schussler. 1984. *Bread not Stone: The Challenge of Feminist Biblical Interpretation*. Boston: Beacon Press.

Forman, Robert, K. C. 1998. *The Innate Capacity: Mysticism, Psychology, and Philosophy*. New York: Oxford University Press.

Fuller, C. J. 1980. "The Divine Couple's Relationship in a South Indian Temple: Mīnākṣī and Sundareśvara at Madura." *History of Religions* 19:321–48.

Gaston, Anne Marie. 1982. *Śiva in Dance, Myth, and Iconography*. Delhi: Oxford University Press.

Geertz, Clifford. 1979. "Religion As a Cultural System." Pp. 167–178 in *Reader in Comparative Religion: An Anthropological Approach*, ed. William A. Lessa and Evon Z. Vogt. New York: Harper and Row.

Gheranda Samhitā. 1980. Sanskrit with English Translation by S. C. Vasu, 1914–15. Reprint, Delhi: Oriental Books.

Gold, Ann Grodzins. 1992. *A Carnival of Parting: The Tales of King Bharthari and Gopi Chand As Sung and Told by Madhu Naisar Nāth of Ghatiyali*. Berkeley: University of California Press.

Goldberg, Ellen. 2001a. "The Haṭhayoga pradīpikā of Svātmarāma and the Rahasyabodhini of Kṛpalvānanda." *Journal of Indian Philosophy and Religion*. 6:10:1–37.

———. 2001b. "Pārvatī Through the Looking Glass." *Acta Orientalia*. Vol. 62. Forthcoming.

Goldman, Robert. 1993. "Transsexualism, Gender, and Anxiety in Traditional India." *Journal of the American Oriental Society* 113:3:374–401.

Gonda, Jan. 1986. *Prajāpati's Rise to Higher Rank.* Leiden: Brill.

———. 1979. "The Śatarudrīya." Pp. 75–91 in *Sanskrit and Indian Studies,* ed. M. Nagatomi, B. K. Matilal, J. M. Masson, and E. Dimock. Dordrecht: D. Reidel.

———. 1977. *Medieval Religious Literature in Sanskrit,* vol. 2. Fasc. 1, *A History of Indian Literature.* Weisbaden: Otto Harrassowitz.

———. 1975. *The Dual Deities in the Religion of the Veda.* Amsterdam: North-Holland Publishing Co.

———. 1965. *Change and Continuity in Indian Religion.* The Hague: Mouton and Co.

Goudriaan, Teun. 1981. "Hindu Tantric Literature in Sanskrit." Pp. 1–172 in *Hindu Tantric and Śākta Literature,* edited by Sanjukta Gupta and Teun Goudriaan. Wiesbaden: Otto Harrassowitz.

———. 1979. "Introduction, History and Philosophy." Pp. 3–47 in *Hindu Tantrism,* edited by Sanjukta Gupta, Jan Dirk Hoens, and Teun Goudriaan. Leiden: Brill.

Gross, Rita. 1996. *Feminism and Religion.* Boston: Beacon Press.

———. 1993. *Buddhism after Patriarchy: A Feminist History, Analysis, and Reconstruction of Buddhism.* Albany: State University of New York Press.

Guenther, Herbert V. 1995. *The Life and Teaching of Naropa.* 1963. Reprint, Boston: Shambala.

———. 1993. *Ecstatic Spontaneity: Saraha's Three Cycles of Dohā.* Berkeley: Asian Humanities Press.

Gupta, Sanjukta. 1992. "Women in the Śaiva/Śakta Ethos." Pp. 193–210 in *Roles and Ritual for Hindu Women.* Edited by Julia Leslie. Delhi: Motilal Banarsidass.

———. 1981. "Tantric Śakta Literature in Modern Indian Languages." Pp. 173–214 in *Hindu Tantrism,* ed. Sanjukta Gupta, Jan Dirk Hoens, and Teun Goudriaan. Leiden: Brill.

———. 1979. "Modes of Worship and Meditation." Pp. 121–186 in *Hindu Tantrism,* ed. Sanjukta Gupta, Jan Dirk Hoens, and Teun Goudriaan. Leiden: Brill.

Handelman, Don, and David Shulman. 1997. *God Inside Out: Śiva's Game of Dice.* New York: Oxford University Press.

Haraway, Donna. 1991. *Simians, Cyborgs, and Women: The Reinvention of Nature.* New York: Routledge.

Harlan, Lindsey and Paul B. Courtright, eds. 1995. *From the Margins of Hindu Marriage. Essays of Gender, Religion, and Culture.* New York: Oxford University Press.

Harman, William P. 1989. *The Sacred Marriage of a Hindu Goddess.* Bloomington: Indiana University Press.

Hart, George L. 1999. "Woman and the Sacred in Ancient Tamilnadu." Pp. 229–54 in *Women in Early Indian Societies,* ed. K. Roy, New Delhi: Manohar.

———. 1975. *Poems of Ancient Tamil: Their Milieu and Their Sanskrit Counterparts.* Berkeley: University of California Press.

Haṭhayogapradīpika. 1972. Sanskrit text, commentary, and translation. Madras: Adyar Library and Research Center.

———. 1974. Text and commentary. Swami Kṛpalvānanda. Pransali: Kṛpalu Muni Mandal Trust Ashram.

Hawley, John Stratton, ed. 1994. *Sati, the Blessing and the Curse. The Burning of Wives in India.* New York: Oxford University Press.

Heilbrun, Carolyn, G. 1980. "Androgyny and the Psychology of Sex Differences." Pp. 258–266 in *The Future of Difference*, ed. Hester Eisenstein and Alice Jardine. New Brunswick: Rutgers University Press.

———. 1973. *Toward a Recognition of Androgyny*. New York: Knopf.

Heilijgers-Seelen, Dory. 1994. *The System of Five Cakras in Kubjikāmātātantra 14–16*. Groningen Oriental Studies, vol. IX. Netherlands: Groningen.

Hewitt, Marsha A. 1993. "Cyborgs, Drag Queens, and Goddesses: Emancipatory-Regressive Paths in Feminist Theory." *Method and Theory in the Study of Religion* 5-2: 135–55.

Hiltebeitel, Alf. 1978. "The Indus Valley 'Proto-Śiva' Reexamined through Reflections on the Goddess, the Buffalo, and the Symbolism of Vāhanas." *Anthropos* 73: 769–97.

Hoens, Dirk Jan. 1979. "Transmission and Fundamental Constituents of the Practice." Pp. 71–120 in *Hindu Tantrism,* ed. Sanjukta Gupta, Dirk Jan Hoens, and Teun Goudriaan. Leiden: Brill.

Hoeveler, Diane Long. 1990. *Romantic Androgyny: The Woman Within*. University Park: Pennsylvania State University, Press.

Ingalls, Daniel H. H. 1965. *An Anthology of Sanskrit Court Poetry: Vidyākara's* "Subhāṣitaratnakośa." Cambridge, Mass.: Harvard University Press.

Inglis, Stephen R. "Suitable for Framing: The Work of a Modern Master." Pp. 51–75 in *Media and the Transformation of Religion in South Asia,* ed. Lawrence A. Babb and Susan S. Wadley. Delhi: Motilal.

Irigaray, Luce. 1989. "Equal to Whom?" *Differences* 1:2:59–76.

———. 1987. *Sexes and Geneologies*. Translated by Gillian C. Gill. New York: Columbia University Press.

———. 1985a. *Speculum of the Other*. Translated by Gillian C. Gill. Ithaca, N.Y.: Cornell University Press.

———. 1985b. *This Sex which Is Not One*. Translated by Catherine Porter by Ithaca, N.Y.: Cornell University Press.

Jacobsen, Knut A. 1996. "The Female Pole of the Godhead in Tantrism and the *Prarkti* of Sāṃkhya." *Numen* 43:56–81.

Jagadep, N. 1989. "Contributions of Hindu Women in Tamil Society." *Journal of Tamil Studies* 36:63–66.

Jamieson, Stephanie W. 1996. *Sacrificed Wife/Sacrificer's Wife: Women, Ritual, and Hospitality in Ancient India*. New York: Oxford University Press.

Jayakar, Pupul. 1990. *The Earth Mother: Legends, Goddesses, and Ritual Arts of India*. San Francisco: Harper & Row.

Jeffery, Patricia. 1998. "Agency, Activism, and Agendas" Pp. 221–43 in *Appropriating Gender: Women's Activism and Politicized Religion in South Asia*. ed. Patricia Jeffery and Amrita Basu. New York: Routledge.

Jeffrey, Patricia and Roger Jeffrey. 1998. "Gender, Community, and the Local Stgatge in Bijnor, India," Pp. 143–166 in *Appropriating Gender: Women's Activism and Politicized Religion in South Asia,* ed. Patricia Jeffrey and Amrita Basu. New York: Routledge.

John, Mary E., and Janaki Nair. 1998. *A Question of Silence: The Sexual Economies of Modern India*. New Delhi: Kali for Women.

Joshi., N. P. 1998. *Tāpasvinī Pārvatī: Iconographic Study of Pārvatī in Penance*. New Delhi: New Age International.

———. 1984. "Early Forms of Śiva." Pp. 47–61 in *Discourses on Śiva: Proceedings of a Symposium on the Nature of Religious Imagery*, ed. Michael W. Meister. Philadelphia: University of Pennsylvania Press.

Jung, C. C. 1977. *Mysterium Coniunctionis*. Translated R. F. C. Hull. 1955–1956. Reprint, Princeton, N.J.: Princeton University Press.

Kakar, Sudhir. 1981. *The Inner World: A Psycho-analytic Study of Childhood and Society in India*. 1978. Reprint, Delhi: Oxford University Press.

Kalidos, Raju. 1996. "Naṭarāja As portrayed in the *Tēvāram* Hymns." *Acta Orientalia* 57:13–56.

———. 1994. "Vāmācara Viṣṇu in Hindu Iconography: A Problem in Sociological Values." *East and West* 44: 2–4:275–91.

———. 1993. "The Twain-Face of Ardhanārī." *Acta Orientale* 54:68–106.

———. 1989. "Yoninilaya—Concept and Application in South Indian Art." *East and West* 39:1–4:115–43.

Kandasamy, P. 1994. "Ardhanārīśvara: Samples of Cola Masterpieces." *East and West* 44:2–4:491–96.

Kapur, Ratna, and Brenda Cossman. 1996. *Subversive Sites: Feminist Engagements with Law in India*. New Delhi: Sage.

Kapur, Ratna and Brenda Cossman. 1995. "Communalising Gender, Engendering Community: Women, Legal Discourse and the Saffron Agenda." Pp. 82–120 in *Women and the Hindu Right: A Collection of Essays*, ed. Tanika Sarkar and Urvashi Butalia. New Delhi: Kali for Women.

Karlekar, Malavika. 1993. *Voices from Within: Early Personal Narratives of Bengali Women*. Delhi: Oxford University Press.

Katz, Steven T. 1983. "The Conservative Character of Mystical Experience." Pp. 2–61 in *Mysticism and Religious Traditions*. Ed. Steven T. Katz. New York: Oxford University Press.

Kaviraj, Gopinath. 1968. *Aspects of Indian Thought*. Burdwan: University of Burdwan.

Khandelwal, Meena. 1997. "Ungendered *atma*, Masculine Virility, and Feminine Compassion: Ambiguities in Renunciant Discourses on Gender." *Contributions to Indian Sociology* 31:1:79–106.

Kinsley, David R. 1986. *Visions of the Divine Feminine in Hindu Religious Tradition*. Berkeley: University of California Press.

Klein, Anne C. 1985. "Primordial Purity and Everyday Life: Exalted Female Symbols and the Women of Tibet." Pp. 111–138 in *Immaculate and Powerful: The Female in Sacred Image and Social Reality* ed. Clarrisa W. Atkinson et al. Boston: Beacon Press.

———. 1995. *Meeting the Great Bliss Queen: Buddhists, Feminists, and the Art of the Self*. Boston: Beacon Press.

Knott, Kim. 1996. "Hindu Women, Destiny and *Strīdharma*." *Religion* 26:15–35.

Kondos, Vivienne. 1986. "Images of the fierce goddess and portrayals of Hindu women." In *Contributions to Indian Sociology*. 20, 2: 173–97.

Kosambi, D. D. 1981. *The Culture and Civilization of Ancient India in Historical Outline*. 1970. Reprint, New Delhi: Vikas.

Kramrisch, Stella. 1988. *The Presence of Śiva*. Reprint, Delhi: Motilal. 1981.
———. 1960. *Indian Sculpture in the Philadelphia Museum of Art*. Philadelphia: University of Pennsylvania Press.
———. 1959. "Traditions of the Indian Craftsman." Pp. 18–24 in *Traditional India: Structure and Change*, ed. Milton Singer. Philadelphia: American Folklore Society.
———. 1924. "The Vishnudharmottaram." *The Calcutta Review* X:331–86.
———. 1922. *The Vishnudharmottaram. Part III: A Treatise on Indian Painting and Image-Making*. Calcutta: Calcutta University Press.
Krishnamurthi, C., and K. S. Ramachandran. 1960. "Ardhanārīśvara in South Indian Sculpture." *Indian Historical Quarterly* 36:69–74.
———. 1964. "Hermaphorditism and Early Ardhanārīśvara Figures in India." *Vishveshvaranand Indological Journal* 2:123–25.
Kristeva, Julia. 1982. "Women's Time." Pp. 31–54 in *Feminist Theory: A Critique of Ideology*, ed. Nannerl O. Keohane, Michelle Z. Rosaldo, Barbara C. Gelpi. Brighton, Sussex: Harvester Press.
———. 1974. *La Revolution du language poetique*. Paris: Seuil.
Kṛpalvanānda, Swami. 1995. *Rahasyabodhini: Commentary on the Haṭhayogapradīpika*. Sanskrit and Hindi. Translated by Swami Vinit Muni and Ellen Goldberg. Unpublished manuscript.
Kumar, Krishna. 1975. "A Dhyāna-Yoga Maheṣamūrti and Some Reflections on the Iconography of the Maheṣamūrti-Images." *Artibus Asiae* 37:105–20.
Kumar, Nita. 1994. "Introduction." Pp. 1–26 in *Women As Subject: South Asian Histories*, ed. Nita Kumar. Charlottesville: University Press of Virginia.
Kumar, Pushpendra. 1974. *Sakti cult in ancient India*. Varanasi: Bhartiya Publishing House.
Kūrma Purāṇa. 1972. English and Sanskrit. Translated by Abhibhushan Bhattacharya (and others). Ed. Anand Swarup Gupta. Varanasi: All India Kashi Raj Trust.
Lawson, E. Thomas. "Cognitive Categories, Cultural Forms and Ritual Structures." Pp. 188–206 in *Cognitive Aspects of Religious Symbolism*, ed. Pascal Boyer. Cambridge: Cambridge University Press.
Lerner, Gerda. 1986. *The Creation of Patriarchy*. New York: Oxford University Press.
Leslie, Julia, ed. 1992. *Roles and Rituals for Hindu Women*. New Delhi: Manohar.
———. 1989. *The Perfect Wife: The Orthodox Hindu Woman according to the Strīdharmapaddhati of Tryambakayajvan*. Delhi: Oxford University Press.
Liddle, Joanna, and Rama Joshi. 1986. *Daughters of Independence: Gender, Caste, and Class in India*. London: Zed.
Lingapurānam. 1970. Vol. 10. Edited by J. L. Shastri, Delhi: Motilal Banarsidass.
Long, J. Bruce. 1983. "Rudra As an Embodiment of Divine Ambivalence in the *Śatarudrīya Stotram*." Pp. 103–128 in *Experiencing Śiva: Encounters with a Hindu Deity*, ed. Fred. W. Clothey and J. Bruce Long. New Delhi: Manohar.
———. 1970. "Śiva and Dionysos—Visions of Terror and Bliss." *Numen* 17–18:180–209.
Mackay, E. 1935. *Early Indus Civilization*. London: Clay and Sons.
Mahāpātra, Sthāpaka Nirañjana. 1994. *Śilparatnakośa: A Glossary of Orissan Temple Architecture*. Ed. Bettina Bäumer and Rajendra Prasad Das. New Delhi: Indira Gandhi Centre for the Arts and Motilal Banarsidass.

Maity, S. K. 1982. *Masterpieces of Pallava Art*. Bombay: Taraporevala Sons and Co.

Marglin, Frederique Apffel. 1989. *Wives of the God-King: the Rituals of the Devadasis of Puri*. 1985. Reprint, Delhi: Oxford University Press.

Marglin, Frederique Apffel. 1985a. "Female Sexuality in the Hindu World." Pp. 39–59 in *Immaculate and Powerful: The Female in Sacred Image and Social Reality*, ed. Clarissa W. Atkinson et al. Boston: Beacon Press.

———. 1985b. "Types of Oppositions in Hindu Culture." Pp. 65–83 in *Purity and Auspiciousness in Indian Society*, ed. John B. Carman and Frederique Apffel Marglin. Leiden: Brill.

———. 1982. "Types of Sexual Union and Their Implicit Meanings." Pp. 298–315 in *The Divine Consort: Rādhā and the Goddesses of India*, ed. John Stratton Hawley and Donna Marie Wulff. Berkeley: Graduate Theological Union.

Markandeya Purāṇa. 1969. English and Sanskrit. Translated with notes by F. Eden Pargiter. Delhi: Indological Book House.

Marshall, Sir John. 1931. *Mohenjodaro and the Indus Civilization*, vols. 1, 2, and 3. *Being an Official Account of Archaeological Excavations at Mohenjodaro Carried Out by the Government of India between the Years 1922–1927*. Delhi: Indological Book House.

Mathieu, Nicole-Claude. 1978. "Man-Culture and Woman-Nature?" *Women's Studies International Quarterly* 4:1:63–71.

Matsya Purāṇa. 1972. Ed. Jamna Das Akhtar. Sanskrit with English translation. Delhi: Oriental Publishers.

Maxwell, T. S. 1989. "Śilpa vs. Śāstra." Pp. 5–16 in *Shastric Traditions in Indian Arts*, vol. 1, ed. Anna Libera Dahmen-Dallapiccola. Stuttgart: Steiner Verlag Wiesbaden.

McDaniel, June. "The Embodiment of God among the Bāuls of Bengal" in *Journal of Feminist Studies in Religion*. 8:2:27–40.

Menon, Ritu. 1998. "Reproducing the Legitimate Community: Secularity, Sexuality, and the State in Postpartition India." Pp. 15–32 in *Appropriating Gender: Women's Activism and Politicized Religion in South Asia*, ed. Patricia Jeffery and Amrita Basu. New York: Routledge.

Menski, Werner F. 1992. "Marital Expectations as Dramatized in Hindu Marriage Rituals." Pp. 47–68 in *Roles and Ritual for Hindu Women*, ed. Julia Leslie. Delhi: Motilal Banarsidass.

Mitterwallner, Gritli V. 1984. "Evolution of the *Liṅga*." Pp. 12–31 in *Discourses on Śiva: Proceedings of a Symposium on the Nature of Religious Imagery*, ed. Michael W. Meister. Philadelphia: University of Pennsylvania Press.

Misra, R. N. 1989. "Indian Śilpa Tradition, Śilpi and Aesthetics: A Study of Correspondence." Pp. 175–86 in *Shastric Traditions in Indian Arts*, vol. 1, ed. Anna Libera Dahmen-Dallapiccola. Stuttgart: Steiner Verlag Wiesbaden.

Moi, Toril. 1985. *Sexual/Textual Politics: Feminist Literary Theory*. London: Methuen.

Mookerjee, Ajit. 1988. *Kālī: The Feminine Force*. London: Thames and Hudson.

———. 1985. *Ritual Art of India*. London: Thames and Hudson.

Mosteller, John F. 1988. "The Study of Indian Iconometry in Historical Perspective." *Journal of the American Oriental Society* 108:1:99–110.

———. 1987. "A New Approach for the Study of Indian Art." *Journal of the American Oriental Society* 107:1:55–63.

Nath, Radha Govinda. 1953. "The Acintya-Bhedābheda School." Pp. 366–386 in *Cultural Heritage of India*, edited by Haridas Bhattacharyya. 1937. Calcutta: Ramakrishna Mission.

Needham, Rodney. 1973. "The Pre-Eminence of the Right Hand: A Study in Religious Polarity." Pp. 1–31 in *Right and Left: Essays on Dual Symbolic Classifications*, ed. Rodney Needham. Chicago: Chicago University Press.

Nuckolls, Charles W. 1997. "The Dynamics of Desire in Jalari Myth" in *History of Religions*. 36: 357–388.

O'Flaherty, Wendy Doniger (also see Wendy Doniger). 1994. "Speaking in Tongues." *The Journal of Religion* 74:3:320–337.

———. 1982. "The Shifting Balance of Power in the Marriage of Śiva and Pārvatī." Pp. 129–43 in *The Divine Consort: Rādhā and the Goddesses of India*. ed. John Stratton Hawley and Donna Marie Wulff. Berkeley: Graduate Theological Union.

———. 1980. *Women, Androgynes, and Other Mythical Beasts*. Chicago: University of Chicago Press.

———. 1973. *Asceticism and Eroticism in the Mythology of Śiva*. London: Oxford University Press.

Olivelle, Patrick. 1998. *The Early Upaniṣads: Annotated Text and Translation*. New York: Oxford University Press.

Ortner, Sherry B. 1996. *Making Gender: The Politics and Erotics of Culture*. Boston: Beacon Press.

———. 1974. "Is Female to Nature As Male Is to Culture?" Pp. 67–88 in *Woman, Culture, and Society*, ed. Michelle Zimbalist Rosaldo and Louise Lamphere. Stanford, Calif.: Stanford University Press.

Padma Purāṇa. 1988–1992. Translated and annotated by N. A. Deshpande. Delhi: Motilal Banarsidass.

Padoux, Andre. 1990. *Vāc: The Concept of the Word in Selected Hindu Tantras*. Delhi: Sri Satguru Publications.

Pal, Pratapaditya. 1988. *Indian Sculpture*, vol. 2. Berkeley: Los Angeles County Museum of Art and University of California Press.

———. 1985. *Art of Nepal: A Catalogue of the Los Angeles County Museum of Art Collection*. Berkeley: Los Angeles County Museum and University of California Press.

Papa, Regina B. 1994. "Deconstruction of Dualism and the Indian Myth of Ardhanārīśvara." *Journal of the Institute of Asian Studies*. 10:np.

Parikh, Indira J., and Pulin K. Garg. 1989. *Indian Women: An Inner Dialogue*. New Delhi: Sage Publications.

Peterson, Indira V. 1989. *Poems to Śiva*. Princeton, N.J.: Princeton University Press.

Pintchman, Tracy. 1997. *The Rise of the Goddess in the Hindu Tradition*. 1994. Reprint, Delhi: Sri Satguru.

Plaskow, Judith. 1991. *Standing at Sinai: Judaism From A Feminist Perspective*. San Francisco: Harper San Francisco.

Pollock, Sheldon. 1989. "The Idea of Śāstra in Traditional India." Pp. 17–26 in *Shastric Traditions in Indian Arts*, vol. 1, ed. Anna Libera Dahmen-Dallapiccola. Stuttgart: Steiner Verlag Wiesbaden.

Pott, P. H. 1966. *Yoga and Yantra: Their Interrelation and Their Significance for Indian Archeology*. Reprint, The Hague: Martinus Nijhoff. 1946.

Rabuzzi, Kathryn Allen. 1994. *Mother with Child: Transformations through Childbirth*. Bloomington: Indiana University Press.

Ramaswamy, Vijaya. 1997. *Walking Naked: Women, Society, Spirituality in South India*. Shimla: Indian Institute of Advanced Studies.

Rangaswamy, M. A. Dorai. 1958–1959. *The Religion and Philosophy of the Tēvāram: With Special Reference to Nampi Arurar (Sudarar)*. 4 vols. Madras: University of Madras.

Rao, T. A. Gopinatha. 1968. *Elements of Hindu Iconography*, vol. II, part I. New York: Paragon Book Reprint Corp.

Rastogi, Navjivan 1992. "The Yogic Disciplines in the Monistic Śaiva Tantric Traditions of Kashmir: Threefold, Fourfold, and Six-Limbed." Pp. 247–80 in *Ritual and Speculation in Early Tantrism*, ed. Paul E. Muller-Ortega. Albany: State University of New York Press.

Rawson, Philip. 1973. *The Art of Tantra*. London: Thames and Hudson.

Rich, Adrienne. 1976. *Of Woman Born: Motherhood and Experience and Institution*. New York: Norton.

Roy, Kumkum. 1999. "Introduction." Pp. 1–48 in *Women in Early Indian Societies*, ed. K. Roy. New Delhi: Manohar.

———. 1995. "Where Women Are Worshipped, There the Gods Rejoice The Mirage of the Ancestress of the Hindu Woman." Pp. 10–28 in *Women and the Hindu Right*, ed. Tanika Sarkar and Urvashi Butalia. New Delhi: Kali for Women.

Ruether, Rosemary Radford. 1983. *Sexism and God-Talk: Toward a Feminist Theology*. Boston: Beacon Press.

Samanta, Suchitra. 1992. "*Maṅgalmayima, sumaṅgali, maṅgal:* Bengali Perceptions of the Divine Feminine, Motherhood and 'Auspiciousness.' " *Contributions to Indian Sociology* 26:1:51–75.

Sanday, Peggy Reeves. 1981. *Female Power and Male Dominance*. Cambridge: Cambridge University Press.

Sarkar, Tanika. 1998. "Woman, Community, and Nation: A Historical Trajectory for Hindu Identity Politics." Pp. 89–104 in *Appropriating Gender: Women's Activism and Politicized Religion in South Asia*, ed. Patricia Jeffery and Amrita Basu. New York: Routledge.

Schneider, U. 1987. "Towards a Sculptural Programme at Elephanta" Pp. 325–34 in *Investigating Indian Art: Proceedings of a Symposium on the Development of Early Buddhist and Hindu Iconography*. ed. M. W. Meister. Berlin: Museum of Indian Art.

Schouten, Jan Peter. 1995. "The Unconventional Woman Saint: Images of Akka Mahādevī." Pp. 123–150 in *Female Stereotypes in Religious Traditions*, ed. Ria Kloppenborg and W. J. Hanegraaff. Leiden: Brill.

Sen, Amartya. 1992. *Inequality Reexamined*. Delhi: Oxford University Press.

Shah, Priyabala. 1990. *Shri Vishnudharmottara*. Baroda: Oriental Institute.

———. 1961. *Vishnudharmottara-Purāṇa Third Khaṇḍa*, vol. II. Baroda: Oriental Institute.

Shaheed, Farida. 1998. "The Other Side of the Discourse: Women's Experiences of Identity, Religion, and Activism in Pakistan." Pp. 143–166 in *Ap-*

propriating Gender: Women's Activism and Politicized Religion in South Asia, ed. Patricia Jeffery and Amrita Basu. New York: Routledge.
Shaw, Miranda. 1994. *Passionate Enlightenment*. Princeton, N.J.: Princeton University Press.
Showalter, Elaine. 1977. *Literature of Their Own: British Women Novelists from Bronte to Lessing*. Princeton: Princeton.
Shukla, D. N. 1996. *Vāstu-Śāstra: Hindu Canons of Iconography and Painting*. 1959. Reprint, New Delhi: Munshiram Manoharlal.
Silburn, Lillian. 1988. *Kundalini: The Energy of the Depths: A Comprehensive Study of Nondualistic Kasmir Saivism*. Translated by Jacques Gontier. Albany: State University of New York Press.
Singer, June. 1989. *Androgyny: The Opposites Within*. 1976. Reprint, Boston: Sigo Press.
Singh, Madanjeet. 1968. *Himalayan Art*. London: Macmillan.
Singh, Sheo Bahadur. 1973. "Syncretic Icons in Uttar Pradesh." *East and West*. 23:3–4:339–46.
Sinh, Pancham. 1980a. *The Hatha Yoga Pradipika*. Sanskrit with English translation by P. Sinh. 1914–1915. Reprint, New Delhi: Oriental Books.
———. 1980b. *The Gheraṇḍa Saṃhitā*. Sanskrit with English translation by P. Sinh. 1914–1913. Reprint, New Delhi: Oriental Books.
Śiva Pūraṇa. 1986. Ed. J. L. Shastri. 4 vols. Sanskrit with English translation. Reprint, Delhi. Motilal. 1970
Śiva Samhitā. 1979. Sanskrit with English translation by S. C. Vasu. 1914–15. Reprint, New Delhi: Oriental Books.
Śivaramamūrti, C. 1984. "Forms of Śiva in Sanskrit Sources." Pp. 182–90 in *Discourses on Śiva: Proceedings of a Symposium on the Nature of Religious Imagery*, ed. Michael W. Meister. Philadelphia: University of Pennsylvania Press.
———. 1976. *Śatarudrīya: Vibhūti of Śiva's Iconography*. New Delhi: Abhinav Publications.
———. 1974a. *L'art en Inde*. Paris: Edition d'Art Lucien Mozenod.
———. 1974b. *Naṭarāja in Art, Thought, and Literature*. Delhi: National Museum.
Smith, H. Daniel. 1997. "Impact of "God Posters" on Hindus and Their Devotional Traditions." Pp. 24–50 in *Media and the Transformation of Religion In South Asia*, ed. Lawrence A. Babb and Susan S. Wadley. 1995. Reprint, Delhi: Motilal Banarsidass.
Spivak, Gayatri Chakravorty. 1999. "Moving Devī." Pp. 181–200 in *Devī the Great Goddess: Female Divinity in South Asian Art*, ed. V. Dehejia. Washington, D.C.: Arthur Sackler Gallery, Smithsonian Institute.
———. 1988. *In Other Worlds: Essays in Cultural Politics*. Methuen, NewYork: Routledge.
Srinivasan, Doris Meth. 1997. *Many Heads, Arms, and Eyes: Origin, Meaning, and Form of Multiplicity in Indian Art*. Leiden: Brill.
———. 1990. "From Transcendency to Materiality: Paraśiva, Sadaśiva, and Maheṣa in Indian Art." *Artibus Asiae* 50:108–42.
———. 1989. "Significance and Scope of Pre-Kuṣāṇa Saivaite Iconography." Pp. 32–46 in *Discourses on Śiva: Proceedings of a Symposium on the Nature of Religious Imagery*, ed. Michael Meister. Philadelphia: University of Pennsylvania Press.

———. 1987. "Saiva Temple Forms: Loci of God's Unfolding Body." Pp. 335–47 in *Investigating Indian Art: Proceedings of a Symposium on the Development of Early Buddhist and Hindu Iconography*. Berlin: Museum of Indian Art.

———. 1984. "Unhinging Śiva from the Indus Civilization." *Journal of the Royal Asiatic Society* 1:77–89.

———. 1983. "Vedic Rudra-Śiva" *Journal of the American Oriental Society* 103:3:543–56.

Tambs-Lyche, Harald, edited by 1999. *The Feminine Sacred in South Asia.* Delhi: Manohar.

Tharu, Susie, and K. Lalita. 1991. "Introduction." Pp. 1–37 in *Women Writing in India 600 B.C. to the Early Twentieth Century*, vol. 1, ed. S. Tharu and K. Lalita. New York: Feminist Press, City University of New York.

The Bhagavadgītā in the Mahābhārata. 1981. Sanskrit and English. Translated by J. A. B. van Buitenen. Chicago: University of Chicago Press.

The Holy Teaching of Vimalakīrti: A Mahāyana Scripture. 1983. Translated by Robert A. F. Thurman. University Park : Pennsylvania State University Press.

The Hymns of the Rg-Veda. 1973. Ed. J. L. Shastri, translated by Ralph T. H. Griffith. 2 vols. Delhi: Motilal Banarsidass.

Tulpule, Shankar Gopal. 1984. *Mysticism in Medieval India.* Wiesbaden: Otto Harrassowitz.

Van Buitenen, J. A. B., trans. 1981a. *The Bhagavadgītā in the Mahābhārata.* Sanskrit with English translation. Chicago: University of Chicago Press.

———. 1981b. *The Mahābhārata.* 3 vols. Chicago: University of Chicago Press.

Varenne, Jean. 1989. *Yoga and the Hindu Tradition.* Reprint, Delhi: Motilal Banarsidass. 1973.

Varma, Ravi, A. 1956. "Rituals of Worship." Pp. 445–463 in *The Cultural Heritage of India*, vol. IV, ed. H. Bhattacharya. Calcutta: Ramakrishna Mission.

Vasu, Sri Candra. 1979. *The Śiva Saṃhitā.* Sanskrit with English translation by S. C. Vasu. 1914–1915. Reprint, New Delhi: Oriental Books.

Vaudeville, Charlotte. 1997. *A Weaver Named Kabir.* 1993. Reprint, Delhi: Oxford University Press.

Vayu Purāṇa. 1970. Vol. 39–40. Ed. J. L. Shastri. Delhi: Motilal Banarsidass.

Visnu Purāṇa. 1989. Sanskrit and English. Translated by H. H. Wilson. Vol. 1-2. 1980. Reprint, Delhi: Nag Publishers.

Wadley, Susan. 1991. *The Powers of Tamil Women.* New Delhi: Manohar.

———. 1977. "Women in the Hindu Tradition" *Signs: Journal of Women in Culture and Society* 3:1:113–125.

Wadley, Susan, and Doranne Jacobson. 1992. *Women in India: Two Perspectives.* Columbia: South Asia Publications.

Wayman, Alex, and Hidek Wayman, trans. 1976. *The Lion's Roar of Queen Śrīmāla: A Buddhist Scripture on the Tathāgatagarbha Theory.* New York: Columbia University Press.

Weil, Kari. 1992. *Androgyny and the Denial of Difference.* Charlottesville: University of Virginia Press.

Whicher, Ian. 2000. *The Integrity of the Yoga Darśana: A Reconsideration of Classical Yoga.* Albany: State University of New York Press.

White, David Gordon. 1996. *The Alchemical Body: Siddha Traditions in Medieval India*. Chicago: University of Chicago Press.

———. 1984. "Why Gurus Are Heavy." *Numen* 33:40–73.

Williams, Joanna 1987. "An Ardhanārīśvara-Linga." Pp. 299–314. in *Kusumanjali: New Interpretation of Indian Art and Culture*, vol. II, ed. M. S. Nagaraja Rao. Delhi: Agam Kala Prakashan.

Yadav, Neeta. 2001. *Ardhanārīśvara in Indian Art and Literature*. Delhi: D. K. Printworld.

Yocum, Glenn E. 1982. *Hymns to the Dancing Śiva: A Study of Manikkavacakar's Tiruvacakam*. Columbia: South Asia Books.

Zimmer, Heinrich. 1955. *The Art of Indian Asia: Its Mythology and Transformations*. New York: Bollingen Foundation.

Zvelebil, Kamil Veith. 1985. *Ānanda-Tāṇḍava of Śiva Sadanṛttamūrti*. Tiruvanmiyur: Institute of Asian Studies.

———. 1974. *Tamil Literature*, vol. X. Fasc. 1, Weisbaden: Otto Harrassowitz.

Index